CW00684401

All In Good Time

ALL IN GOOD TIME
Growing up in 1950s Wakefield

Keith G. Barraclough

All in Good Time
Keith G. Barraclough

Published by Aspect Design 2012
Malvern, Worcestershire, United Kingdom.

Printed by Aspect Design
89 Newtown Road, Malvern, Worcs. wr14 1pd
United Kingdom
Tel: 01684 561567
E-mail: books@aspect-design.net
Website: www.aspect-design.net

All Rights Reserved.

Copyright © 2012 Keith G. Barraclough

Keith G Barraclough has asserted his moral right
to be identified as the author of this work.

The right of Keith G. Barraclough to be identified as the
author of this work has been asserted in accordance with
Section 77 of the Copyright, Designs and Patents Act 1988.

This book is sold subject to the condition that it shall not,
by way of trade or otherwise, be lent, resold, hired out or
otherwise circulated without the publisher's prior consent
in any form of binding or cover other than that in which it
is published and without a similar condition including this
condition being imposed on the subsequent purchaser.

A copy of this book has been deposited
with the British Library Board

Cover image:
Photograph of the River Calder and the new power station,
Wakefield, 1956. R. H. BARRACLOUGH

ISBN 978-1-908832-15-3

Dedicated to the next generation:
Thomas, Heather and Daniel,
and the next: Halle and Harrison.

CONTENTS

PREFACE

I always wanted to write something completely different from the technical reports and publications that were the outputs of my working life, so when I retired I decided to combine quite a good memory with hoards of supportive material, such as diaries, photographs and various memorabilia, to write about life in the 1950s. My story is set against the background of major changes in the economic, political and social development of Britain in that period. Rationing ended as the austere post-war years of the 1940s were transformed into a sustained period of economic growth and consumerism. The decade of the fifties marked a clear decline in Britain's influence as a world power, yet it was also the dawn of the new Elizabethan age when pioneering post-war social reforms started to flourish. It was a period of few changes in social attitudes, especially towards minority groups and towards sex and sexuality, but a completely new social group, teenagers, emerged, demanding recognition and independence from their old-fashioned parents' generation.

I was six years old in 1949 when I moved to Belle Vue, south of the city of Wakefield, from a small Yorkshire mill town, Uppermill, on the west side of the Pennines, and with a predominantly Lancashire culture. Unlike me, Wakefield was very sure of itself: it was the administrative capital of the West Riding of Yorkshire; it had a proud history and a self-confident population in full employment, knowing what it liked and disliked – people speaking with a Lancashire accent came into the latter category! A diverse industrial economy was dominated by coal mining, with textiles and engineering also playing significant roles. Smoke and steam were everywhere; Belle Vue was home to one of the biggest steam locomotive sheds in the north of England, next to Wakefield's new coal-fired power station built in the mid-fifties. Churches, chapels, pits, pubs and cinemas abounded. Wakefield's ten cinemas were still a main source of entertainment, but they were gradually giving way to the new medium of television. I had first-hand experience of Wakefield's education system, a flagship model of the 1944 Education Act, based on secondary modern, grammar, and technical schools, entered by a selection process that was far more complex than the common misconception of a one-off, pass/fail examination at eleven plus. Wakefield's sporting heritage was firmly based on cricket and rugby league; a backstreet cricket pitch was outside my Belle Vue family home, which was also within a stone's throw of the rugby ground of the famous Wakefield Trinity club. As a fervent young supporter, I saw 'the Trinity' gradually develop into one of the most successful teams in the history of rugby league. I soon learned that hard graft and physical effort were key ingredients of both work and play.

The outcome is a sort of 1950s journal of personal, local and social history. My father would probably have dubbed my book as 'neither nowt nor summat', which I was tempted to use as its title, but eventually settled on one that reflects both a happy childhood and the 1950s ethos of delayed gratification when waiting for reward was the norm, usually after hard work and saving up: 'All in good time'.

Keith G. Barraclough

FOREWORD

Keith Barraclough's book is no typical work of local history. Rather it captures in vivid detail what it was actually like to live in Wakefield in the 1950s as a quite ordinary boy in the Belle Vue of the time. It records a way of life rarely preserved and now lost. Here is home life in a terrace house with its coal fire, its outdoor privy, its front room kept for best, and the challenge of tuning the living-room wireless. Here are the sights and sounds experienced by the young Wakefield Trinity supporter or patron of the local flea-pit cinema. Here are the smells and struggles of learning to swim at the 'old' Almshouse Lane baths. The big national events – the death of George VI and the Coronation of the present Queen – are recorded as they were marked by ordinary people in Wakefield. Individuals, as they were encountered at home, at school, or in the church choir or scout group, are brought sharply into focus: the no-nonsense mother, the straight-laced spinster aunts, the corner-shop keeper, and stern schoolteachers still made in the Victorian mould. Especially memorable is Barraclough's father, with his skills and eccentricities, his delight in taking things apart to discover the secrets of their manufacture, and his loving ritual of preparing his pipe. It was a world where the majority longed for an invitation from a privileged neighbour to watch the television. Although only half a century ago, the culture and ethos reflected here were very different from today, perhaps encapsulated in the contrast between 'You can't have it yet' and 'You've never had it so good'. The changes that have taken place in Wakefield itself in the intervening fifty years are most usefully noted in the concluding chapter. Whilst this book must be of special interest to those who know Wakefield, its compelling record of a bygone way of life will have a much wider appeal.

Kate Taylor
Local Historian, Wakefield

CHAPTER ONE

Introduction and the Move to Wakefield – 1949

The period of initial rejoicing, then relief, that followed the end of the Second World War was tempered by the reality that many families were suffering permanently from the impact of the conflict: some men had never returned home, some had returned badly injured, and even those who had returned safely in one piece had to re-establish relationships with their family, often without success. Many families had also lost their homes and material possessions, especially in the large bomb-damaged cities, and there was a continuing need throughout the country to house an increasing population. For many, life was never the same again; for the fortunate, the most significant problem was rationing.

I was one of the fortunate ones. My father had joined the police force in the 1930s and, despite having to work long and awkward hours in a reserved occupation during the war, he was always close to home and available for his family. My sister, Elaine, had been born four months before the war started; I was born in the middle of the war in December, 1942. We spent the 1940s as a family unit living relatively undisturbed in a small mill town called Uppermill, in the district of Saddleworth on the west side of the Pennines, close to the Lancashire town of Oldham. At that time the Saddleworth district was within the West Riding of Yorkshire but its culture and traditions were characteristic of the Northwest region. The

Whit Friday Walk, Uppermill, *c.*1947. The author's sister, Elaine, is the second girl from the right. R. H. BARRACLOUGH.

locals spoke with a strong Lancashire accent that had quite different vowel sounds from those spoken in the rest of Yorkshire, further east. Whit Friday was Saddleworth's biggest day of the year, when shops and schools were closed for the Northwest tradition of Whit walks, a public celebration of Pentecost, the birth of the Christian church. Members of the local churches in the district would 'walk out' behind their own church banner, carried behind a marching brass band.

Whit Friday was the day new clothes were first displayed, and I can recall my mother kitting me out in new trousers and a white blouse that she had run up for my first Whit walk with other Sunday school kids in about 1947.

In the 1940s some women made their own clothes whilst those who could afford to buy a new outfit had to save up the coupons from their clothing ration book for the big day. After the morning parade, everyone congregated in the village square for a united service. There were children's

First Whit Walk for the author (centre), Uppermill, *c*.1947. R. H. BARRACLOUGH.

sports and games in the afternoon then a brass band competition in the evening, contested by the top bands of the day such as Brighouse and Rastrick, CWS Manchester and the famous Black Dyke Mills band of John Foster's mill in Queensbury.

I was too young to remember the war years in Uppermill, but my parents would often talk about the German VI 'Doodlebugs' when they had droned westwards across the night sky towards their targets in the nearby cities of Oldham and Manchester; in particular they spoke about the surprise attack on Christmas Eve, 1944. Apparently, the odd VI did cut out too early over Uppermill and there was the occasional local tragedy but, overall, there was very little bomb damage compared with the havoc wrought in the larger towns and cities further west.

All my early recollections are post-war events and, naturally, represent those extremes of anguish and pleasure which are impossible to erase from the memory, compared with the routine of daily life. Being hit by a spade on the forehead and scarred for life by a young 'friend' was a particularly memorable incident. Failing to attract the attention of my teacher that I needed to go to the lavatory during my first day at school had unforgettable consequences! But there were many pleasurable moments too, especially in about 1947: riding in Dad's police car for the first time, playing in the thick snow, the first taste of ice cream after having my tonsils out in Oldham hospital and a family holiday at my Auntie Olive's Blackpool boarding house in the summer following that harsh winter.

Dad, Reginald Harrison Barraclough, was born in Shelley, near Huddersfield, in the West Riding of Yorkshire in 1908, the youngest of seven children. He had started work just after his fourteenth birthday with little education, although he could read and write very well, despite having suffered beatings from a masochistic teacher in the local village school. Dad was close to the next youngest brother, Harry, and youngest sister, Maggie; his other brothers and sisters were much older and more distant. Brother Gordon had been killed in a coal mining accident before I was born, and I had been named after him. Dad followed his father and most of his family into one of the local mills near Shelley but he had greater ambitions. A good all-rounder with considerable sporting and musical talents, he had played in trial games for Huddersfield Town AFC in the late 1920s when they were a top class team in the football league. He sang in the local Shelley church choir, composed music and played in a local Shelley Brass Band. During this time he was also paying for singing lessons with John Fletcher Sykes, a professional musician and conductor of Huddersfield's Philharmonic Society and Vocal Union.

Dad would not have realised until 1939 that fate had dealt him a very lucky hand when his application to join the army as a bandsman six years earlier was turned down, and his subsequent application to be a policeman in the West Riding Constabulary was successful. He had been able to call on a good reference to his varied talents from an influential mill owner, and it seems this made all the difference with the police force. George Norton of nearby Bagden Hall, owner of Nortonthorpe Mill and a well known local philanthropist had 'put a word in', although how he came to know my father at all remains a mystery. It seems that Norton's daughter Mabel was involved in some way because she wrote to Dad on 27 December 1933 stating that, 'my father had a word with the Chief about you and he was hopeful you would get the appointment …' It's not what you know, it's who you know, and surprise, surprise, Dad's application was successful. After a period of initial training, his first stint on the beat was in the Rotherham District of Wickersley before being posted to Uppermill, Saddleworth, as a member of the Huddersfield Road Traffic Division in 1937. He had married in the same year and started a family two years later.

Mum, Violet Muriel Howard Tait, was born in Foston, near York in 1911, and had a genteel but strict upbringing. She was the youngest of four sisters – the others were Florence (Flo'), Edith and Olive – and she grew up in Kirkburton, about a mile from Shelley. Mum's father, Thomas Tait, was in-service as a gardener and chauffeur to T. J. Dyson, a solicitor of the Huddersfield firm Laycock, Dyson & Laycock. My maternal grandmother, Margaret, was a strict Victorian lady who ruled the roost of their humble home, Hartley Cottage, which was close to the Dyson's in Kirkburton. After leaving the local village school, Mum worked as a shop assistant at the Maypole in Huddersfield before marrying and raising two children. Mum was very conservative and lived by the Victorian maxim: Cleanliness is next to godliness. A lot of her mother had rubbed off on her, and she had a no-nonsense approach to everything – some would say 'typical Yorkshire'. Mum's favourite word was 'muck' which she used to describe most undesirables. However, she was not averse to getting her hands dirty to help a united cause. 'Mucking in' was seen as a great Christian virtue and brought with it staunch friends, or 'muckers', as a result of the collective effort. I was still very small when I realised that 'muck' was a complicated business in this part of the world. Mum had learned housework and needlework from her mother and was good at sewing, knitting and mending; her cooking was plain but wholesome, considering the difficult times of food rationing. Mum was tough and unsentimental. Having to cope with a boy for the first time in her life was obviously going to be a real challenge and not without conflict!

Dad's desire to succeed was fuelled by his earlier lack of opportunities;

nothing stood in his way once he had set his goals. Like many men of his generation he was largely self-taught, very adaptable and creative, but this package came with a considerable amount of eccentricity which would often embarrass his wife and, eventually, his children. Dad had acquired woodworking and metalworking skills, mainly through networking with experts. He made a lot of my early toys and a lot of the furniture for the marital home, a police house in Uppermill. Although basically a shy man, he had spent hours in a furniture shop in Huddersfield pretending to be interested in buying a bookcase and bureau whilst painstakingly measuring their dimensions, inspecting their dovetail joints and mentally dissecting the intricate details of a complex lid-folding mechanism in order to faithfully reproduce them back home in his own workshop without the benefit of any detailed drawings.

Dad would often berate himself for having to fathom everything out for himself without the basic knowledge which he claimed a grammar school education might have given him. He had an unblemished record in the police force and had been rapidly promoted to Sergeant, but he had no great career

Family snap, Uppermill, *c*.1948.
R. H. BARRACLOUGH.

ambitions beyond doing his duty to pay the bills and fund his obsessive hobbies. By the late 1940s Dad had become totally engaged in a new hobby, photography, which he was to pursue relentlessly for the next ten years, with his own blend of tenacity, sensitivity and artistic talent.

My parents' marriage was typical of their generation. Dad was the breadwinner and he decided on the general way the family should be managed, rather like a director of a small company. Like most women at the time, Mum had ceased work to become a full-time housewife when she had started a family. Mum was the homemaker and Dad's 'operational manager', looking after all the day-to-day tasks of running a household, including domestic chores, the operational budget and dealing with the children's daily needs. This arrangement usually functioned adequately, and there was rarely a need for the director to intervene on day-to-day operational matters. As far as bringing up their children was concerned, they were totally consistent in their approach to firm discipline, the application of Christian principles, and the teaching of right from wrong. Both my parents also believed that doing anything, particularly any activity related to 'getting on' in life, should be pursued with honest endeavour and 100 per cent effort. I soon became familiar with the exhortation, 'Get stuck in!' Boredom wasn't in my parents' vocabulary so I didn't know the meaning of the word either. The fruits of success from hard work had to be harvested in a reserved and self-effacing manner. Neither Mum nor Dad could tolerate loud boastful ('brussen') behaviour. In their younger days they had both won various awards and medals for a range of activities, but these had been stuffed away in a bedroom drawer, certainly never to be worn and not even proudly displayed to us at home. When I asked about them they were blandly dismissed as 'nowt', so that was that.

In the summer of 1949, Dad was posted to the Wakefield Headquarters of the West Riding of Yorkshire Constabulary as a member of its Advanced Driving School which had been formed in 1944 to train police drivers to the standards laid down by the Home Office. The Wakefield Driving School had developed a high reputation and trained many officers from across the country. In typical fashion Dad had taught himself to drive just before the introduction of the mandatory test. He told the tale of how as a single young man in April 1935, he had bought a second-hand Morris Minor in Wickersley for £25 and driven it home to Shelley without having been in a car before! By 1949 he had many years of practical experience with motor vehicles and was now recognised as an expert. I believe he saw the move to Wakefield as an opportunity, not for his own career particularly, but for his children's future. Mum saw it differently: this was an unwelcome change but something she just had to get on with.

Through the centuries, the *de facto* county town of Wakefield had exploited its natural resources and geographical location at the edge of the Pennine foothills on the River Calder. It had prospered from the corn trade and its thriving markets, including one of the largest cattle markets in the North of England. Drovers would bring beasts from miles away to the surrounding fields where the cattle would be grazed to fatten them up for the market. The district had at least three Graziers Inns. Coal had been mined for centuries, and Wakefield had also developed a key role in the textile trade, becoming the largest centre for wool stapling in the West Riding by around 1800. From the early eighteenth century Wakefield had become established as an important inland port, and the gradual construction of a more extensive canal system meant that raw materials such as wool, corn and lime could be transported into the industrial towns of Lancashire; coal, cloth and other manufactured goods could be carried by water as far as London. By the early nineteenth century, Wakefield had ceded its prominent position in textiles to the towns of Bradford, Huddersfield and Halifax, further west. It continued to develop as an industrial mining town exploiting its rich coal seams, and in the Victorian era had diversified to embrace other industries such as glass making, chemicals and dye manufacturing, engineering and iron foundries. Wakefield had also become one of the largest malt producing centres in England. By the middle of the nineteenth century, the availability of steam power had enabled Wakefield to regain a position in textile manufacture, notably in worsted spinning rather than cloth manufacture; in 1949 woollen mills were still a significant source of employment in the city. The railways also became hugely important by the second half of the nineteenth century, with Wakefield becoming a node in a complex rail transport network running the length and breadth of the country. Not surprisingly, the population grew rapidly in the Victorian age, and this increasingly busy and diverse town expanded into the surrounding areas: towards Outwood to the north; Eastmoor and Primrose Hill to the east; Belle Vue and Agbrigg to the south.

By 1949 Wakefield still had a relatively small population of about 60,000, but it had established itself as a seat of power and authority: in

1856 it had become the location for the headquarters of the new West Riding Constabulary, eight years after its own force had been formed; it had enjoyed city status since 1888 when the fourteenth century parish church of All Saints became a cathedral in a new diocese. A year later in 1889 Wakefield's status was further enhanced when it became the administrative centre of the West Riding County Council in the face of strong competition from its larger neighbour, Leeds. By the end of the nineteenth century, the capital of the West Riding of Yorkshire boasted appropriately bold examples of

Wakefield Cathedral. *WAKEFIELD EXPRESS.*

Victorian architecture to complement the earlier Greek Revival Georgian Court House in Wood Street, notably a grand County Hall, complete with an elegant dome, and an imposing Town Hall, complete with an ornate clock tower. The cathedral had the tallest spire in Yorkshire and was a landmark for miles around. Within the city there were also fine examples of elegant Georgian architecture in the town houses of former wealthy merchants, notably in Westgate and around St John's Square, where there was also a handsome Georgian church. By the early seventeenth century Wakefield had its own House of Correction, which eventually became Wakefield prison, within Victorian buildings close to the city centre. South of the city centre stood Wakefield's only surviving chantry chapel, the tiny St Mary's, built as part of a medieval bridge on the River Calder, originally one of four chapels standing at the principal entrances to the town. It was now one of only four surviving chantry chapels in the whole country. Further south in the district of Sandal, the stone ruins of the thirteenth century Sandal Castle were awaiting serious excavation, perhaps to reveal more about its role in the Battle of Wakefield in 1460 when Richard, Duke of

York, had met his death in the Wars of the Roses. Nearly five hundred years later, Lancastrians were still unpopular in this part of the world, largely as a result of an intense rivalry in various other 'Wars of the Roses', i.e. sporting contests such as cricket.

The move from Uppermill to Wakefield on 14 June 1949 seemed like a move to a different planet, despite being within the West Riding of Yorkshire and less than 30 miles away. Shortly after we arrived in Wakefield, HRH Princess Elizabeth and the Duke of Edinburgh visited the city and the nearby Yorkshire Show at Lupset on the 27 July. I cannot remember joining the crowds in Wood Street and nearby streets of the city centre to welcome the royal party, but my sister can. Apparently, Dad knew the best place to stand, since his police duties included escorting royalty and he had inside information on the planned route of the cavalcade.

Wakefield had virtually full employment in 1949 and offered many different types of work, especially for men. Typical of the times, opportunities

Dad (right) and his boss, John Morton of the West Riding Constabulary stand to attention for Royal Escort duty in *c.*1949. The car is a post-war (*c.*1947) Mk IV Jaguar, with front-opening 'suicide doors' but without Jaguar's 'leaping cat' bonnet mascot – at that time an optional 'extra'. R. H. BARRACLOUGH.

One of the many collieries in the Wakefield District, Parkhill. CITY OF WAKEFIELD MDC LIBRARIES PHOTOGRAPHIC COLLECTION.

for women were somewhat more restricted, although there was plenty of work in the textile mills and as clerks and secretaries in numerous offices of both local government and the professions such as law. Coal mining and its related industries were the core activities of the area, with the city encircled by the winding gear of many collieries in the outlying districts, now tunnelling for coal beneath the city itself. The National Coal Board, NCB, had been formed by the Labour government in 1946 and Wakefield would soon be the administrative Headquarters of NCB Area 7 with offices in Newton Hill, north of the city.

Coal mining was supported by an infrastructure of local heavy engineering industries manufacturing a variety of robust tools and equipment to mine, convey and transport coal. Prominent amongst these were the British Jeffrey Diamond Company, manufacturers of coal cutting tools, and Richard Sutcliffe Ltd., manufacturers of gigantic material handling conveyors.

Wakefield was also home to many other engineering industries. Notable amongst these were world leading enterprises created by Victorian entrepreneurs such as Joseph P. Rhodes in the field of machinery for sheet metal working, and Edward Green who had patented his famous fuel economisers, which used the exhaust gases from boiler heaters to pre-heat the water. The Spencer Wire Company Ltd. was busily making iron, steel, copper and aluminium wire; the Wakefield branch of Williams & Womersleys Ltd. manufactured specialist machines and power transmissions; Slater and Crabtree Ltd. made press tools. Amongst the major textile manufacturers were: M. P. Stonehouse Ltd., Alfred Hayley & Co., Harrap Brothers (Sirdar Wools Ltd.), Harold Holdsworth & Co., George Lee & Sons and Patons & Baldwins. Breweries were prominent amongst a range of other local industries. There was plenty of work in Wakefield's construction industry following the Second World War, especially in housing. A new power station was also being planned for Wakefield following the nationalisation of the electricity supply in 1947.

The service industry provided many jobs in the retail and transport sectors. There were many bus companies servicing Wakefield by 1949 but the main operator in and around the city was the West Riding Automobile Company which, in 1950, would become the country's largest independent operator by taking over the business of J. Bullock & Sons, based in nearby Featherstone. Green and cream-lined single and double-decker buses, mainly Leyland and Guy types, connected Wakefield to outlying towns and villages, whilst red buses serviced more local routes. The latter had been purchased to replace the local trams in 1932, and by 1949 a swish new fleet of some fifty-five bright-red and cream-lined AEC Regent III double-deckers was running regularly in and around the city. A number 10 connected the city with Leeds and Sandal on a north–south route; a number 20 connected the city with Ossett to the northwest and Agbrigg to the southeast. These had been the two main tram routes established in 1904 by the Wakefield City and District Light Railway Company, which was acquired by the Yorkshire (West Riding) Electric Tramways Company in 1905. The red buses were distinguished by a wide side entrance with a central grab pole and twin staircases to the front and rear of the top deck; the green double-deckers had a normal rear corner entrance and single stairway to the top deck.

An AEC Regent III West Riding bus, BHL 902, heads towards Westgate End, Wakefield, with Westgate Station's clock tower in the background. Photo taken in the 1960s. COPYRIGHT AND COURTESY OF THE JOHN BANKS COLLECTION.

Many of the local West Riding buses were garaged at their largest depot, in Belle Isle, south of the city on the A61 Barnsley Road. This was originally a tram depot built in 1904, generating its own electricity from steam-fired generators using boilers fed with water from the nearby River Calder, and a fuel economiser supplied by E. Green & Sons. Congestion of the streets from parked buses was becoming a problem in 1949 and a new bus station would soon open in 1952 next to the Bull Ring in the city centre at a cost of £60,000.

Wakefield's complex railway network was now under the new, nationalised British Railways organisation. One of the largest engine sheds in the North of England was located in Belle Vue, southeast of the city, and there were two main line railway stations within the city itself: Westgate Station, servicing north–south traffic on the former London and North Eastern Railway (LNER) line; Wakefield Kirkgate Station handling east–west traffic on the former London Midland & Scottish (LMS) line,

Picking rhubarb in the dark forcing sheds. WAKEFIELD COUNCIL MUSEUM COLLECTION.

originally known as the Lancashire and Yorkshire Railway (LYR). In addition to the normal movement of people and goods, particularly coal, a special train would regularly travel to London and the South laden with 'forced rhubarb', a succulent delicacy grown indoors in damp, dark sheds in a huge area known as the Rhubarb Triangle between Wakefield, Morley and Leeds.

New shops were soon to be built around a refurbished Bull Ring in the city centre, more modern and fashionable than the corner shops in the outlying districts which catered for normal day-to-day needs. Of course, there was no shortage of post offices in local communities, which also had a proliferation of fish and chip shops, the only providers of 'takeaway' food, wrapped in copious amounts of newspaper.

There had been relatively little Second World War bomb damage in the city, apart from some areas to the south, in Belle Vue and Thornes, where six people had been killed. A number of housing estates had been built

An early 1950s photo of new shops in the Bull Ring, and the new Bus Station.
WAKEFIELD COUNCIL MUSEUM COLLECTION.

before the war on the outskirts of the city in Lupset, Eastmoor and parts of Portobello but, like most parts of the country, there was an urgent housing shortage as a result of the post-war baby boom. Many of the older houses lacked adequate facilities, as we were soon to find out. Owner occupation was still quite rare; most occupants paid rent of some form.

The 1944 Butler Education Act had set the standard for state education in the country, particularly by raising the school leaving age to fifteen and creating the requirement for three types of secondary schools, freely available to all children but entered by a selection process. Wakefield met these requirements in offering secondary modern, grammar and technical schools within its catchment area. Entry into the three grammar schools in Wakefield was determined by the competitive eleven plus scholarship selection process. The all-boys grammar school had been established in 1591 by Royal Charter in the reign of Queen Elizabeth I and still bore her name as the Queen Elizabeth Grammar School, known locally as

'QEGS'. The all-girls Wakefield Girls' High School was formed in 1878 in response to the growing movement demanding the social and educational emancipation of women. A third grammar school, Thornes House Secondary (Grammar) School was formed much later in 1921 and educated boys and girls separately until 1941 when it became co-educational. Thornes House was the city grammar school supported by the local authority, catering for pupils who had passed the eleven plus examination. It had no fee paying pupils, unlike QEGS and Wakefield Girls' High School, which were Direct Grant Schools, funded by both the state and private fees. Private education was also available at the all-boys Silcoates School in Silcoates House, Wrenthorpe, which had been established as a grammar school for dissenters in 1820, and twelve years later as the Northern Congregational School, mainly for the sons of non-conformist ministers.

Unlike the centrally located QEGS and Wakefield Girls' High School, Thornes House Grammar School was based outside the city centre in an elegant, late eighteenth century Georgian mansion set in Thornes Park, adjoined by Clarence and Holmfield parks, in a vast garden of pleasure. Here, the citizens of Wakefield could enjoy playgrounds, playing fields, beautiful gardens, a lake, many trees, shrubberies and brass band performances in a fine bandstand within about a mile of the city centre. An imposing statue of Queen Victoria was soon to be removed from its prominent position in the middle of the Bull Ring in the city centre to a rather inconspicuous site on the edge of the park near Denby Dale Road, where she would have looked even more disconsolate if the council's original plan for Thornes Park had come to fruition. On purchasing Thornes House and its 112 acre estate for £18,500 in 1919, Wakefield County Borough Council had planned a huge estate of some 750 council houses for most of the land, beyond the twenty acres needed for the new secondary school. However, the plan foundered when the Borough Council was unable to obtain support from the Housing Commissioner who had expressed concerns at the money already spent on the development of the Portobello housing estate! Thornes Park opened officially in 1924, thereby stitching the final patch to the green quilt of Wakefield Park, started by Clarence Park in 1893, then Holmfield Park in

1919. Meanwhile, other options for a housing estate had to be considered, notably in the nearby Lupset area, further west.

There was a variety of places for recreation and entertainment in 'the Merrie City' of Wakefield. Theatre had a long history since the days when 'Mystery Plays' were performed in the streets hundreds of years previously but by 1949 only one live theatre, the Essoldo (formerly the Opera House) in Westgate had survived. There was a much greater demand for the more popular 'silver screen', provided by ten cinemas in and around the city, of which the Carlton, Playhouse, and the Palace in Belle Vue dated back to the early part of the century, before the Great War of 1914–18. The most modern cinemas were the Regal in the city centre, built in 1935, and the Savoy built in early 1936 to service the new Lupset housing estate on the outskirts of the city. There had always been intense competition amongst cinema owners for the cinema-going public, and in 1949 little heed was paid to the imminent competition from a different medium, television, which was already available in the Home Counties but not the North of England. That was soon to change.

Wakefield had a particularly high density of pubs, many with men-only bars. Dance bands played live music in the local commercial dancehall, the Embassy Ballroom; dances were also held in Unity Hall and the Music Saloon. Swimming was a popular post-war pastime in Wakefield, and the city had two pools of contrasting vintage and style: the old Victorian baths in Almshouse Lane, affectionately known locally as 't'owd' baths; and the rather swish Art Deco style baths which had been built in 1938 just beyond the Regal cinema in Sun Lane, simply known as 't'new' baths.

Keen hobbyists could benefit from a range of clubs and associations. Dad joined the Wakefield Camera Club and soon started to network with other members and to enter its various competitions and exhibitions. As might be expected in a tough mining area, the fine arts were rather inconspicuous, although Wakefield did have an art gallery in Wentworth Terrace and a museum in the park at Holmfield, by now commonly known as Holmfield House. The area had produced two sculptors: Wakefield-born Barbara Hepworth and Castleford-born Henry Moore. By 1949 they had

Wood Street, Wakefield, 27 July 1949. HRH Princess Elizabeth and Prince Philip listen to the choir of Thornes House Grammar School from the balcony of the Town Hall. THORNES HOUSE SCHOOL WEBSITE.

both earned an international reputation for their abstract art, although it would be fair to say that their work was little understood or appreciated by most folk of the Merrie City at that time. By contrast, music thrived in various forms, particularly choral singing and local performances by the Yorkshire Symphony Orchestra. During her visit in the summer of 1949 HRH Princess Elizabeth had made a special request to hear the choir of Thornes House Grammar school whose command performance in Wood Street was said to be one of the highlights of her West Riding tour.

Many sports were played and watched, but cricket and rugby league were, by far, the most popular. In the summer cricket was played with intense passion in the back streets, in school playing fields and in many local grounds of the local amateur leagues and semi-professional district leagues of the Yorkshire League. The pinnacle of this activity was the Yorkshire county team whose players were worshipped like gods. Dad and Uncle Harry would adopt an almost religious tone when describing the exploits of their childhood heroes, Wilfred Rhodes and George Hirst, cricket legends of Yorkshire and England, both from the Kirkheaton District of Huddersfield. The local Wakefield hero of the same generation had been David Denton, an attacking batsman during his heyday as an England cricketer before the Great War and a Yorkshire county player until 1920. By 1949 the local hero was Johnny Wardle who was worshipped as much for his Yorkshire wit as his ability to fool opposing batsmen with his cunning left-arm spin bowling. The most fervently worshipped of the modern gods in the county team was opening batsman Len Hutton, who was still the holder of the world record score of 364, clocked up in the Oval Test match against the Australians in 1938. However, by its own high standards and the high expectations of its keen followers, the Yorkshire county team had only a moderately successful season in the summer of 1949 when it had to share the county championship with those 'southerners' from Middlesex. Meanwhile, the competitive lower league system continued to produce new talent. In the summer of 1949 two eighteen-year-old youngsters dropped off its endless conveyor belt to make their debuts in Yorkshire's first XI without undue fuss and ceremony: Frederick Sewards Trueman and Dennis Brian Close. In his first season Close not only did the double of scoring a 1,000 runs and taking 100 wickets, he also became the youngest cricketer to play for England.

Unlike many neighbouring towns and cities, Wakefield did not support a professional association football team, and soccer was not usually played in the local schools. Thornes House Grammar School was one notable exception and there were also many amateur soccer teams in the locality. Wakefield had started to become a rugby stronghold in 1873 when a group of young men from the Holy Trinity Church in George Street formed the Wakefield Trinity club. Initially, rugby was just one of many sporting activities of this group of young men and they were not the only rugby club in the locality, but gradually they developed a fine rugby tradition throughout the land and became known for their high standard of play and sportsmanship. In the early days the Trinity played on various fields, including Heath Common and a field behind the Alexandra public house in Belle Vue, southeast of the city. In the 1878/79 season they played their first game on a field next to St Catherine's School and St Catherine's Church in Belle Vue. This site became their headquarters and permanent home when in 1895 the Wakefield Trinity Football and Athletic Club passed a

One of the earliest photos of a Wakefield Trinity squad of players, about two years after the club's formation in 1873. WAKEFIELD COUNCIL MUSEUM COLLECTION.

resolution to buy the ground, which was eventually purchased in 1896. The ground was gradually developed and by 1898 had terracing for up to 12,000 spectators, a wooden grandstand and a track around the rugby pitch to cater for cycling events. In 1895 Wakefield Trinity was one of the twenty two founding members of the Northern Union which severed links with the amateur Rugby Football Union following a bitter dispute over payments for players. At that time, most northern working class players needed 'broken time' payments from their clubs to compensate for lost earnings from their regular jobs, particularly when playing matches away from home. The strictly amateur Rugby Football Union could not tolerate the encroachment of professionalism and an acrimonious split occurred.

Professional rugby did not happen overnight but it eventually became official, and rugby league gradually evolved into a different game from the strictly amateur code of rugby union, with different laws and fewer players per team (thirteen compared with fifteen in rugby union). By 1949, rugby league was widely played at amateur level in the district and in most junior and secondary modern schools, although QEGS and the private school Silcoates continued to play rugby union. The local district supported two rugby union clubs, Wakefield and Sandal. Keen supporters of the Trinity in 1949 were still talking about the dramatic 13–12 defeat of Lancashire rivals, Wigan, in the first post-war Rugby League Challenge Cup Final at London's Wembley Stadium in 1946, when the Trinity captain, Billy Stott, had won the game by kicking a long range penalty goal with only 90 seconds of the game remaining. Few people in Wakefield either knew or cared that their hero Stott was actually an Oldham-born Lancastrian. By 1949 there was less to cheer about when Wigan defeated Trinity 37–2 in the second round of the Rugby League Challenge Cup. The Trinity team was now entering a rather lean period.

It was too early to judge the achievements of the ambitious National Health Service (NHS) which was only one year old in 1949, although some statistics did not auger well for Wakefield at that time. According to an NHS Patients' Guide, published in 1948, Wakefield had only eighteen general practitioners (GPs) which meant that it had an exceedingly high average number of patients per GP (3,513) – the so called 'list' – much higher than the average list for the whole of England and Wales (2,461), and those of comparable industrial areas such as Leeds (2,438) and Bradford (2,610). The non-industrial area of Harrogate had an average list of 1,351. Hospital care was in better shape in Wakefield, which had three general hospitals: The County General, Clayton and Pinderfields, now within the new NHS scheme. There was also a maternity hospital in Manygates and a mental hospital, Stanley Royd, which had been established in 1818 as the West Riding Pauper Lunatic Asylum.

In 1949 treatments for many illnesses were still very crude, and the use of drugs to treat diseases was still in its infancy. The application of a hot poultice seemed to be the cure for many illnesses, especially anything relating to the respiratory system! Penicillin and streptomycin were available but their interaction with the body was little understood. However, there had been a post-war boom in the development of new drugs and, with costs increasing, the Labour government agreed to the principle of prescription charges in 1949, although this policy was not actually implemented until later in the fifties.

The average life expectancy in the UK for males of my father's age, forty-one, in 1949 was a further thirty-one years, but it was probably much lower in Wakefield. Respiratory diseases such as pneumonia, bronchitis, whooping cough and tuberculosis (TB) were still quite common, especially in this mining community. Although the number of deaths nationally from these diseases was in gradual decline by 1949, deaths from cancer, especially lung cancer, were continuing to increase. Outbreaks of poliomyelitis – often known as infantile paralysis because of the vulnerability of young children to the virus – were occurring throughout the country in the late forties without any prospect of a vaccine, which would take a further six years to develop. Contraceptive pills, pacemakers and vaccines against measles were also unheard of in 1949.

Of course, hindsight is the only exact science; most people were blissfully ignorant of the limitations imposed on their health and well-being. It was supposedly an austere period but people were just getting on with their lives and grateful that the whole country was gradually recovering from the war effort. I didn't know at the time, but I had been fortunate to move to Wakefield, a city which provided many diverse opportunities for a young boy, although they were within a tough, uncompromising and highly competitive environment.

References and Further Reading

Not so Merry Wakefield, Kate Taylor, ISBN 1-903425-72-7, Wharncliffe Books, 2005.

The Making of Wakefield, 1801–1900, Kate Taylor, ISBN-978-1-845630-78-2, Wharncliffe Books, 2008.

Theatres and Cinemas of the Wakefield District, Kate Taylor, ISBN 978-0-7524-4281-3, Tempus Publishing Ltd., 2007.

Wakefield District Heritage, compiled by Kate Taylor, published by Wakefield European Architectural Heritage Year Committee, 1976, Wakefield Library.

The National Health Service: Patients' Guide, Ministry of Health, London: HMSO, 1948.

West Riding Automobile Co. Ltd., David W. Allen, ISBN 1-8987432-95-3 Venture Publications Ltd., Glossop, Derbyshire.

Thornes Park, Richard Bell, ISBN 1-902467-03-5, Willow Island Editions, 1999.

Aspects of Wakefield: Discovering Local History, edited by Kate Taylor, ISBN 1-871647-41-X, Wharncliffe Publishing, 1998.

CHAPTER TWO

Introduction to Belle Vue
and 52 Regent Street, circa 1950

Belle Vue is about a mile south east of Wakefield city centre, but it seemed a lot further than that in 1950, and we usually travelled home on one of the regular West Riding buses servicing the outlying districts. Occasionally, it would be a long-distance green bus such as a number 85 from Holmfirth, via Wakefield, to Pontefract, but it was usually the regular number 20 red bus from Ossett to Agbrigg, a district adjoining Belle Vue further south, which in the past had been part of the former meeting place of a huge wapentake, dating back to the Danelaw when the Vikings ruled this part of the country.

The bus would trundle down Kirkgate, past the numerous pubs and shops, towards the railway bridge advertising a local drinks manufacturer, Crystal Spring Ltd., in huge lettering. On emerging from the gloom under Kirkgate railway bridge, the road continued over a wide bridge spanning the River Calder. This 'new bridge' had retained its name following construction in 1933 to relieve the nearby medieval Wakefield Bridge, on which stood the tiny Chantry Chapel. Although the new bridge was a bland, modern, concrete structure compared with the narrow stone bridge, its construction had been essential to cope with the increasing road traffic to and from the south of Wakefield, even in pre-war days.

The Chantry Chapel on the old Wakefield Bridge – used to promote Wakefield Camera Club in the early fifties. R. H. Barraclough.

The Chantry Chapel stood rather forlornly to the side of the modern bridge, yet it also appeared proudly defiant of all the industrialisation around it. On some days, white, frothy soap suds from up-stream effluent would be swept up by the breeze from the nearby river weir and dance around the bridge and chapel, giving the whole area a rather surreal appearance. Some locals said that the soapsuds could only be seen on Tuesdays, the day after Wakefield housewives did their weekly wash – because it took a day for all the soapy water to drain into the river!

Beyond the south side of the new bridge, previously known as Bridge End, the road forked into the A61, Barnsley Road, running almost due south, and the A638, Doncaster Road, running approximately southeast. The White Bear hotel stood exactly at the road fork and was a well known local landmark. Its name was somewhat of a misnomer: in the past the hotel building had obviously been rendered white, but the passage of time and the smoke-filled atmosphere had taken their toll, rendering the building with a distinctly grey and grimy hue.

The Graziers on Doncaster Road at the junction with Denmark Street, Belle Vue.
MARTIN WRIGHT.

Beyond the White Bear, our bus would follow the Doncaster Road over a bridge spanning Fall Ings Cut, past Sugar Lane which forked off to the right due south, with Wakefield Cemetery on its left. The Graziers hotel and Denmark Street on the right hand side of Doncaster Road gave way to a cluster of shops and buildings, indicating that we had entered the district of Belle Vue. We would alight at the Alexandra Hotel, known locally as t'Alec, at the far end of the shops on the left hand side.

The number 20 bus would continue its journey down Doncaster Road for about 500 yards before turning sharp right into the straight Agbrigg Road, past the hastily constructed semi-detached houses on the left hand side, known locally as the 'cardboard villas'. Agbrigg had several streets feeding into its main artery, which also had numerous corner shops and terraced houses along its length. After about 600 yards, the number 20 bus would eventually terminate at yet another famous pub landmark, the Duke of York Hotel (t'Duke) opposite a small piece of ground known as Agbrigg Common, where there was a funfair every autumn.

The Alexandra on Doncaster Road at the junction with Clarion Street, in a modern setting of 'street furniture'. BRIAN DAVIDSON.

The Duke of York at the junction of Belle Vue Road and Agbrigg Road. MARTIN WRIGHT.

Doncaster Road, and particularly t'Alec, defined a boundary in Belle Vue which had more than a whiff of class snobbery about it. The area 'back o' t'Alec' (north and east) was generally seen to be a less desirable place to live by those with residences on the other (south) side. There had been some Victorian housing developments 'back o' t'Alec', but in 1919 Wakefield's first corporation houses had been built there, around Elm Tree Street. 'Back o' t'Alec' was also industrialised. It was home to railway engine sheds when the Yorkshire and Lancashire Railway Company moved their facility from an area near Kirkgate Station to Belle Vue in 1893. Originally a dead-end, ten-road shed, the LMS railway made it a through-shed and added further modifications, including a 70-foot turntable, coaling and ash disposal facilities, and staff accommodation. Belle Vue was now home to one of the largest engine sheds in the North of England, and after the 1948 nationalisation of the railways, it was allocated 140 locomotives by British Railways. By the 1950s there were around 700 local men employed in the Belle Vue sheds, including several hundred footplate workers, (drivers and stokers) around 200 shed staff, and 35 men in management and administration.

Belle Vue Engine Sheds and terraced houses 'back o' t'Alec'. Steve Armitage.

There were also hundreds of local men employed at the two main factories 'back o' t'Alec': Slater and Crabtree's, and Joseph Rhodes Ltd., the latter having moved to an eight acre site in Elm Tree Street in 1921. By 1950 Joe Rhodes was enjoying a post-war boom in the manufacture of sheet metal presses for export throughout the world, fully justifying the company trademark of a Colossus.

I am sure Mum took great solace from the fact that we lived on the 'right side' of Belle Vue, which had a lot of its origins in the late nineteenth century Victorian period. Our home was about halfway up Regent Street, south of the junction with Oxford Street, but any similarity with the street owned by the Crown Estate of His Majesty, King George VI in the heart of the nation's capital was in name only. Regent Street, Belle Vue, had one corner shop at the junction with Oxford Street and joined the south side of Doncaster Road at an acute angle below the bus stops. We would usually take a short-cut home by immediately crossing Doncaster Road and nipping up a narrow passage, known as Round Street, which led into Oxford Street. Alternatively, if Doncaster Road was busy, we might cross higher up via a zebra crossing to an unmade dirt road which also provided access to some of Belle Vue's key amenities: the blackened stone building of St Catherine's Church on the left, an array of turnstile entrance doors to the Trinity rugby ground straight ahead, and the dirty brick buildings of the Conservative Club and the Palace cinema on the right. As we carefully picked our way to Oxford Street, via the short, narrow dirt path between the Conservative Club and the entrance to the Palace, we would ignore the beckoning smiles of film stars on the tired, ragged posters peeling off the cinema's walls; it was far more important to focus on side-stepping the collection of puddles and dog turds which usually lay in wait for unsuspecting pedestrians. From Oxford Street we would turn left into Regent Street, towards number 52 on the right hand side.

Properties in Regent Street, Oxford Street and around Denmark Street had been built in the 1870s in what was originally known as 'the Great Old Field near Quaker Houses in the Parish of Sandal Magna', where cattle were grazed next to the Graziers inn before being taken to the large market

A pre-Second World War photo of Oxford Street, Belle Vue taken from the top of Denmark Street showing Wesley Street Chapel on the right, and the junctions with Back Regent Street and Regent Street in the distance. Note the gas lamps and iron railings. City of Wakefield MDC Libraries Photographic Collection.

in the city. The streets consisted of rows of brick-built terraced houses of varying design, some of which were set back from the road by a few feet of tiny front gardens. Some of the grander terraced houses at the top of Regent Street had elegant front bay windows and steps up to the front door; our house lower down had a plain front window and only one step to the front door. Many houses, including ours, had been graced with decorative railings on the low front wall, but these had been removed when iron was desperately needed by the country during the Second World War. Evidence of the crude way in which these elegant railings had been hastily severed from the wall was still painfully clear.

The largest manifestation of Victorian Belle Vue was Wakefield Cemetery, which had been the private estate of local mill owners, the Naylors of Belle Vue House. The next owner of the property, Sir Lionel Pilkington, demolished the house and for £5,000 sold the land to Wakefield Corporation for use as a much needed cemetery where the first burial took place in 1859. Twin chapels of rest had been designed and constructed in the middle of the cemetery, one for the Established Church and the other for Nonconformists. By 1950 this blackened stone edifice dominated the vast twenty acre L-shaped site, bounded on the east by the terraced houses south of Doncaster Road, and by a red brick wall on the west side, running the full length of Sugar Lane towards Belle Vue Road and t'Duke pub in Agbrigg.

The south side of Belle Vue was the focus for entertainment and worship; there were no large industries here. Sometimes the margins between entertainment and worship became rather blurred. For about nine months of the year the Wakefield Trinity rugby ground

The twin chapels of rest, Wakefield Cemetery. CITY OF WAKEFIELD MDC LIBRARIES PHOTOGRAPHIC COLLECTION.

would regularly attract thousands of local worshippers of professional rugby league, who also demanded entertainment for their entrance fee. The Palace was an early purpose-built cinema established in 1914. It was initially known as the Trinity Picture House, presumably because of its close proximity to the Trinity rugby ground, but by 1950 everyone knew the Palace as t'Spit or t'Spit and Whistle, derived from notices in the cinema forbidding spitting and whistling!

St Catherine's Church School had been built in 1871 as a mission room for St Helen's Church, Sandal, and was used as both a school and a place of worship before a separate church building was erected nearby on Doncaster Road, in response to the supposed needs of the growing population of Belle Vue. The stone building of St Catherine's Church had been designed in the Early English style by Wakefield architect, William Watson, and was consecrated in 1876 by the Bishop of Ripon after the foundation stone was laid by the Mayor of Wakefield in 1875. A mission room associated with St Catherine's Church had also been built 'back o' t'Alec' in Clarion Street and had provided services since around 1890. Round the corner from us, at the junction of Oxford and Wesley Streets, a Wesleyan Chapel had been

St Catherine's Church, Doncaster Road, Belle Vue. St Catherine's Church.

built in 1870, and there was also a Victorian Methodist Chapel along the north side of Doncaster Road, at the junction with Dunbar Street.

The housing around Regent Street, Denmark Street, Oxford Street, and the churches, chapels, Trinity ground and cemetery, are all readily seen on the 1893 Ordnance Survey map of Wakefield (South). By contrast, the 1854 map of the same area shows none of these developments; only a few large houses can be seen, notably Belle Vue House, the Quaker Houses, Maybush House, the Graziers and a public house on the site of the Alexandra.

Regent Street ended at Maybush House which in 1950 housed some of Wakefield's rare GPs. Dr Donald Downie, a Scot, had lived and practised there for about thirty years and by 1950 was close to retirement. Dr Alexander Jacob and our family GP, a young blond-haired Scot, called Dr Douglas Gavin Scott, also practised from this grand house, which was some 150 yards from our house, set in its own grounds and suitably well hidden from its neighbours. Agbrigg, to the south, was readily accessible via a public footpath through the grounds of Maybush House. The straight 350 yard journey from the bottom of Regent Street on Doncaster Road to Maybush House represented a sort of linear progression up the social ladder, from the working-classes of lower Regent Street, to the upper-working/aspiring lower-middle-classes of middle Regent Street (us), to the middle-classes in their modern semi-detached houses at the top end of Regent Street, to the doctors ensconced in Maybush House. And, if Dr Scott's profession and house did not set him apart, then his car certainly did. The number of private cars in Belle Vue could probably be counted on the fingers of one hand in 1950. Dad's job no longer required him to have a police car on a regular basis and he travelled to Wakefield on the bus like most people who worked in the city. Apart from the odd wagon and van delivering to local shops, most of the traffic was confined to Doncaster Road. Dr Scott's huge black Ford Pilot limousine attracted a lot of attention as it swept out of the grounds of Maybush House into the unmade part of Regent Street in a cloud of dust, hurtling past our house at speeds which Dad always grumbled were far too dangerous. But he never said anything. After all, one needed 'to keep in' with the doctor.

Our house had been built in about 1879 to the same design as about eight others in the terrace to the south of Oxford Street. It had been acquired recently by the West Riding Constabulary as living accommodation for its staff and we were its latest tenants, following on from various occupants, including a few railway men. There was little to distinguish number 52 from its neighbours, apart from the etched pattern of the two upper glazed panels of the front door, which always imparted a characteristically loud cracking noise when the door was closed. Mum always worried that I would break the glass, but I never did. Diffuse daylight from the front door, and artificial light from an electric light bulb dangling from the ceiling on a thin twin flex cable, were both incapable of dispelling the gloom in the narrow front entrance, made worse by the dark brown 'Lincrusta' wallpaper which looked as if it had been there since the house was built. It was not a welcoming hall – just a means of entering the rest of the house.

Beyond the middle of the hall, on the left-hand side, there was a door into t'front room which was always kept closed; it didn't have a 'no entry' sign, but that was the intention. At the far end, on the left of the passage, a steep, narrow flight of stairs led to a small landing. This landing provided access to my parents' front bedroom, as well as my sister's bedroom and my tiny bedroom, both over the living room and with windows looking out on to the back yard. Above the bedrooms there was an attic, reached by a

Doncaster Road cuts through Belle Vue, past the Alexandra at the junction with Clarion Street (bottom left), past Elm Tree Street and 'back o' t'Alec' (left), past Agbrigg and Agbrigg Road further south, (top right). Although this aerial photo was taken in the 1960s, it still shows many fifties landmarks: the zebra crossing leading to St Catherine's Church and t'Spit cinema in front of Wakefield Trinity's rugby ground, with St Catherine's Church School behind its long East Stand. Regent Street runs from bottom left to mid right, crossing Oxford Street, past our house and Wakefield Cemetery (right) as far as Maybush House. Belle Vue Engine sheds are just visible in the top left corner. COPYRIGHT © ENGLISH HERITAGE, NATIONAL MONUMENTS RECORD AEROFILMS COLLECTION.

wooden stairway just outside my bedroom door. Downstairs, a door at the end of the passage opened onto the square-shaped living room, the largest room in the house. In the far left corner of the living room a door led to the narrow scullery which projected out from the room. Since it was the only place in the house with running hot and cold water, the scullery served as kitchen, bathroom and washroom, but there was no lavatory in the house.

The outside lavatory was housed in its own little brick building at the bottom of the back yard, next to the dustbin, both approached via a slabbed path leading from the back door. In wet weather, care had to be taken to avoid brushing against a lilac tree which had been strategically planted next to the lavatory entrance. However, its role as an air freshener could only be enjoyed for a few weeks in the spring; during the rest of the year it always seemed to be so wet that it fulfilled the role of shower quite well. The outer wall of the lavatory building formed part of the rear boundary of the property, alongside a tall back gate which opened onto Back Regent Street. I don't think I was particularly unhappy with our new abode, but Mum reflected that our nice police house in Uppermill was brand new circa 1937 with an upstairs bathroom, including a lavatory. Apparently, we had moved down in the world, but at least the house was on the right side of Doncaster Road!

Showing great fortitude following her initial disappointment, Mum had issued an enamelled potty, known as a po, for each bedroom, with the strict instruction that they should only be used for dire emergencies, and certainly never for 'number twos'. Fortunately, I never experienced the degree of urgency which might have tested the boundaries of this rather ambiguous set of instructions, even though I was scared to visit the lavatory in the dark: it did not have an electric light and was home to some rather large spiders. Mum did her best to make the lavatory clean and respectable, and the wooden pine lavatory seat was regularly scrubbed until it was nearly white. In order to make the lavatory experience as hygienic and pleasant as possible Mum even installed the latest technology: Izal Medicated Toilet Roll. Many folk in the area 'made do' with newspaper, torn into appropriately sized sheets and secured to the wall with a nail. Sometimes, shrieks could be heard from a nearby lavatory for emergency paper to be dispatched down the yard. This instruction was sometimes followed by further shrieks if that particular newspaper or comic was not deemed ready for the recycling process. Dad called the lavatory the 'Nessy', presumably derived from the word necessary. This was a more accurate descriptor than Mum's 'Privy'; private it certainly wasn't!

Actually, I was not particularly impressed by Mum's profligate approach. Izal Medicated Toilet Roll was less than paper-thin and readily tore at critical moments. It was also obvious, without knowing any physics, that the coefficient of friction of both the shiny side and the rough side was totally unsuitable to manage the job in hand. However, a fresh piece of Izal Medicated Toilet Roll paper made some interesting noises when tautly placed over a comb and blown. My friends and I had great fun playing tunes on these novel musical instruments, and when this craze was at its height I supplied all the kids in Regent Street with sheets of our lavatory paper, until the store manager of number 52 found out.

T'front room was redundant for about 364 days of the year. It had a fireplace for a coal fire but one was rarely lit, except perhaps for one or maybe two days around Christmas time when my aunts and uncles might visit. Apart from those special occasions, t'front room was virtually out of bounds for me. Of course, I would sneak in occasionally just to see if anything new had been installed, and to get an update on the progress of our social statement. I soon cottoned on to the fact that the whole point of a front room was to display the current state of family wealth, its history and respectability, including family photographs and records of distant places visited, preferably abroad. No matter where you were on this sliding scale of success, t'front room of most aspirants in the neighbourhood followed this general guideline.

The furnishings in t'front room were the smartest we owned. A pre-war three-piece suite (two armchairs and a two-seater settee), draped in white antimacassars, showed no signs of wear and occupied most of the available space in front of a non-existent fire. A display cabinet exhibited souvenir mugs from bygone coronations, as well as a range of wedding presents, including sherry glasses, and a complete tea service that, as far as I recall, were all there for display purposes only, never to be used. The mantelpiece was home to an array of miniature brass animals but the overall effect was spoiled because they were not to a uniform scale. Family photographs were carefully aligned on most available surfaces to face prospective viewers at the correct angle. A 1937 wedding photograph showed a young, thin, happy version of my mother, arm in arm with her man, whose other cupped hand attempted to conceal a much needed cigarette. Snaps of happy holidays on Blackpool beach had recorded uncles paddling in the sea with grey flannel trousers rolled up to their knees, and 'gallasses' (braces) hoisted over gleaming white shirts. My sister and I beamed from every surface in various poses and stages of childhood development. A model of Blackpool Tower and similar mementos from the distant Isle of Man completed the show.

But, apart from close family, there were very few onlookers. The vicar and doctor might be ushered in on those rare occasions when Mum declared that the living room was 'not fit to be seen', but friends and neighbours who were sufficiently close and confident enough to 'pop in' to a policeman's house were led straight into the living room, never t'front room. Perhaps keeping them guessing about the contents of t'front room was all part of a strange social game? After all, we had not seen theirs either. Even from the outside, it was impossible to see through the veil provided by net curtains in all the front windows down the street. Most people in the neighbourhood kept themselves to themselves; there was less association with neighbours than some historians would lead us to believe.

The living room was the warmest place in the house, but its temperature gradients were huge. A coal fire burned in the grate for most of the year except during the peak of summer; it was the focal point of the room. Lighting the fire would be Mum's routine task in the morning before the rest of us got up. A home-made hearth rug fashioned from clippings of differently coloured spare cloth and rags provided a place to loll in the warmth of the fire playing with my Dinky toys. The rug had an oily smell which reminded me of the inside of the weaving shed where my aunties worked; the rug's

Playing with Dinky Toys in the living room of 52 Regent Street, *c*.1950. R. H. BARRACLOUGH.

random mix of bright colours was a striking contrast to the pale brown, patterned linoleum which covered most of the floor. Mum would scrub the lino every Thursday, with occasional help from Elaine who by now was rapidly discovering the disadvantages of being a girl. Facing the fire were two easy chairs which were not specifically designated as parents' chairs but I rarely sat in them; they were certainly not as comfortable as the bouncy suite in t'front room.

The centre of the living room was dominated by a polished oak dining table and four oak dining chairs which had been bought from a proper furniture shop and were of good quality. Elaine and I would sometimes chase each other around this central island until Mum called a halt by threatening us with the 'strap', a piece of leather attached to Dad's old

Dad's 'office' – his home-made bureau and bookcase. R. H. BARRACLOUGH.

police truncheon which he no longer used. Fortunately, the mere threat of this punishment had the desired effect. We were rarely smacked by either parent. A threat from Mum, just a glare from dad, at most his raised voice, were usually enough to make us behave.

Dad's home-made oak bureau was the administrative centre of the household, where stationery and important papers were stored and where all correspondence and important business were attended to. This was Dad's 'office' and I was not allowed to enter but, of course, I would occasionally root around. Above the bureau, the family collection of literature was stacked in the matching home-made oak bookcase, which had hinged doors made of individual leaded lights, immaculately reproduced from the original design in the Huddersfield furniture shop. The house library contained a few novels by unknown authors and the odd classic, but most books related to more important practical matters such as needlework and home health. There was a very fat red dictionary which Dad would consult occasionally when drafting important letters. Issues of *Amateur Photographer* magazine were now starting to be collected and stored in the bookcase. By 1950 Dad had already converted the attic into a dark room for developing and printing his own photographs; later he would add a little studio with various spotlights and floodlights for indoor portraiture.

There were lots of knitting patterns around the living room, and always some article of knitwear under construction that could be worked on during a spare moment. If Mum wasn't cleaning, shopping or cooking she was knitting. Naturally, Elaine also became a high-speed knitter and, not to be left out, I nagged them to teach me as well. I managed to knit less than a quarter of a scarf, but was painfully slow and soon gave up.

We had a dark brown, upright Stainer piano with matching stool, the folding seat of which included storage for manuscripts of pre-war songs and ballads. *Francis and Day's 54th Album* contained Mum's favourite songs which Dad might be persuaded to play occasionally. More serious music such as Haydn's *Creation* and Dad's other classical music scores were kept in his home-made, polished oak music cabinet which, on the basis of its workmanship and occasional use, merited pride of place in t'front room. Elaine had started learning to play the piano but it was a brief and unhappy relationship. A series of false notes, a loud crash of the hinged keyboard lid and a tearful squawk would usually herald the end of a short practice session. Elaine soon gave up the piano in preference to ballet and tap dancing classes run by a young lady, Audrey Stephenson, who lived locally at number 29 Maybush Road. The dancing classes were held in a room above the Liberal Club on Doncaster Road, and the group would perform at various shows in

Members of Audrey Stephenson's dancing class perform at Thornes vicarage in the early fifties. R. H. BARRACLOUGH.

Wakefield dressed in fancy costumes made by Audrey's mother, May, funded by weekly contributions from members of the class.

The piano was on the back living room wall between the hall entrance door and the door to the cellar head. Some foodstuffs might have been kept cool down in the cellar but its main function was to store coal supplied from an outside chute in Regent Street. A tall cone-shaped metal coal scuttle was used to transfer coal from the cellar to the living room fire. A gas meter was in the far corner of the cellar and this had to be regularly fed with shilling coins (bobs), kept in a jam jar at the top of the cellar steps. A gradually diminishing flame on the cooker would be the signal to rush down into the cellar to feed the meter with a bob coin before the gas went out. Needless to say, Mum managed the cash flow so that the jam jar was never empty, thereby avoiding a financial enquiry from the director of the household.

The HMV wireless set was the entertainment centre of the household, positioned under the living room window. It was a late 1930s/early 1940s table-top model, encased in a beautiful shiny walnut cabinet, and the source of great wonder and amazement to me. I would often peer through the curved, interlaced wire speaker grille to try and understand what magic lay inside, but there was nothing really discernible at all. Squinting through the back I could see orange things glowing, like dimly lit light bulbs – I did not know what a valve was at the time, neither did I know that the thing that would eventually replace them had already been invented. When the set was switched on it would take almost half a minute for the valves to warm up before the crescendo of a loud hum gradually gave way to faint speech or to music.

Sometimes, when my parents were absent from the living room, I would try to tune into one of the distant foreign stations indicated on the dimly lit tuning indicator screen, but I never heard a word from places such as Hilversum or Warsaw, although there were plenty of cat-like yowls of variable frequency, and noises that sounded like distant hailstones on a tin roof. Dad's sensitive ear would instantly recognise that 'someone had been fiddling with the wireless again', and with expert precision he would ceremoniously carry out the procedure of tuning the wireless back to its original setting, by turning the dial very slowly with his right hand while his large left ear was flattened against the speaker grille to detect the exact position at which the maximum desired signal was being received with the minimum of noise. As with all procedures requiring a steady hand and maximum mental concentration, tuning the wireless could not be accomplished without a smoke of his pipe, which protruded from his mouth at an angle that did not compromise any aspect of the whole operation. Every syllable of the news on the *Home Service* or Wilfred Pickles and the contestants in *Have a Go* on the *Light Programme* had to be captured with the minimum of ambiguity.

In modern parlance the scullery had a 'multi functional role'. However, there were no modern gadgets such as a vacuum cleaner, refrigerator or washing machine to accommodate, only a gas cooker, sink and bath. Limited amounts of food, cooking materials and utensils were kept in wooden cupboards and on shelves; there were no 'storage units'. A huge bath was cleverly hidden below a large, hinged wooden board which could be held upright by a hook attached to an eye on the wall. This seemed like a rather innovative idea at first, but it proved otherwise. Inevitably, the board also served as a work top, so the procedure of having a weekly bath had to be preceded by a major reorganisation of the scullery. Sometimes Elaine and I would wash in a bowl of hot water in front of the fire: it was warmer and spared valuable hot water from the back boiler arrangement, which could barely cope with the volume needed for the larger bath.

I hated Mondays, especially during winter. Monday was always washday, come what may, rain or fine weather. After Mum had scrubbed, 'possed', rinsed and mangled the clothes, the only option for completing the drying process in winter was in front of the coal fire in the living room. A huge wooden clothes drier would be hauled down from the ceiling via a rope and pulley mechanism to occupy the warm zone, thereby creating a damp atmosphere throughout the house.

The bedroom might have been one place to escape to, but in 1950 bedrooms were extremely cold in winter and mine was only a box room, measuring, at most, eight feet long and six feet wide; it had been formed from the adjacent bedroom by the introduction of a dividing wall. There was just about room for a bed and a bookcase which had to store many of my treasures, as well as an increasing collection of books. So, going to bed meant exactly that; it wasn't a place to loiter or play. The trick was to undress at great speed and to get completely under the bedclothes and shiny green eiderdown as quickly as possible, remembering to take tomorrow's clothes into the bed to maintain their warmth. Creation of a well insulated, airtight tent would soon warm the bed up, and it was then possible to poke my head out in reasonable comfort, perhaps to read a book, listen to the music on the wireless down below in the living room or chat to my sister through the thin dividing wall. The poor sound insulation was quite useful as we recounted various tales and I tried to teach her to burp.

Mum and Dad had already met Frank Lockwood and his wife Mary, of 69 Regent Street, during one of their house cleaning expeditions from Uppermill before we moved in to number 52, so Elaine and I soon got to know their children: Trevor, the same age as Elaine; Judith, the same age as me; and Gillian, a couple of years or so younger than me. We played together around the Trinity ground in the summer of 1949 and jointly celebrated Guy Fawkes Night of 1949 and 1950 with a few fireworks and traditional food: home-made toffee and parkin. We soon became acquainted with Frank's unmarried sister, another Mary Lockwood, who lived next door to us at number 50. The straight-backed and straight-laced Mary Lockwood would have been a commanding figure where she worked in the Drawing Office of the Town Hall in Wakefield, but I didn't know at the time that she was also caring for her mother, Caroline, also resident at number 50. There seemed to be quite a few spinsters in the immediate neighbourhood, all apparently living alone – or were they? Our other neighbours were married couples, John and Violet Hill at number 54 and Dennis and Margaret Ryan at number 56. Three doors down from us at number 46 lived Stephen and Sybil Crowhurst. They had two sons, Michael who was a year or so older than me and John who was my age. For some unknown reason they had acquired the respective nicknames, 'Big Tish' and 'Little Tish'. Both were sporty and we soon became friends. I recall being most interested in the fact that in the summer their dad was involved with cricket, initially as a player, then later as an umpire.

All the back rooms of Regent Street looked out on to the backs of the terraced houses in the next street, Wesley Street, the first few houses of which were also joined on to a small group of houses in Back Regent Street, known as back-to-backs. All these houses had outside lavatories in little brick buildings at the bottom of their back yards, forming a mirror image of Regent Street. Back Regent Street separated the two sets of back yards and was about fifteen feet wide, giving rear access to houses in Regent, Back Regent and Wesley Streets; below ground ran the main sewer pipe for all those lavatories. Colin and Hilda Tattersall lived across the street from us at 11 Wesley Street; their son David ('Tatto') was my school age. David (I should say his dad) had a model railway which was the envy of the neighbourhood, and sometimes I would be invited into Mr Tattersall's attic to marvel at the intricate details of his O-Gauge layout. I always thought this was a much better use of attic space than a darkroom and store for smelly chemicals. Next door to the Tattersalls at 9 Wesley

Street lived Jimmy and Geoff Stephenson, two of the four sons of Harry and Olive Stephenson. Jimmy was my school age; Geoff was the same school year group as Elaine. Lower down at 2 Back Regent Street lived Fred and Marjorie Booth who had a lad, Johnny, a year or two younger than me. William and Elizabeth Gott lived at 6 Back Regent Street. Mrs Gott had already achieved legendary status amongst the local lads, for it was said that in the past she had been engaged in an almighty fight with another woman in the locality.

I soon settled into the neighbourhood, with many friends and a natural playground, Back Regent Street. Gradually, I got to know other kids further afield from my links at school. My parents had chosen Sandal Magna Primary and Junior School in Agbrigg, rather than Belle Vue Infants and the local church school, St Catherine's close by, probably on the recommendation of the Lockwoods whose children were already going to Sandal Magna. My school was less than ten minutes' walk away, either via the 'Doctors' Path' and Maybush Road to Agbrigg or my preferred route through the cemetery and down Sugar Lane, past the old men toiling in their allotments on the right hand side and the tall brick cemetery wall on the left. My sister Elaine was also enrolled in Sandal Magna Juniors and she was given the responsibility of escorting me to my new school on my first day in June 1949; few parents walked their infants to school.

At first, school seemed to consist mainly of playing around, dancing, and even supposed sleeping, which I did not particularly enjoy. Surprisingly, I preferred the more serious stuff of reading and arithmetic, especially the chanting of multiplication tables. I found that I could manipulate numbers quite easily from lots of inadvertent practice in playing and scoring various games such as cards, dominoes, darts and cricket. Reading also came fairly easily, so at that time there was no pressure on me at school and I took it in my stride. Elaine, on the other hand, was not so fortunate. She had to sit the eleven plus scholarship examination in 1950 after having experienced a new school and new teachers for less than a year. She had done reasonably well in her previous school and under normal circumstances might have passed the eleven plus, but the rapid change to a new system gave her little time to adjust and she failed. In September, 1950, Elaine started at Manygates Secondary Modern School which at that time had a rather mediocre reputation in the classroom but a rather good one on the rugby field.

I recall 1950 as a very happy period and in the summer our family would spend a lot of time together exploring the countryside around Sandal, Heath Common, Newmillerdam, and Nostell, usually on Sundays when we were not allowed out to play and we had to go for walks after church. Dad also used these occasions as photo opportunities. In the late summer of 1950 we spent two memorable weeks in Staithes, a picturesque fishing village nestled in a cleft of steep cliffs which formed a natural harbour on the North Yorkshire coast.

Staithes had been one of the largest fishing ports in the North of England and home to the famous explorer, James Cook. Its breathtaking beauty had also attracted many Victorian artists, known as the Staithes Group of Artists. I suspect this is also why a keen amateur photographer might have chosen it in 1950. Fishing was now quite a small activity in this peaceful little village, where Dad had rented a house next to the Cod and Lobster Inn on the harbour front. It was such a contrast to Belle Vue, waking up to the noise of the pounding sea, the squawking seagulls and the smell of the sea air and seaweed. Everyday a woman in traditional dress would feed the gulls on the slipway between our rented house and the Cod and Lobster. She wore a frilly bonnet and I didn't know at the time that the dark colour

Staithes in 1950 showing the harbour (left) and the author with friends in the coble Mizpah (right). R. H. Barraclough.

of her dress and bonnet meant that she was in mourning, probably for a husband or son lost at sea.

I soon befriended some local lads and we would clamber on the huge rocks around the harbour, looking for sea urchins and samples of jet that were supposed to be available in the area. The Staithes fishermen were a friendly group, and sometimes they took me out to sea in their cobles, the Brothers and Mizpah, small two-man wooden boats that could be launched directly from the shore.

On one memorable occasion the sea was extremely rough and we were tossed around so much at the narrow harbour entrance that the fishermen nearly abandoned this dangerous manoeuvre in favour of the more amenable Runswick Bay round the corner. We eventually managed to enter Staithes harbour and, although I was slightly apprehensive, I didn't fully appreciate the dangers of this expedition. At that time I couldn't swim and I didn't wear a life jacket. Had I gone overboard my woollen pullover, tweed jacket and Wellington boots would have rapidly filled with water and dragged me down. No wonder Mum looked extremely relieved on the edge of the shore as we entered the relative safety of the harbour. I expect Dad was elsewhere, taking pictures.

References and Further Reading

St Catherine's Church Wakefield, 1951 Publication of 75th anniversary 1876–1951.

Private Communication, Chris Leach, Lancashire and Yorkshire Railway Society.

Working for the Railway: The Wakefield Locomotive Sheds and their Workpeople, John Goodchild, Wakefield Historical Society Journal, 2008.

CHAPTER THREE

Exploring Belle Vue and Beyond, circa 1951

Belle Vue was, largely, a working class district but in Mum's eyes it was behaviour rather than class *per se* that was usually the discriminator. 'Mucky' folk, such as those who failed to 'donkey stone' their front doorstep on a regular basis, were readily identified, whatever their 'class'. Another discriminator was the more subtle deviation from normal folk like us towards either 'common' or 'posh'. Much has been said and written about the characteristics of these two extremes but, from my own recollections, they seemed to be very much in the eye of the beholder, especially the female beholder of other females.

To Mum, 'common' sometimes applied to the local women who readily allowed themselves to be seen in public doing various things, which even she might do occasionally, but only within the confines of her own home, out of sight. Women who smoked in the street and publicly displayed their hair curlers came into this 'common' category, for example. Many of these transgressions had little sexual appeal, but anything that appeared to be an obvious attempt to attract a man, such as dyed blonde hair ('straight out of a bottle'), heavy make-up ('put on with a trowel'), bare legs ('you'd think she can't afford stockings') and loud-coloured clothing, particularly reds and purples, ('you can see 'er comin' a mile off') warranted the label 'common as muck', which was about as bad as any woman could get, especially if she was already married. This label was also reserved for women who swore incessantly, by affixing the adjective 'bloody' to every noun which 'folk like us' never did.

'Posh' people did not swear, did not wear loud-coloured clothing, only occasionally dropped their aitches, and spoke in a confident manner not dissimilar to folks on the wireless ('la de dah'), using a sequence of flowing sentences rather than simple one-liners. Posh women might be housewives or employed in some professional capacity, often as teachers or in an office, but not just as typists. On the male side, vicars, doctors and engineers were obviously posh. There were a few posh folk around Belle Vue but the district of Sandal was much 'posher'. Posh folk had obviously 'got on' via a decent education at a grammar school and maybe college or university as well. Both Mum and Dad, like many parents in Belle Vue, harboured an aspiration for their children to have an education, which they had missed out on during the 1920s and thirties. However, to Mum it often seemed that having 'gumption' (common sense) was just as important as a formal education. Dad was not interested in the way people spoke or the common/posh discriminator, but he would often implore me to work hard at school to avoid ending up like him, 'uneducated'.

As a believer in hard graft, Dad had no time for those who were obviously 'lakin', i.e. pretending to be ill and not working. Men who seemed to earn a lot of money without appearing to do much for it were implicitly mistrusted and often referred to as 'spivs'. Men who wasted their money drinking in t'Alec and gambling at the bookies, 'back o' t'Alec' were also not Dad's type; neither were those who 'fancied themselves' as 'ladies' men' by 'dressing up'. Dad beavered away at work and his new hobby: by January 1951 he was already winning prizes at the Annual Awards of the Wakefield Camera Club and exhibiting his winning prints in the Wakefield Art Gallery.

There were a few young men around Belle Vue dressed in khaki uniforms in 1951. National Service was still seen to be necessary and in 1950 had been extended from eighteen months to two years, as post-war political problems continued throughout the world. Some local soldiers of the KOYLI (King's Own Yorkshire Light Infantry) had been in Malaya since 1947, and now there were serious problems in another Far Eastern country called Korea.

Fat people stood out from the crowd; most folk around Belle Vue had a lean and hungry look, resulting from plenty of exercise and years of food rationing. The points system of rationing had ended in 1950 and Mum could readily buy bread and some vegetables in local shops. Arthur Winter, a local dairyman, kept us regularly supplied with milk, but cream, cheese, butter, tea, sugar, meat and, most importantly as far as I was concerned, sweets and chocolates, were still rationed in 1951. I can remember the euphoria in Uppermill when sweets came off ration in early 1949, but they were rationed again a few months later when demand exceeded supply.

Belle Vue had a wide range of food shops on Doncaster Road, including a butcher (Miller's), bakers (Beggs's and also Barnes's), grocers (John S. Driver Ltd. and CIS), and there were many general stores in the locality. Along Elm Tree Street, there were Pearson's, Creighton's on the corner with Albert Street and Ormiston's on the corner with Dunbar Street. Annie Ormiston was the sister of Miss Mary Lockwood, our next door neighbour. There was also a 'house shop' at 14 Pear Tree Street (originally named William Street) run by Susan Dwyer. I was more familiar with the general stores closer to home on the south side of Doncaster Road, especially Ratcliffe's in Denmark Street and Lambert's at the corner of Oxford Street and Regent Street, no more than 30 yards from our house.

Women were prominent in running many local stores and they appeared formidable figures in their standard uniform of hairnets, cardigans and 'pinnies'. A defensive posture of folded arms, supported on the shelf of a large bosom, signalled a lack of tolerance of any mischief-making from local kids, but that was usually no deterrent. Poor old Mary Lambert must have tired of having her sole means of marketing regularly defaced when her carefully whitewashed prices on the shop window were converted to lower values by grubby fingers of local rascals, who would mischievously change an 'eight' or a 'six' to a 'zero' or, perhaps, a 'seven' to a 'one'; but she never caught us. Eliza Ratcliffe was more alert; there were no flies on her, but plenty stuck to the flypaper dangling from her shop ceiling at number 27 Denmark Street. Ratcliffe's seemed intent on capturing the broad market for all local requirements and was jam-packed with a range of goods that not only blocked the available illumination but also the narrow shop entrance; sometimes the odd onion or potato would find its way onto the pavement or the gutter. This 'Aladdin's cave', was deceptive, however. Although the range of offerings was very large, there were usually only one or two items of anything, since the whole shop was not much bigger than our front room.

I would occasionally run errands for Mum to Ratcliffe's and Lambert's but she used these shops only in emergencies, preferring the shops on Doncaster Road, especially Driver's, part of a bigger grocery chain. I would often run errands to the Doncaster Road shops, especially those on the south side, readily accessible without crossing the busy road. The Post Office near the corner of our side of Regent Street was very handy and I might be sent to M. G. Wilson Ltd., the chemist near the bottom of Round Street. When sweets eventually came off ration, I was also a regular visitor to Freddy Fisher's sweet shop on the south side of Doncaster Road. Freddy took the prize for the smallest shop in the neighbourhood: his tiny cubicle was easily filled with just one adult customer. Walls ice cream wafers from Freddy Fisher were eventually a family treat on Sunday afternoons, and I usually volunteered to fetch them so that I could hare back up Round Street before they melted. I can also recall buying blue iced lollipops from Ratcliffe's and being fascinated when they turned my pee blue. Once I had been trained in road safety, I would cross Doncaster Road to visit the newsagents, (t'paper shop), opposite the bottom of Regent Street or Gill's, opposite the bottom of Denmark Street. Off-licences were quite common in the vicinity: Pybus's and Wise's at the bottom of Denmark Street and White's on the corner of Pear Tree Street and Elm Tree Street. However, none of these businesses would have survived had they depended on trade from number 52 Regent Street; my parents drank alcohol only at Christmas.

Fish and chip shops were everywhere in Belle Vue: down Denmark Street, along Doncaster Road and 'back o' t'Alec'. However, I suspect Mum thought that only 'common folk' ate fish and chips on a regular basis, so they were not part of her weekly menu. The proprietor of the nearest fish and chip shop in Denmark Street, Jack Hickman, was treated with the same apprehension as the local one-legged window cleaner: 'Fish Jack' had three fingers missing from one hand. We were allowed chips only as a special treat, usually on the way home from either the Autumn Fair in Agbrigg or the Easter Fair on Heath Common, when we would call at one of the shops along Agbrigg Road, usually either Lovatt's or Taylor's, for 'two penneth' of chips. Taylor's did a roaring trade during the Agbrigg fair, with customers from the nearby fairground often forming a long queue outside the shop on the corner with Altinkool Street.

Meat was scarce before it came off ration in 1954, so Mum introduced alternatives. Her *pièce de résistance* was raw tripe, served every Friday for tea. I normally ate everything put in front of me, but I really struggled with raw tripe. My more fickle sister flatly refused to eat it, and neither of us knows to this day how she got away with such a defiant stance. Raw tripe bounced off teeth like rubber balls bounced off the walls of Back Regent Street. I didn't know then that normal people ate tripe cooked with onions, reputedly quite a tasty dish. The bland taste of raw tripe could only be improved by the addition of lots of vinegar but this had no effect on its rough, serrated texture. It was tripe or nothing. Had I known that I was actually chomping at the inside of a cow's stomach, I think perhaps I would have joined my sister in protest. Or would I? I was always hungry!

Apart from making sure he had enough tobacco ('baccy), Dad rarely shopped, although I can recall him sneaking off with Elaine down Denmark Street to Norman Tower's electrical shop on the north side of Doncaster Road to buy Mum's Christmas present, a hairdryer. At a stretch he might also 'pop' to Sowdon's (formerly known as Dixon's) to have some shoes repaired but, like most men, Dad left most of the shopping to the homemaker.

The local Belle Vue kids spoke a weird dialect in a strange accent, quite different from my Lancastrian one. They would 'lake' (play) games such as 'taws' (marbles); they would 'guzzle' (gobble) 'spogs' (sweets) when they were available. Sometimes they would 'fratch' (argue) and 'chuck mackers' (throw stones) at each other, often resulting in someone being 'copped' (caught) and 'brayed' (beaten up). Life was very territorial and there was great rivalry between kids in different streets, especially before 5 November when they would go 'chubbin' to seek wood for their bonfires.

I had been accepted by the lads in and around our street, but had been 'brayed' in the snicket between St Catherine's Church and the rugby ground by a group of lads from 'back o' t'Alec'. After all, I was intruding into border territory, I had a policeman for a father, and I spoke with a strange Lancashire accent. Both Mum and Dad instructed me in no uncertain terms that the only way to treat bullies is to fight one's corner but I lacked the confidence at that age; the lesson learned from the whole experience was to avoid trouble by not standing out from the crowd. I became very conscious of anything that might make me different from my peers, such as dress, attitude and my accent. I couldn't do much about my dad's job but I cultivated a Yorkshire accent very quickly, became more sensitive about what I wore, and developed a keen awareness of danger, particularly when alone. This was a key moment in my development: it was the first time I can

St Catherine's Church, *c.*1951. Sᴛ Cᴀᴛʜᴇʀɪɴᴇ's Cʜᴜʀᴄʜ.

recall taking my own decisions on how to deal with an external situation, independent of my parents. If I were to survive in this environment, I would have to adopt a pragmatic approach and somehow fit in.

That said, I was supposed to be learning how to fight the good fight at St Catherine's Church. Mum was already 'mucking in' with the Mothers' Union and the Young Wives' Association, taking part in their various meetings, outings and fund-raising events. My joining Sunday School, then later the church choir, obviously had a certain inevitability about it. Elaine

There are lots of hats and handbags on display for this Mothers' Union outing in the early fifties. Mum is standing behind the little boy. R. H. BARRACLOUGH.

was also enrolled in Sunday School, then later the Crusaders for children over twelve. It was via St Catherine's Church that Elaine met some of her friends: Janet Carr, the daughter of Harry and Elizabeth Carr who lived next to Maybush House, at number 91 Regent Street; and Anne Sutton, the daughter of George and Edna Sutton from Dunbar Street. George Sutton, a quiet gentle man, was also a churchwarden.

Dad did not attend church except on special occasions. I suspect he was normally too engrossed in his photography or, maybe, he thought that the music was not up to scratch. The year 1951 was the seventy-fifth anniversary of St Catherine's Church, and from 30 September to 8 October there were various events, some of which I think Dad did attend. All groups of the church made some contribution to the celebrations, not least a joint

Mrs Edna Sutton prepares to throw a dart during a Young Wives' fete in the early fifties. Mum is at the back on the extreme right. R. H. Barraclough.

effort by the Mothers' Union and Young Wives' Group in a Pageant of Bible Women involving thirty-one ladies in a huge cast, with Mum as Magdalene which, with hindsight, was an interesting bit of casting. My contribution to the Pageant along with other Sunday School kids was to sing 'Away in a Manger', three months ahead of Christmas.

Being a choirboy in about 1952 was exciting and something new to try out, but I soon realised that it used up a lot of time which could be better spent. The only consolation was that my local friends, 'Little Tish' and 'Tatto' had also joined the choir at the same time, and I felt the burden was being shared. We would often attend church three times on Sunday and there was a regular choir practice on Wednesday night led by Leslie Vokins, the organist and choirmaster, who kept a watchful eye on his choristers from a huge mirror above the organ keyboard. Dressing up in a cassock and surplice was fun at first but it soon palled. I started complaining that the starched ruffs rubbed on my neck and made it sore, but that made no impression at home. The tall, lean vicar, the Reverend Thomas Bartlett Summers, was a kind, gentle man but his sermons were in a language that I didn't understand, and my mind soon wandered as he droned on. Nice old Bill Sharpe, who walked with a limp and had a quavering tenor voice, used to give us sweets to suck during the sermon; Percy and Olive Murgatroyd gave us words of encouragement when they sensed we needed more down-to-earth support than the offerings from the pulpit. Colin Tattersall also sang in the choir so 'Tatto' had to be on his best behaviour. The pinnacle of my days as a chorister came when Mr Vokins

St Catherine's Church choirboy. R. H. BARRACLOUGH.

ordered me to sing the part of the page boy in Good King Wenceslas during a Christmas carol service, but nerves got the better of me as I strained to stay in tune and project a thin voice towards Mum and Dad seated in the distant congregation. I had been taken aback to see my friend Brian Perkin sing the part of the King instead of Percy Murgatroyd who had a sore throat and persuaded Brian to take his place at the last minute.

We would 'play out' around Back Regent Street: cricket, football, and hopscotch (using chalked up squares and bits of broken tiles) were popular games, as was 'killer' in which being 'killed' involved being hit by a soft ball from the person 'on'. Bows and arrows were made from string and canes; stilts were constructed from bits of wood or treacle tins and string. Playing cricket in the narrow Back Regent Street was like playing in the nets. One boy batted whilst the rest of the players, sometimes as many as ten boys, each with his own ball, would queue to take turns to bowl at the batsman. The wicket was notionally the iron grate in the centre of the street opposite our back gate, and it was a decision of the majority if the ball was judged to have bowled the batsman out by passing over the grate; there were no stumps. It was great batting practice, made harder by the uneven cobbled stones in the centre of the street, which provided an unpredictable bounce of the ball. The game had its own simple rules: 'corkies', hard cork balls, were banned, a rule imposed by the women in the locality; any balls

Playing in the back yard of 52 Regent Street. R. H. BARRACLOUGH.

hit into the nearby back yards had to be retrieved by the batsman. Often this involved scrambling over gates that happened to be locked, such as Mary Lockwood's. Sometimes, older lads would attempt to slog the ball over the roof tops in Oxford Street. On the rare occasion when this was achieved, the batsman had to forfeit his own ball to compensate the bowler for the lost ball, which would end up somewhere in one of the many back yards in a neighbouring territory behind Denmark Street

We also played in the nearby cemetery, but would avoid the mortuary chapels next to the path leading to Sugar Lane because we thought they were too spooky. Children were not supposed to deviate from the cemetery path and we thought it very daring to be in the middle of the cemetery, hiding behind the gravestones from the grave diggers. We would then make ourselves visible to them and race off before they could catch us. At the time I imagined they gave chase, but now I am not so sure! The cemetery walls had not had their railings removed during wartime, and I can remember my sister spearing her thigh when hastily climbing a spiky railing bordering the cemetery at the top of Regent Street. Mum was not pleased, particularly since this incident occurred the day before we went on holiday, necessitating an emergency visit to Dr Scott.

Fishing at Newmillerdam.
R. H. BARRACLOUGH.

The holiday in Staithes had ignited an interest in fishing and model boats. My friends and I would fish on various ponds, and at Newmillerdam. By now I was also friends with Fred Jackson, a local joiner and funeral director who had a workshop on the corner of Oxford Street and Arthur Street. I would spend hours watching Fred at work, both of us ankle deep in wood shavings, as he transformed boards of plain wood into beautiful polished coffins, complete with shiny metal handles. The morbidity of the fruits of his labours was not given a second thought: I was focused on learning how to shape wood and hoping I would be able to scrounge some off-cuts as the starting point for my latest design of model boat.

Our 1951 summer holiday in Skegness was a huge disappointment compared with Staithes. Mum took an instant dislike to our boarding house where, much to Dad's annoyance, she whispered her complaints to avoid being overheard by the landlady and other lodgers. It was the sort of establishment where a list of 'do nots' had been stuck to the inside of the wardrobe doors, quite different from our past visits to Auntie Olive's Blackpool boarding house where there were no strict rules and we had the run of the place. Perhaps that is why I summoned up the courage to try and change the atmosphere of the dismal Skegness abode by secretly placing an imitation dog turd in the middle of the dining room floor. I had been fascinated by many offerings in a local joke shop but couldn't resist the realism of 'Naughty Fido', quite a work of art, superbly crafted in *papier maché*. The other highlight of the week was the ease with which I squandered the remains of my pocket money in an amusement arcade, feeding coins endlessly into the 'Laughing Sailor' in the hope his compulsive laughter would cheer me up. There was little to cheer about when the landlady presented Mum with our week's bill for £8 and threepence. This included the agreed deal of £7 for 'beds' but it was the charge for 'sundries' that didn't go down too well with Mum, especially nine shillings for milk and one shilling for 'use of cruet'. To add insult to injury the landlady accused Elaine and me of having torn some lace curtains, but we, and presumably our family budget, were stoutly defended by Mum who took great pleasure in pointing out that the said curtains were already rotten. The weather in Skegness had also been rotten, not even 'bracing', as the brochures had led us to believe. We were all relieved to return from our Skegness 'digs' to home comforts in the afternoon of Saturday 14 July; little did we know that two tragic and mysterious incidents were about to unfold later that evening.

Around midnight, officers of the West Riding Constabulary surrounded the farmhouse of a suspected burglar, Alfred Moore, in Kirkheaton, Huddersfield. During the incident Detective Inspector Duncan Fraser and PC Arthur Gordon Jagger were shot. Fraser died from his wounds at the scene; Jagger died two days later in Huddersfield Royal Infirmary. Dad was devastated by the tragic loss of two colleagues and, like many at the time, seethed that the killer should be 'strung up' in accordance with the law. Moore had been arrested shortly after the shots had been fired and was found guilty of murder, for which he was eventually hanged in Armley Prison, Leeds, in 1952. The common belief at the time was that justice had been done. Coincidentally, during the same weekend and apparently within the same time frame, the beautiful Georgian building of Thornes House Grammar School was destroyed by fire, following a Saturday evening performance of *A Midsummer Night's Dream* by members of the Wakefield Amateur Theatre Guild, who were using the building as dressing rooms. 'Accidents will happen!' was the common cry, but was it really an accident?

The fire at Thornes House, July 1951. *WAKEFIELD EXPRESS.*

I first went to t'Spit cinema in the early Spring of 1951. The children's programme was scheduled on Saturday afternoons and cost four pence. It was quite surprising how many kids would queue outside the corner entrance before the doors were opened for the 2 p.m. performance. T'Spit had been advertised under various names in its thirty-seven-year history but all were completely inappropriate. Perhaps the name, t'Expectorate would have been a good compromise between t'Spit and all its other incongruous names such as Palace, Palace de Luxe and Cosy Cinema? The rectangular brick building was badly spalled and hardly palatial. Once inside, even with 'lights up' it was extremely dark and it had a characteristic smell of body odour, smoke and dust, not exactly *de luxe.* For the children's programme only the cheap bench seats in front of a wooden barrier were made available: behind the barrier were rows of individual seats used by adults and youths during the evening performances (at a price of one shilling). Some of the seats in the back were doubles, designed for courting couples, perhaps giving some justification to the 1951 advertised name of Cosy Cinema. I didn't know at the time but some young couples would have canoodled in these seats for the last time, perhaps the night before the young man went off to fight for his country, maybe never to return …

As with all gatherings of excited children there was a loud hullabaloo of high pitched talking and screaming before the performance started, and the noise became louder as it dawned on us that there was virtually no adult supervision. The person notionally in charge was a thin man in dark blue uniform, boasting extravagant gold braid. He also wore a peaked hat, giving the impression of a brass bandsman. However, his only instrument was a rather weak torch which he used to attempt to illuminate available seats to latecomers. His proper name was Dews but everyone in Belle Vue knew him as 'Teacake'. As soon as 'Teacake' gave the signal that everyone was seated, the dim lights would go completely out, the talking would gradually subside amid shushing noises and the show would begin. Suddenly the screen would burst into life from a powerful beam of projected light that was also very effective at illuminating the dancing dust particles in its path. Or were they fleas?

All the films were in black and white, and the show would usually start with the crowing cockerel and fanfare music of the latest Pathé News. Each news clip was accompanied by background music and a non-stop commentary, both designed to match the mood of the story. Sombre orchestral music and a grave tone would accompany the latest news on the King's health, while lighter music and a light-hearted commentary, often interspersed with weak jokes, supplemented the images of various film stars and celebrities of the day. A lot of the political news went over my head but I did pay particular attention to the sports news, especially the big football and cricket matches. However, much to my annoyance, these clips were extremely brief and usually only showed the winning goal or winning run. It was as if each clip of sports news was designed to last for just a few bars of the accompanying brass band music, which was played at a high tempo. I also saw my first images of London and the Festival of Britain which had opened there in the summer of 1951, with the aim of promoting the best of post-war Britain and projecting an image of a less austere era; at least that was the gist of the very patriotic commentary. Elaine had visited the Festival of Britain with a party from Manygates School that summer, but much to my disappointment I failed to spot her on the newsreel in t'Spit. The news would often be followed by a 'cowboy', such as Roy Rogers, and a short comedy, usually an offering from an endless series made by the Three Stooges, but the real entertainment would be provided by the audience.

The film projector would frequently break down. There was initially only a murmuring of disappointment, but as the delay went on the noise would intensify to a protest. In defiance of t'Spit's well known request, shrill whistles would start from older boys who had mastered this difficult art: the rest of us stamped our feet and howled our derision. If the repair was not carried out in this critical period then all hell would break loose. One Saturday afternoon the repair took so long that 'Teacake' was forced to make an appearance to quell the uprising, but his intervention was hopeless in the dim light, and his very presence made matters worse. Emboldened by the safety of the gloom, the more confident kids started to chant his name, mockingly. 'Teacake' would then brandish his torch in a vain attempt to pick out the culprits. On one occasion a brave urchin, oozing with much more confidence than I could ever have mustered, grabbed his opportunity for the limelight, stood up in the front and made Tarzan noises whilst simultaneously beating his chest, much to the amusement of the audience, who appreciated the performance as befitting the silver screen itself. Again, before 'Teacake' could identify the perpetrator, 'Tarzan' had disappeared into the jungle of bodies. Order could only be restored by a successful repair to the film.

I soon became disenchanted by my Saturday afternoon visits to t'Spit, not because of the disorderly conduct of the audience – this was exciting and no doubt I played some part – but mainly my dislike of the Three Stooges films which I did not find funny at all. Perhaps I was too young to appreciate their humour, but I found many of their antics very frightening. I can remember one particular film in which their crazy attempts to extract teeth were so real and upsetting for me that I actually walked out. From that moment on I feared visiting the dentist who was frightening enough anyway. Known as 'Googley Eyes', the school dentist would peer down at his hapless victims with piercing eyes on stalks as he wielded a mechanical drill driven by a complex pulley arrangement; of such images are nightmares made. Fortunately, something far more pleasurable was distracting me from the dentist and the Saturday afternoon performances of the Three Stooges. Very loud cheering noises would occasionally penetrate the walls of the cinema, beckoning further investigation. And they weren't coming from St Catherine's Church.

I was smitten with rugby league the day I first entered the Wakefield Trinity ground. Initially I went in free when the gates were opened at half-time, but when I stopped going to t'Spit I would queue at the turnstile for children and old-age pensioners to pay to enter the ground and watch the whole match. We lived round the corner from the main entrance of the ground which was on the corner of Arthur Street and Anderton Street, and I would normally leave home at five minutes to three on Saturday afternoon and be in the ground in time for the kick-off at three. The hub of the ground was the main stand next to the main entrance, straddling the half-way line on the west side. Underneath were the players' changing rooms, accessed by a central tunnel connected to a rear tunnel which ran the full length of the stand. The long tunnel led spectators to both ends of the ground known, for obvious reasons, as the St Catherine's End to the north and the Agbrigg End to the south. The main stand was a handsome late Victorian structure with an air of permanency about its slate pitched roof, supported by regularly spaced columns and decorated with an elegantly shaped wooden fascia board. Occupants of the main stand, including well-heeled local dignitaries and officials of the club, were afforded the best view of the match from an elevated position, but I never envied them, for it must have been extremely cold up there in winter, despite the presence of large glazed windows on the sides. Some of the older supporters had rugs wrapped around their knees.

My preference was to move around the ground to get close to the action, especially the end the Trinity were supposed to be attacking. I

An early fifties match at Belle Vue. Frank Mortimer of the Trinity attempts a conversion kick from the touchline in full view of the main stand. R. H. BARRACLOUGH.

would usually start watching the game at one end, then change ends at half-time by walking through the tunnel under the main stand. It was quite a frightening experience in the tunnel because there was always a crush of spectators trying to move in both directions in a very confined space. As the centre of the tunnel was approached, the strong smell of oil of wintergreen liniment would fill the air from the nearby changing rooms; the noise of the spectators' feet moving around the wooden floorboards above could also be heard.

Both the St Catherine's End and the Agbrigg End of the ground were open terraces with steel safety barriers for standing spectators. Ground improvements had been carried out in 1950 at the St Catherine's End which now had smart, white looking concrete terracing and a single-storey club office at the top of the northwest corner, set against the background of the

The St Catherine's end (also known as the Doncaster Road end) of Belle Vue rugby ground in 1950 on completion of new terracing by volunteers. The inset figures were key club members in 1950: top left, Herbert Goodfellow, Trinity captain and long standing scrum half; top right, John Tom Wood, club secretary; bottom right, James Bullock, club president. WAKEFIELD TRINITY WILDCATS.

dirty brick gable end of the adjacent t'Spit cinema. Fencing in the form of arched metal railings at each end was supposed to deter spectators from getting on to the sacred turf, but they could have been readily hurdled by those with that intent. However, pitch invasions were almost unheard of in 1951. Despite the hostile environment, there were usually only one or two policemen strolling around the perimeter of the pitch, seemingly glad to have the opportunity to watch the match whilst on paid duty. The original cycle track around the pitch had long gone.

At the top of the terracing at the St Catherine's End, the south side of the huge pitched roof of the neighbouring St Catherine's Church provided a drab, grey backcloth to a large, navy blue wooden scoreboard. A ladder up to a high platform enabled the scores for the Visitors and Wakefield to be manually updated with white numerals on dark rectangular metal plates, large enough for everyone in the ground to see at a glance. Those not in the ground could also get a quick glimpse of the latest score from the top of a double-decker West Riding bus, as it trundled into the city past the Doncaster Road entrance.

Two massive loudspeaker horns were mounted on each side of the scoreboard as part of the public address (PA) system, but most of the crowd at the opposite Agbrigg End struggled to hear the faint announcements. There was usually a lot of consultation amongst the crowd concerning announcements relating to last minute changes to the Trinity team, interspersed with loud groans if a crowd favourite had been suddenly withdrawn. The top of the scoreboard was the only place in the whole ground sporting a sizeable advertisement: 'MELBOURNE ALES' was in huge capital letters below the distinguished trademark of the Leeds and Wakefield Breweries Ltd. This company logo took the unusual form of a bowing courtier dressed in frock coat, wig, knee breeches and high-heeled shoes, a reminder of a gentler era and almost certainly the only dandy present in this macho crowd, whose members clad themselves in the more practical attire of cloth caps, scarves, belted coats and heavy, laced up footwear to combat the cold, damp terraces. A regular advertisement for 'MELBOURNE ALES' in the match programme claimed that they were obtainable wherever this trademark sign could be seen, but neither Melbourne Ales nor any other alcoholic beverage was widely available in the ground in 1951. The usual liquid refreshment was either hot tea or E. P. Shaw's fizzy pop obtainable from the wooden refreshment hut next to the large sliding doors of the main entrance.

Opposite the main stand the low east stand ran along most of the length of the pitch. This was inferior to the main stand in every aspect and appeared to be a cheaper construction, but had cost upwards of £4,000 when it was built as a covered terrace in 1924 – a lot of money for those days. By the early 1950s a few rows of narrow wooden bench seats had been fitted and were probably nowhere near as comfortable as the individual seats in the grandstand opposite. Dad always called the east stand 't'scrattin' shed', presumably due to its similarity to the typical rickety sheds he, and men of his generation, built for hens to scratch ('scrat') around in. I rarely sat in the east stand: it cost extra and the view was not very good even from the top, particularly when a low winter sun managed to poke through the clouds.

It was amazing that such a small ground would hold more than 30,000 spectators, but in the early fifties the attendance was usually much less than half that number, even for a big match. I would attend as many games as possible, including the reserve team ('A' team) games which were usually played in front of only a few hundred spectators. However, 'A' team games were useful for acquiring information about up-and-coming players and trialists who masqueraded under the name of 'A. N. Other' and might be signed on by the club if they showed promise; true supporters of the Trinity kept an eye on such important matters. My faithful support also extended to the acquisition of a wooden rattle which I embellished with a tiny blue-red-blue band representing the Trinity's colours. I would always buy a match programme (printed by John Lindley, Son and Co. of Almshouse Lane) at a cost of about threepence, and would later read it from cover to cover, several times over, in order to be in a position to recite the scoring statistics of individual players at a moment's notice.

The Trinity team ran out from the tunnel under the main stand, sometimes to the appropriate tune, 'Entry of the Gladiators', if the man in charge of the PA system had remembered to play the scratchy record. I always thought that the dull appearance of the Trinity jersey in dark blue, with a single red band, gave opposing teams with lots of white on their jerseys such as Wigan, St Helens and Bradford Northern a psychological advantage, because they looked bigger and more imposing. Size and weight were important in the forwards, the main ball carriers; the backs tended to be leaner and much quicker, but all players had to be brave in the tackle. Occasionally, before the proper kick-off, a local 'celebrity', usually an attractive winner of a local beauty contest such as 'Miss Coal' or 'Miss Trinity', would be introduced to the crowd, who would provide appropriate wolf-whistles as she gave a notional start to proceedings by kicking the ball a few yards in her high heels. She would then be escorted from the pitch to a ripple of polite applause from the crowd, now anxious for the real thing to get underway.

I was immediately struck by the pace and power of rugby league, which was always played in a highly competitive atmosphere, generated by the fierce roar of a passionate crowd. Inevitably, referees were highly criticised for any decision against the home team; for some spectators, shouting insults at the referee seemed to be the sole purpose of their presence. By now it was no surprise to me that referees from Lancashire were particularly vulnerable to taunts from the Belle Vue crowd. However, all referees had a difficult job: individual discipline of some players was often poor, and those with short tempers were very susceptible to being 'wound up' by the opposition. Brawls were frequent and, occasionally, players would be sent off for fighting.

Injuries were quite common in this brutal physical contest. Treatment of injuries on the field was usually limited to the 'magic sponge', administered by a track-suited team trainer. For Trinity, Johnny Malpass would dart onto the pitch from one of the two white painted concrete 'dugouts' straddling the half-way line beneath the main stand. It took me some time to realise that the 'magic' released by the sponge was actually cold water, and if this did not do the trick, the injured player was either taken off, sometimes on a stretcher carried by the smart, black-and-white uniformed men of the St John's Ambulance Brigade, or sometimes consigned to hobble on the wing for the rest of the match. There were no substitutes, and the occurrence of injuries often determined the outcome. Rugby league was uncompromising and unpredictable, and I loved every minute of it.

Trinity had a mediocre team in the early fifties, although they were good enough to win the knock-out Yorkshire Challenge Cup in October 1951. As paid professionals the players had to live up to high expectations from the critical home crowd who had parted with good money to watch them play; to be condemned as 'war 'n' nowt' (worthless) was one of the biggest insults the crowd could hurl at the players. The performance of the Trinity forwards around this time was particularly disappointing and

Try or not? There's no video camera but the linesman has a good view of this incident in the northwest corner of the Belle Vue ground during a match against Huddersfield, *c.*1951. It was certainly a cold day, judging from the caps and coats worn by members of the crowd! WAKEFIELD COUNCIL MUSEUM COLLECTION.

they would be angrily exhorted by the crowd to 'get stuck in', as if they weren't trying. When bawling at individual players, there was ample scope in the Trinity line up for plenty of aitches to be dropped, especially in the forwards. During a single match, 'orner, 'owes, 'udson, 'iggins and 'ughes in the forwards as well as full back 'irst, might be urged to 'frame thy sen'. However, try as they might, Trinity were usually no match for the top teams in the league, especially those from Lancashire and Cumbria, which not only had big tough forwards but could also boast world-class backs as well. At this time Gus Risman (Workington), Brian Bevan (Warrington) and Willie Horne (Barrow) were prominent stars, alongside many top-class Australians who had been lured to the leading clubs in the immediate post-war period. One of these, Lionel Cooper of Huddersfield, scored a record number of ten tries in one match against Keighley on 17 November 1951, and I was constantly reminded of this amazing feat by Uncle Harry who was an ardent Huddersfield supporter. Cooper was not only a fast winger, but big and strong as well. By contrast, Trinity's right winger Johnny Duggan, and left winger Dennis Boocker, were rather lightweight and usually no match for the likes of Cooper, although they were both crowd favourites. Apparently, when Trinity signed their first Australian, Dennis Boocker, in 1947, the great excitement in the city had been suddenly muted when it was discovered that he had actually been born in Wales and had emigrated to Australia at the age of two. In the world of rugby league, the men from Wales did not rank anywhere near as highly as those from 'Down Under'!

I started to collect autographs and after the match would hang around the tunnel under the main stand with other young enthusiasts, waiting for the players to emerge from the steamy changing rooms. After a long wait, a group of visiting players would suddenly appear in the tunnel all at the same time, wet hair plastered down and shining faces glistening with cuts and bruises. The name of the game was to be the first to recognise the most illustrious star and in deferential silence poke the autograph book and pen under his nose before anyone else. Battered and bruised, this was probably the last thing the players wanted and, although they were generally very obliging, some would be very peeved as they were pursued and harried as far as the team coach, parked outside the main entrance on Arthur Street. I was awestruck to be in the presence of 'supermen'.

Travelling to away matches was quite unusual, except for the local derby games against Featherstone Rovers and Castleford. If the Trinity were playing away from home, the quickest way of finding out the result was by reading 't'green un', the *Yorkshire Evening News* sports paper that came out early Saturday evening. This was preferred to 't'pink un', the *Yorkshire Post* version which was too biased towards soccer in its reports. Every Saturday I would dash down Regent Street to t'paper shop on Doncaster Road to discover the fate of the Trinity from 't'green un' if they were playing away, or to check whether the match report of the home game agreed with my own on-the-spot analysis.

By the time the new school year had started in September 1951 I was rugby mad. We would regularly play proper thirteen-a-side rugby league games in the school field and also 'touch and pass' – without tackles – in the school playground, coached and supervised by Mr G. A. Patterson, the sports master. Eventually, my enthusiasm and insatiable appetite for rugby league were rewarded by my being selected for the school team at just over nine years of age, two years younger than many lads in the team. At the end of the 1951/52 season, on the morning of Saturday, 29 March 1952, just before the Easter holidays, Mr Patterson had arranged a rugby match against a team representing the city of York. Nine of us travelled to York in a van driven by David Barnsley's dad; the rest travelled in a car. Dad also came along to offer practical help and moral support as I donned the bright green jersey of Sandal Magna County Junior School's rugby team for the first time.

York, Saturday morning, 29 March 1952. Sandal Magna County Junior School's rugby league team before a match against a representative team from York: back row, left to right: Brian Perkin, John Shepherd, Jack Harrison, Jeff Sidebottom, Ronnie Blewitt, Keith Barraclough, Bob Guiry; front row, left to right: Michael Haworth, Colin Hammond, Keith Oldroyd, David Barnsley, David Pedley, Michael Holliday. R. H. BARRACLOUGH.

Action shots from the rugby match in York: Sandal Magna County Junior School, Wakefield are in white shorts and have possession of the ball; Mr G. A. Patterson is the referee, dressed in double breasted suit, white shirt, tie and leather shoes. R. H. BARRACLOUGH.

We won the match quite easily by about 30 points and afterwards, for the first time in my life, I had a shower. Normally, we would troop home after a game at our Victorian school without the luxury of either a bath or shower. After the match in York we went to the Castle Museum and then to the York–Wakefield Trinity match, which Trinity lost 9–6.

My 1952 equivalent of 'street cred' had gone up a few notches in Belle Vue and I was on top of the world. A few weeks earlier, however, my little world had been turned upside down.

References and Further Reading

St Catherine's Church Wakefield, 1951 Publication of 75th anniversary, 1876–1951.

Dreadnoughts – A History of Wakefield Trinity Football Club, 1873–1960, D. W. Armitage and J. C. Lindley, November 1960, published by the Wakefield Trinity FC Programme Committee.

CHAPTER FOUR

Smoke, Smells and Transport, circa 1952

I cried when the King died. He had passed away peacefully in the early hours of Wednesday, 6 February 1952, and the sad news started to break locally around lunchtime. I remember first hearing about it at school, where lessons suddenly took on a different tone: the teachers were very sombre and we had to be even quieter than normal. Flags flew at half mast and the bell of Wakefield Cathedral solemnly tolled. Most recreational and social activities were cancelled on the Wednesday night, including concerts and dances; cinemas and theatres also closed. At home the normal wireless programmes were cancelled, so by the evening it was becoming very apparent that this had been an extraordinary day. This was my first experience of death and it seemed to be associated with the end of the world, so when I went to bed that night I had a little cry in my 'tent'. I cannot remember my exact feelings for the late King – maybe the tears were forced because crying was what I was supposed to do – but for the first time in my life I cried about the loss of someone I had never met and never known.

During the next few days mass mourning could be observed on an unprecedented scale. Dad came back from work in the city centre with reports of photographs of the late King displayed in shop windows, some of which were draped in black ribbon. Many local people wore black armbands, including our milkman, Arthur Winter. The Saturday, 9 February edition of the *Wakefield Express* contained a huge article: 'Nation Mourns King George VI,' which was also appropriately framed in black. I think I probably read this article before checking if my name was amongst the prizewinners of the children's painting competition in Auntie Marion's Corner, and before my usual close examination of the latest opinions of Pinder on Wakefield Trinity. The mayor, Councillor Ernest Borkwood, had sent his condolences on behalf of all the citizens of Wakefield by midday on Wednesday. At a special meeting of the City Council on Friday, the *Wakefield Express* reported that its leader, Alderman Alfred Carr, J. P. moved:

> That this Council do present a Loyal and Dutiful Address containing expressions of condolence to our Most Gracious Sovereign Lady Queen Elizabeth, the Dowager Queen Mother and all the Royal Family upon the death of our Beloved and Most Gracious Sovereign Lord King George VI, and of loyalty and devotion to the person of her Majesty upon her accession to the Throne and that the Common Seal of the Council be affixed to such address.

Needless to say, such a comprehensively loyal proposal had been hastily seconded and passed unanimously by the City Council. The death of King George VI was the only news for days leading up to the funeral on the 15 February. Locally, two communion services were held at St Catherine's Church on the 16 February. But there was one thing missing in all the details of this tragic event, and I couldn't get an answer from either the *Wakefield Express* or from my parents. Why did the King die?

Although the King had reportedly died of 'heart failure', (don't we all?) it transpired that the basic cause was lung cancer. However, it seemed that the word, 'cancer' was hardly ever spoken or written in 1952. It took years before Mum would silently mouth the word, as she did for anything that she regarded as both detestable and incomprehensible. The few taboo words in this category were usually related to fatal illnesses – tuberculosis, TB, was an unspeakable in the early fifties and only earned promotion to the quietly spoken category when the disease became more widely understood and manageable. 'Lung cancer' was a two-word unspeakable in 1952, at least at number 52 Regent Street.

The King's health had been deteriorating for some time, necessitating lung surgery on 23 September 1951, although reports carefully avoided any specific medical details. Of course, I had seen the newsreel at t'Spit, but I had not taken in most of the report. Commentator, Bob Danvers-Walker, had gravely informed us during the shot of the surgeon driving away from Buckingham Palace that: 'In the skilled hands of one surgeon, Clement Price Thomas, lay the King's life.' I am now quite sure that practically all cinema goers throughout the country completely missed the tragic irony of this statement. At the very moment of its utterance, the brief news clip had shown that something else lay in the surgeon's skilled hands, as well as the steering wheel of an imposing Rolls Royce: it was an elegant cigarette holder complete with burning fag.

King George VI's chest surgeon, Clement Price Thomas, has a quick fag after operating on the King in 1951. British Pathé Ltd.

The first case-control studies indicating a relationship between the smoking of tobacco and lung cancer had already been reported in the British Medical Journal two years earlier in 1950. However, these studies were by no means conclusive and made next to no impact. A significant fraction of the nation continued to smoke, oblivious to any likely dangers to their health including, apparently, King George VI and his chest surgeon. In about 1950 around 80 per cent of men aged between 35–59 were smokers. It was still seen as glamorous to smoke and some cigarette manufacturers even appealed to the intelligence of the smoker. A regular advertisement in the *Wakefield Express* in 1952 was placed by Godfrey Phillips Ltd. for Minors cigarettes, (a packet of twenty cost two shillings and eight pence) which were promoted to the reader by the rather unconvincing slogan: 'With Intelligent Folk it's save and smoke'. Smoking was a habit enjoyed across the whole of society from royalty to surgeons, to politicians, policemen, miners, housewives, factory girls and even some top sportsmen of the day. Our own local GP was also a cigarette smoker.

The King smokes a cigarette at the 1946 FA Cup Final. British Pathé Ltd.

In the 1950s smoking was accepted in many public places such as shops, cinemas, telephone boxes, pubs, the upper deck of buses, sports stadia and even some areas of hospitals. Notable exceptions were churches and the downstairs of local double-decker buses. When tobacco smoke was confined to enclosed spaces in which there was also a damp atmosphere from wet clothing (e.g. telephone kiosks and upper decks of buses on a rainy day) then a pleasant aromatic flavour would rapidly change to an acrid stench. Smoking on a mass scale could always be seen within large crowds. As a well supported Trinity match drew to a close in the dusk of a winter Saturday at Belle Vue, I would often gaze into the dense crowd on the terraces at the St Catherine's End, fascinated by the continuous display of twinkling lights, formed by individuals lighting up their cigarettes and pipes at slightly different times.

Mum and Dad both smoked but only Dad was a true smoker. Mum had the odd cigarette at home but was obviously not a serious convert, judging from the way she puffed the smoke out immediately once it had been drawn into her mouth (an 'exhaler'). True addicts would linger, eyes half closed, as they experienced the pleasure of their indulgence. An expert would demonstrate complete mastery of the art by blowing perfect smoke rings or by redirecting the smoke up the nose for onward transmission to the lungs. I was always fascinated by the newspaper man selling the *Yorkshire Evening News* at the top of Westgate: with hands full of newspapers, his cigarette was just an appendage to the mouth and was rarely removed until it became too hot to continue, whereupon it would be rapidly replaced with a fresh one. These incessant smokers talked, worked and went about their daily business always with a fag drooping from their lips. In order to redirect the continuous smoke from their squinting eyes, their faces took on a permanent contortion, giving the impression that their appendage was more a nuisance than a pleasure! In this strange way some individuals would readily consume up to sixty cigarettes per day, often Woodbines or Park Drive which were smaller but much cheaper than other popular brands, such as Senior Service and John Player.

Dad's pipe smoking was associated with the paraphernalia and rituals

Self-portrait.
R. H. Barraclough.

characteristic of a serious smoker. He was very choosy about his tobacco but did change brand occasionally. Ogden's St Bruno flake probably had the longest run but Erinmore and Balkan Sobranie were also in favour at various times during the 1950s. He had a selection of pipes in a wooden rack on the living room mantelpiece, and they were all regularly summoned to contribute to the ritual, although I could never quite work out the procedure governing the change from one pipe to another, if there was one at all. Pipes were mysteriously classified according to the quality of smoke they generated, but only Dad knew how to rate them, so his surprise presents on his birthday and at Christmas were confined to simpler items such as 'woolly fur' – coated wire pipe cleaners, tobacco pouches and hand tools for cleaning ('broddling') the pipe and prodding down the tobacco in its bowl. The loading of fresh, hand-rubbed flake tobacco into his tobacco pouch was a regular ritual, but the really skilled aspect was the filling of the pipe to produce the correct density of rubbed tobacco and air, which was critical in determining the degree of pleasure and the correct burn rate. A complicated lighting process would be accompanied by a lot of vigorous sucking that made Dad's cheeks hollow from the effort, although it didn't take much in his case. The burning tobacco would also have to be periodically prodded down into the bowl to adjust its density, sometimes with a bare thumb or finger. Even after much practice there seemed to be a lot of lighting and puffing before a satisfactory steady state could be reached. Despite the time required for all these preliminaries Dad would get through about an ounce of tobacco per day.

But Dad's pipe wasn't just for smoking: it was often a teaching aid or a pointer to help reinforce an argument; it would be a stick to be chewed on or something just to hold when in deep thought. Its most common alternative use, however, was as a percussion instrument. Dad couldn't listen to any music on the wireless without taking some sort of active part; he would regularly join in with an orchestra or a brass band by blowing an imaginary trumpet or trombone. Failing this, if there was no appropriate instrumental section for him, he would make do with performing the accompanying percussion. A simple regular beat would be made by one hand on the armchair but more complex rhythms would involve rattling the end of his pipe on his false teeth. Some tunes, such as *The Archers* theme tune, would normally be played by both 'hand and pipe' percussion. If his audience appreciated the performance, Dad would provide an encore by rattling his false teeth with his tongue to produce a sound that was uncannily similar to that generated by a certain type of maracas!

With such a family pedigree, including an insatiable urge to try out new things, I soon had my first smoke. Acquisition of cigarettes was difficult: the cost of even the smallest pack of the cheapest brand, five Woodbines, would have eaten into most of my sixpence-a-week pocket money, but the main problem, of course, was that I wasn't even ten years old. However, an older acquaintance of 'Big Tish' had managed to obtain a pack of five Senior Service cigarettes which were being individually sold down the chain via 'Little Tish', at extortionate marked-up prices. The desire to have my first smoke overcame my instinctive prudence, and I bought the last cigarette for threepence – convincing myself that it was good value at less than the cost of a Saturday afternoon visit to t'Spit. My precious white stick was gently carried to a secluded area on the edge of the school field during school holidays. I was accompanied by 'Little Tish' who had also bought his cigarette and some matches from his big brother. The disappointment of the taste, and the coughing it produced, were especially memorable, and I was in no fit state to complete the process. However, determined to obtain my full threepence worth, the remaining 'tab end' was saved for a later try.

The choice of venue to complete my first smoke was unfortunate to say the least; I now consider it foolish and extremely dim-witted! For some inexplicable reason I thought our outside lavatory would be a safe place, not realising how the smell of smoke could linger. I was so confident I would not be found out that I didn't even monitor the subsequent use of the lavatory by Mum or Dad. After several days nothing was said, so I relaxed in the knowledge that I had got away with it. Then, after about a week, with my guard well and truly down, Mum struck in typical lightning fashion: 'I wonder who's been smoking in the privy, then?' With robotic precision the heads of Mum and Elaine swivelled in perfect unison in my direction and two pairs of eyes bore down on me, just like an interrogation in the films. Interestingly, Mum had timed her strike when Dad was not present, obviously planning to deal with the whole issue herself as an 'operational' matter. By delaying my eventual plea of guilty, it did buy me valuable time to consider the answer to the inevitable follow-up question, 'And where did you get the cigarette?' A truthful answer would have initiated a neigbourhood investigation that would have ruined my 'street cred' and made my life a misery in Belle Vue. By replying that I had smoked a tab end picked up from the street was a lie, but a credible answer in the circumstances. This admission was followed by uproar and the inevitable finger-wagging health and safety lecture from Mum, during which Elaine turned up her nose at the very idea of having to share a home with such a filthy little toad. But my pragmatic approach had worked. I had received a deserved rollicking, but neither Mum nor Dad had actually killed me which, for a moment, I imagined might have been my fate, had they found out about my involvement in a cigarette extortion racket, run by budding members of the local mafia. Dad never said anything so I never knew if he was ever told of the incident.

Dad did find out about my association with other smokers, some of whom were also underage, but he showed no concern at all. One of these, Nigel – known affectionately as 'Nige' – was already an incessant smoker at fifteen years of age. He came from a large Doncaster family associated with a successful haulage business, which took him to towns and cities throughout Britain, including Wakefield. Ever the dandy, Nige always attracted a lot of attention from admirers in his new dark green suit, smartly trimmed in orange and black. Like his father, Sir Nigel Gresley, he also commanded a lot of attention from servants who made sure that he was fed and watered at all times. Nige had a placid nature but when his latent

Class A4 steam locomotive, Sir Nigel Gresley, no. 60007 in all its splendour.
STEVE ARMITAGE.

power was suddenly released he could be frighteningly awesome. I first experienced this change of mood in the summer of 1952 when, standing quite close to him, his quiet, gentle wheeze suddenly exploded into a stuttering roar which made me and other observers instinctively back away in fear. Class A4 steam locomotive, Sir Nigel Gresley, number 60007, slowly pulled out of Wakefield Westgate Station hauling the mid-morning passenger express to London, and that was the moment I became hooked on steam locomotives and trainspotting.

Most means of transport were objects of huge fascination for boys in the 1950s, usually the larger and more imposing the better. Although small boats and barges could be readily seen on the nearby river and canal network, ships of any size were, of course, not accessible in Wakefield and my imagination had to be stirred by photographs in books, and in films at t'Spit. Since I was captivated by the sheer scale of the giant liners, I would often try to draw pictures of the Queen Mary and the Queen Elizabeth, and I would certainly have been completely smitten by big ships had I actually been in their presence, but I had to wait years to see one in a coastal port.

By 1952 I cannot recall having been within earshot of an aeroplane, something else that had to wait. The maiden commercial flight of the De Haviland Comet jet airliner, heralding the dawn of a new travel age, went more or less unnoticed until the series of highly publicised air accidents and disasters led to its eventual withdrawal from service, when it gradually dawned on the authorities that this particular design of aircraft was a highly dangerous form of transport. I can recall sketching older Second World War fighter aircraft, Spitfires and Hurricanes, from pictures in books and comics, attempting to reproduce the subtle differences in wing shape but, since I had never touched, smelled or heard an aeroplane, I had no 'feel' for this mode of transport at all.

Officers of the West Riding Constabulary and some of their black police cars, all British makes, *c.*1950. From left to right: Standard, Vauxhall, Wolseley, Austin.
R. H. BARRACLOUGH.

Cars continued to hold considerable fascination for me. The traditional black saloons, such as those driven by the police, were gradually giving way to a range of brightly coloured models on the main roads.

Many of these new cars bore their original British marque: Austin, Morris, MG, Riley and Wolseley, although by 1952 these had all been merged into one giant conglomerate, the British Motor Corporation. I was always very keen to have a ride in a car but there were few opportunities.

The West Riding Police Road Safety team demonstrates how not to drive at a local Agricultural Show, early 1950s. R. H. BARRACLOUGH.

Members of the West Riding Police Road Safety demonstration team, early 1950s: back row, left to right: George Heywood, Bill Fish, Fred Rummery, John Morton, and Geoff Greaves. Dad is on the extreme right of the front row with the two supporters of an unknown 'lady'. R. H. BARRACLOUGH.

On some occasions in the summer, however, Dad would pick me up on Doncaster Road in a police car on the way to weekend agricultural shows, where he and colleagues of the West Riding Police Driving School would give demonstrations of road safety, by enacting dangerous manoeuvres in mock scenes involving cars, vans, bicycles and pedestrians. One of the policemen dressed up as a woman pedestrian pushing a pram and crossing the road at the wrong time and wrong place.

It was great fun, but the best part was riding there and back in a car. Without a care in the world I would slither around the shiny front bench leather seat of a Standard Vanguard, completely untethered, while admiring Dad's dexterity as he simultaneously lit his pipe, steered the car and changed gear via the column lever. In-car safety was far from anyone's mind in the early fifties, including police officers responsible for road safety!

The dashboard of a Phase1 Standard Vanguard police car, *c.*1950.
R. H. BARRACLOUGH.

Few of us drooled over the various local buses, which were usually treated as commonplace beasts of burden, transporting us to and from the city centre. Sometimes we would take a number 85 Pontefract–Holmfirth double-decker bus, directly from the stop on Doncaster Road to visit my maternal grandmother and aunts in Shepley, where the bus stopped directly outside their house twelve miles away; we also travelled by bus to visit my aunts and uncles in Shelley. Of more interest were the luxurious private coaches parked on Arthur Street when visiting rugby teams played at Belle Vue.

Steam locomotives commanded my attention above all other modes of transport. I could witness first-hand the imposing scale, power and speed of these huge machines, which had many features characteristic of living creatures. These leviathans breathed, ate, drank, peed, wheezed, coughed and roared. Most of all they had a characteristic body odour, which could only be produced by the complex interaction of coal smoke with the reaction products of steam on hot oil and metal. They were fed and nurtured by other living beings, and many locomotives had their own character and individuality, including unique names and their own combination of mechanical features. Steam locomotives were the gentle giants of 1950s machinery, with the majesty and docility comparable to whales and elephants from the animal kingdom. If someone had told me in 1952 that steam locomotives mated and reproduced, perhaps I would have believed them?

There were hundreds of former LYR and LMS locomotives around the Belle Vue engine sheds, within half a mile of our house. At first these were enthusiastically underlined in my new Ian Allan's trainspotter's book, a catalogue of every locomotive according to its class, number, name and relevant technical details. However, apart from a few mixed traffic, Class Five locomotives ('Black Fives'), many of the local Wakefield locomotives were dirty black goods engines. There were hundreds of these in any one class, making the task of ever spotting them all rather hopeless.

My interest in local LMS engines rapidly waned and I focused on the passenger express trains running on the north–south, Scotland–London (King's Cross) line that had aroused my initial interest, particularly the

A group of former LMS Class 5 locomotives ('Black Fives') outside Belle Vue Engine Sheds. Steve Armitage.

green-liveried Pacifics.[1] My favourites were the Class A4s, designed by LNER chief designer, Sir Nigel Gresley, whose 100th Pacific locomotive built to his design, had been named after him in 1937. A year later, another A4 Gresley Pacific, Mallard attained the world speed record for steam traction, which at 126 m.p.h. was never broken. I spotted all 35 of these beautiful streamlined beasts ('Streaks'), usually from the school playing field, bordering the main line, and numerous trips to Doncaster Engine Sheds.

In the 1950s, smoke from coal fires at home and work was as much a feature as that from tobacco, and steam locomotives. It belched from the chimneys of practically every house and factory in winter. When the air was still, the perfectly aligned plumes of smoke added another dimension to the rows of terraced houses in Belle Vue. Under certain atmospheric conditions, the particles in the smoke combined with the damp, cold air to form a blanket of 'smog' (fog intensified by smoke) which had a nasty

---

1. A 'Pacific' Class steam locomotive is one in which there are four small bogie wheels at the front, six large driving wheels, and two small wheels below the cab, known as a 4-6-2, the arrangement most commonly used for large, mainline passenger express locomotives.

acidic taste and rapidly produced a horrible black mucous in the nose from the soot particles. I thought it great fun turning a nice clean white handkerchief black, by blowing my nose into it.

It was always foggy during and after 5 November, Bonfire Night. By 1952 our gang around Back Regent Street would build our own fire. Once local supplies of spare wood from Fred Jackson's joinery and the cemetery were exhausted, we would spend hours collecting wood ('chubbin') from as far afield as Sandal, then carefully hide it in our back yards to ensure it was not raided by rival gangs from Denmark Street. Each of us had a small, white paper bag containing a few fireworks, (usually made by the Standard Company of Huddersfield) bought over the counter from t'paper shop, but there were never enough Golden Rains, Bangers and Jumping Crackers to form a lengthy display: they would all go up in smoke within a few minutes. The main attractions were the fire, the toffee and the parkin. Having a bonfire in a street as narrow as Back Regent Street was pushing the boundaries of health and safety, especially since the previous year's fire had blistered the paint work of a couple of gates. We all knew that incurring the wrath of Olive Stephenson and Mary Lockwood, not to mention Elizabeth Gott and Violet Barraclough, was not a good idea, so the fire in 1952 was very carefully built and sited in the middle of the street at the maximum distance from all the gates. It had taken quite a long time to light the fire in the damp atmosphere and it was just about ablaze when Gladys Sheard arrived in her little grey baby Austin, expecting to drive home to number 70 at the top of the street: we had never seen a car in Back Regent Street before! Instructions were issued to put the fire out, but this did not happen quickly enough for the impatient driver, who eventually called out the city fire brigade. They soon extinguished the fire, but not without creating lots of smoke. Bonfire night had ended in blackened tears for our gang, and even Mum thought that the lady had been mean spirited, although I suspect all the local women were relieved that the fire had not caused any damage.

The poor visibility from thick fog and smog resulted in hazardous travelling conditions and the postponement of rugby matches. On 8

Playing with fire. Author (left), Michael Crowhurst (centre) and Jimmy Stephenson (right) build a steam locomotive in author's back yard. R. H. BARRACLOUGH.

October, fog had been one of the likely contributory factors to the Harrow and Wealdstone rail crash, Britain's worst post-war rail disaster, in which a pile-up of three trains had resulted in 112 deaths and 340 injured. To a youngster, the lack of visibility and eerie sound-deadening effects produced by thick smog were also slightly frightening. The weekend of 6 December, 1952, was certainly 'smoggy' around Wakefield, where there were a number of car accidents. It was two days before my tenth birthday, my name was in Auntie Marion's Birthday List in that weekend's edition of the *Wakefield Express* and I wasn't allowed to play out in the smog. But it was worse in London which experienced one of the worst 'pea soupers' in its history over the same weekend. Thousands died of respiratory illnesses as a consequence of what became known as the Great Smog. We now know that one of the contributory factors to this nasty yellowish smog was the high sulphur content of the domestic coal, as a result of Britain exporting its high quality, low-sulphur coal to help pay off its war debt! A high sulphur content in the coal led to a high sulphur dioxide content in the smoke, which had produced dangerous levels of sulphuric acid in the smog. The period around my tenth birthday was a turning point when Britain began to realise that something had to be done about its air quality. But it would take years to implement change.

Meanwhile, at 52 Regent Street the living room fire was lit, stoked and fettled by its chief stoker. Mum's responsibility also included the ordering and management of the coal stocks and monitoring their quality. Coals that were not supplied in the requested size were returned in their sacks, forthwith. Coal that 'spat' or didn't burn properly was classified as 'muck', and the coalmen were informed of its poor quality in no uncertain terms. It was certainly true that the quality of house coal from the local seams was starting to deteriorate around this time, and at a price of around £4 per ton the situation merited close monitoring by the local stokers. Mum was probably not aware then of Britain exporting its best coal to foreigners, but she always suspected that certain local households were delivered more 'muck' than others. There was also some envy of the miners in the street who enjoyed the perk of free home coal, allowing some to keep their fires in all night – their houses were always cosy and warm.

According to Dad, I had not been born in a field and was told firmly to 'put t'wood in t'oyl' (close the door!). However, although doors had always to be kept shut, they had to be closed gently to avoid creating a draught which would redirect smelly smoke from the flue into the living room; I was often admonished for banging the doors shut and creating a living room full of smoke. On cold days it was only adequately warm around the hearth, so hobbies were still best carried out within a few feet of the fire. By now I had moved on from Dinky toys to building models in Meccano, which Dad had managed to acquire second hand, with parts supposedly equivalent to those of a very advanced set. Of course, it was really his toy, and he eagerly helped me build various models, despite the frustrations of some missing parts and the poor quality nuts and bolts which often cross threaded.

Encouraged by both Mum and Dad, I was also learning to play the piano. Reading music was essential for the choir and I enjoyed memorising the position of notes on the musical scales, using various acronyms which I thought were wonderful (Every Good Boy Deserves Favours, etc). Piano lessons were held after tea on Fridays, when I would gulp down my tripe before running down the snicket between the Trinity Ground and the rear gardens of the semi-detached houses at the top end of Regent Street, to the tiny front room of Maggie Ramsden's terraced house at 48 St Catherine's Street, Agbrigg. This front (and only) sitting room was accessed directly from the street and, because of its size and the welcoming fire burning in the grate, was always extremely cosy. It was a tight squeeze for piano lessons, with just enough space for the outside door, an internal door to the back scullery, an upright piano on the back wall, a double piano stool for Mrs Ramsden and her pupil, and a settee under the front window where the next client would be seated to wait his or her turn. I always dreaded it when the next pupil turned up early and could eavesdrop on my feeble efforts! One such pupil was Geoffrey Stanley, a cheerful red-haired lad from Sandal whom I later befriended. I also became acquainted with a fascinating device, the metronome, and was disappointed that, although Mrs Ramsden had two beautiful wooden-encased instruments perched on the top of her piano, she rarely set them off in my lessons. She would usually beat time with a pencil on the side of the stool. I soon found out that the pencil was also handy for tapping pupil's fingers when they were playing a wrong note.

Mum always 'aired' t'front room at Christmas by lighting a fire in the grate a day before the relatives visited. Actually, there seemed to be less air in the room at the end of the process than at the beginning – I certainly can't recall any window being opened at that time of the year. The room was warmer after a day or so, but a rather innocuous damp smell was gradually transformed into a distinctively unpleasant odour, not dissimilar to that characteristic of second-hand furniture stores. Of course, I didn't know then that all the smelly vapours from interaction of coal smoke and water vapour, with the porous furnishings, were more likely to be released into the 'air' as the temperature rose.

Mum's three elder sisters had never married. One theory was that there was a shortage of eligible men after the Great War; Mum's opinion was that they had been 'too fussy'! By 1952 my aunts were middle-aged spinsters, and they dressed accordingly: sensible lace-up shoes, plain long skirts, buttoned-up blouses, hand knitted cardigans and no make-up. Auntie Edie was a very serious, sophisticated lady who often wore a slightly painful expression on her wrinkled face, as if she was trying to work out some complex mental arithmetic, or as if she was surrounded by something rather unpleasant – I don't think it was the company or the smell of t'front room. Tiny Auntie Flo' was the complete opposite and a perfect foil to Edie. With a lovely carefree nature, Auntie Flo' smiled continuously and agreed with everything that was said ('yes, that's right'); her mission in life was not to offend anyone. An eternal optimism that there is some good to be found in the most hopeless soul had made her an inspired choice as my godmother, although in reality I suspect that this dubious honour had simply fallen on her as the eldest sister, and therefore first in the pecking order. Auntie Olive was actually my favourite aunt and also Mum's best friend – they were the nearest in age. Olive had experienced life beyond home as a member of the NAAFI during wartime and, afterwards, she had run a boarding house in Blackpool. She was good fun and less prim and proper than the other two. Now, as manageress of the local Co-op drapery store in the village of Shepley, she was again living at home. Unlike her two elder sisters, Olive was a cigarette smoker and was glad to be able to enjoy her inhalations in peace when she visited us.

It seemed a lot of effort for such short visits, the duration of which was dictated by the vagaries of both the winter weather and the Christmas timetable of the number 85 West Riding bus service. My aunts came in pairs, leaving one of them behind to look after my grandparents who, by now, never travelled anywhere. For this reason we visited my aunts and grandparents more often than they visited us; no-one ever stayed overnight. There were many cups of tea drunk and home-made mince pies eaten. My aunts were not teetotal but hardly any alcohol was consumed, until it became the in-thing to have a Babycham or the odd glass of sherry. Even then, Auntie Flo' would only contemplate a drink if the other sister was in the mood, and there was always quite a kerfuffle before the final decision was arrived at ('Go on then!'). This would normally be followed by Auntie Flo's up-front apologies in the event of her having to be carried to the bus legless after one glass. We would play lots of games on a rickety card table, and I can remember being roundly reprimanded by both Mum and Auntie Edie for attempting to have a sneaky look at their cards. A rueful smile and a jocular comment from Auntie Flo' ('ee, I don't know!') would be her attempt to smooth things over, but I was learning where the boundaries between fair and foul play were.

The entertainment took on a different slant when my uncles visited. Dad would always engage Harry and Auntie Maggie's husband, Freddie Gill, in anecdotes of their younger days, which they would recount in an outrageously broad Yorkshire dialect, whilst the rest of us would try to guess the gist of what had been said. Of course, one would try to outdo the other and they would have us in stitches with their particular form of charade – much more fun than the Three Stooges! The villages around Huddersfield had developed their own local dialect, made popular in the fifties by articles written phonetically in the local newspaper, the *Huddersfield Examiner,* by 'Owd Joss' who lived in the Kirkburton area. Harry and Freddie were tickled pink when Dad put them on a par with 'Owd Joss'.

Smoke, steam and oil were not the only smells of Belle Vue in the fifties. Many dogs continuously roamed the streets, unleashed and seemingly ownerless. Fouling of the footpaths was quite common, especially in areas of Belle Vue where I wandered – I should say ran, for that was the problem. Mum's sardonic comment that, 'You never look where you are going!' was absolutely correct because I ran everywhere, eyes fixed a few yards ahead, rather than immediately in front of me. Quite often I would trip and fall, and I can confirm that the streets of Belle Vue were certainly not paved with gold in the early fifties. I could never understand why Mum always asked the question, 'Who's trailed dog muck into the house?' when she always knew the answer.

There are many nostalgic smells that immediately take me back to my Belle Vue home in the fifties: mothballs and Elliman's embrocation in my parents' bedroom; the smell of Dad's chemicals in the attic; the sweet scent of lilies of the valley flowers outside the back door and of the lilac tree at the bottom of the back yard; the paraffin lamp in the lavatory during winter; a cup of hot Oxo in the scullery after a bath; hot poultices and, of course, Bakelite, (phenol formaldehyde), which seemed to be everywhere. In an era before the development and mass uptake of durable plastics, quite a lot of consumer goods, including some kitchen utensils, wireless and telephone components, certain toys, cheap cameras and fountain pens, were still being made of a synthetic material based on Bakelite and its derivatives, which were mechanically hard and electrically insulating, but quite brittle, especially when fabricated into complex shapes. Bakelite produced a bitter tar-like smell from the phenol (carbolic acid) when warm – as in a wireless set – and also when it fractured, which it did far too easily. Many Christmases were ruined by broken Bakelite toys; my first Bakelite fountain pen broke a few days after I received it as a birthday present. The smell still lingers from the time in the early fifties when I cursed the day Bakelite was ever invented.

CHAPTER FIVE

Big Events and Massed Choirs but no TV, 1953

I yearned for a television set, long before the Coronation of Queen Elizabeth II in June 1953 made this wonderful new device so popular, seemingly to everyone except my parents. TV sets appeared in the Wakefield shops around 1950/51 but they were unable to show clear pictures until the summer of 1951, when a new transmitter on the moors at Holme Moss was built to beam television to viewers in the North of England, on both sides of the Pennines. These magic waves had a distance of less than twenty miles to travel to Wakefield and the first test transmissions were a huge success: the live pictures of Sylvia Peters on 15 August 1951 were reported in the *Wakefield Express* three days later: 'as almost as good as the cinema'. Television arrived officially in Wakefield when the Holme Moss transmitter opened on 12 October 1951, but watching television in the comfort of my own home was a different matter altogether. What I now understand as the great virtue of delayed gratification was a period of extreme frustration for me until my parents eventually succumbed to 'the box' many years later. Meanwhile, my television viewing was dependent on others.

I knew two people who had a television set in 1952, but they were not such close friends that I could readily inveigle my way into a seat in front of 'the box'. Perhaps by divine intervention, these two blessed acquaintances came via my association with St Catherine's Church: kind Christian souls who occasionally took pity on me. Nice old Bill Sharpe from the choir had a TV, and I saw my first televised football match at his house in Agbrigg. The other set was owned by Arthur Hargrave, a lay reader, whose son Noel also sang in the choir. They lived close to us at the top of Denmark Street and I would occasionally be invited to watch *Children's Hour* and *Muffin the Mule* there. However, I missed many rugby matches, including the first televised Rugby League Challenge Cup Final at London's Wembley stadium, between Featherstone Rovers and Workington Town; actually, this was also the last televised Rugby League Cup Final for six years, because the authorities were becoming concerned about the effect of live TV broadcasts on the match attendance.

In 1953 the Rugby League Challenge Cup Final at Wembley was a Yorkshire–Lancashire affair between two big, well supported clubs, Huddersfield and St Helens, in front of 90,000 spectators, and I was there. I had never been further south than Skegness until that memorable day of 25 April 1953, when Uncle Harry and I set off for London from Wakefield Westgate Station on a train pulled by an A3 Pacific, Harvester, number 60074. I knew the main route off by heart from my railway books: Doncaster, Retford, Newark, Grantham, Peterborough, London, but I didn't know that there would be so many tunnels on the approach to London; we seemed to be plunged into darkness for ages. On arriving at King's Cross Station I felt very small in the huge crowds, and there was no need for Uncle Harry to remind me that I had to 'stick close' to him: I was petrified of getting lost.

The tiniest detail of the Underground railway that any Londoner took for granted made a huge impression on a ten-year-old boy on his first visit from the West Riding of Yorkshire: the tiled walls of the tunnels; the sudden rush of stale, warm air smelling like the inside of t'Spit, silently announcing the approach of a train from a gloomy tunnel, long before it could be heard or seen; the dim lighting (also like t'Spit); the frightening way in which the sliding doors rapidly closed automatically before the train accelerated away; the discarded cigarette ends trapped between the wooden laths on the carriage floor; having to hold on tight to a slippery pole to avoid being thrown off my feet as the train lurched at high speed somewhere beneath the vast capital city where I could get lost forever; the fact that everybody except me seemed to know where they were going in this vast underground maze!

Fortunately, Uncle Harry also knew the way – or perhaps he just followed the crowd – and we emerged from the Bakerloo Line at Wembley Park Station to see the famous Twin Towers of Wembley Stadium ahead. I had seen these on the black and white film clips on Pathé News and so I was half expecting them to be coloured grey, instead of a lightish brown! Uncle Harry bought a programme for one shilling and we entered the ground long before the kick-off. We had a standing position behind the goal posts on a vast open terrace which seemed miles away from the immaculately prepared playing surface below us. The massed bands of the Coldstream Guards and the Welsh Guards were already entertaining the thin crowd when we entered the stadium, then a man in a white suit, Arthur Caiger, confidently strode onto the pitch to conduct the community singing, culminating in an emotional rendering of 'Abide with Me'. The crowd had now swollen to around 90,000, and we all obediently sang our hearts out before vigorously waving our *Daily Express* song sheets on cue. It was all so different from Belle Vue, as the two teams ceremoniously walked out in brand new kit to be presented to the Duke of Norfolk: Huddersfield in their classy claret and gold hoops; St Helens in dazzling white with a red band.

The game itself was a rather tense and ill-tempered affair, with St Helens applying some dubious tactics that were certainly not appreciated by Uncle Harry and the other Huddersfield supporters, who booed a lot, especially when one of Huddersfield's three Australian stars, Johnny Hunter, was carried from the field as a result of an 'off the ball' incident. However, Huddersfield was the eventual winner by 15–10, following two tries by man of the match, nineteen-year-old stand-off half, Peter Ramsden.

Afterwards, Uncle Harry took me to see the sights around Buckingham Palace, and again it was the size and scale of everything that amazed me: the width of the Mall, the size of St James's and other parks in the very heart of the city and the massive stonework of Buckingham Palace. I also noticed the ongoing preparations for the Coronation taking place around the Mall and the Palace. The Big Day was only five weeks away.

Plans for the televised broadcast of the Coronation of Queen Elizabeth II were already well underway in 1952. Local shops, Robbs, Isherwoods, Powells and Lodge Radiovision were selling and renting TV sets that were predominantly British makes: Decca, HMV, Bush, Murphy, Ekco, G.E.C., Pye and Ferguson. A 14-inch set cost less than £100, but my parents refused to buy one. Dad begrudged the large amount of purchase tax payable on luxury goods, such as television sets, at that time. Although the Conservative government had reduced purchase tax to 50 per cent from

This is what all the fuss was about – a typical early TV set. On the Air Ltd.

the 66·7 per cent rate imposed by the 1951 Labour government, Dad was still not prepared to 'fork out' so much of his hard-earned pay in tax. He was firmly against renting, and any mention of hire purchase would trigger a pipe-pointing lecture on the evils of what was becoming known as the 'never-never'. 'Earn it before you spend it' was Dad's maxim; the alternative was to go without.

According to Mum, television showed a lot of 'muck', not suitable for children of my age. Any reasonable defence against such an irrational judgement would move her to play the health and safety card by implying that TVs were also far too dangerous. I wasn't aware then that some of the early TV sets had caught fire, but it turned out to be less than one in a thousand. Mum's basic problem with television was that it represented a step change in home routines with which she was unsure how to cope. This behaviour was really no surprise considering that her Victorian mother flatly refused to have a TV, washing machine or any new gadget in her house throughout the fifties and sixties.

The city of Wakefield staged a range of events marking the Coronation from May to late autumn, 1953. In Coronation Week special entertainment was laid on in the city, including a 'Mammoth Coronation Fair' in Northgate. One particularly novel attraction for me was Syncopating Sandy, 'the Musical

Genius of the Century' who was attempting to play the piano non-stop for 132 hours, thereby breaking the world record of 130 hours held by a German. My own 'tickling the ivories', as Dad called it, was progressing reasonably well under his watchful eye and I was passing the elementary exams, but the very thought of playing the piano non-stop for more than five minutes, let alone 130 hours, was quite incredible to me. For a fee of one shilling for adults and sixpence for children it was possible to witness this amazing feat during the hours of 11 a.m. to 11 p.m. Sandy Strickland of Bolton was a well known character who toured many northern towns and cities in the 1950s to attempt various piano playing records, but the exact conditions under which he and his rivals made these attempts were always the subject of great controversy. A friend of Dad had paid his shilling and observed that, even with a few days to go, Sandy had appeared rather ill and close to collapse. Some sceptics thought that this was just part of the drama to entice more spectators and make more money, although Sandy's strange diet may have had something to do with it. According to the 6 June 1953 edition of the *Wakefield Express,* 'Sandy had stopped eating, but was smoking 150 cigarettes and drinking 2

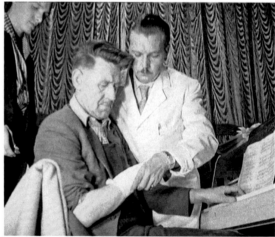

Syncopating Sandy was a major attraction in Wakefield during the Coronation celebrations of 1953 (left), but he endured considerable hardship during his record piano playing attempts – as shown here (right) on a separate occasion when a physician had to bandage his right wrist whilst he kept on playing! City of Wakefield Coronation Souvenir Brochure (left) & British Pathé Ltd. (right).

gallons of tea and 12 bottles of lemonade daily.' Local company E. P. Shaw & Co. Ltd. supplied the minerals. Despite the lack of appropriate food, not to mention the practicalities of relieving himself of all that pop, Syncopating Sandy claimed the record of 132 hours non-stop piano playing at 11 p.m. on Saturday, 6 June. It was said that Sandy and his promoter Bernard Wooley made 'quite a few bob' from various record attempts, long after the event in Wakefield.

There was a special Coronation Exhibition in the art gallery on Wentworth Terrace, including a film show about Wakefield past and present, and a schoolchildren's art exhibition. A Technical and Industrial Exhibition was also held in the Technical College to display to parents and young people 'the great effort which the firms in the Wakefield area are making towards the Nation's need.' There were various special sporting events during the weekend before the big event, including a rugby league match between Trinity and Featherstone Rovers on the Saturday, and a cricket match between Wakefield and a West Indies XI on the Sunday. Special church services were also held on the Sunday, including a combined Coronation Service and Mayor's Civic Sunday Service in the Cathedral. On the Monday there was a celebration tea at school and I arrived home with a souvenir mug to add to the family collection in t'front room. The general consensus was that the mug was of inferior quality to those from earlier coronations, ('things aren't what they used to be') especially since the image of the young Queen made her look rather plain and middle-aged. However, these imperfections were trivial compared with those that aroused public complaints about the coronation mugs supplied by the West Riding authority to children in nearby Horbury. Many of these mugs were oval-shaped. Some even had the Queen's head the wrong way up and were inscribed as Elizabeth I! This incensed local councillor, J. M. Oddie, who told the *Wakefield Express* in its report of 13 June 1953, that the Horbury Urban District Council must also be mugs for accepting such shoddy goods.

The city had decorated its new Bull Ring shopping centre with red, white and blue pennants, decorative panels and special flower beds on the traffic

Souvenir mugs from the 1953 Coronation of Elizabeth II (left) and the planned Coronation of Edward VIII in 1937, (right) – the one that never happened. MYOTT (LEFT) AND JOHNSON BROS., (RIGHT).

island. Shops were decorated 'to their own taste'. Decorations extended up Wood Street to the Town Hall and County Hall; flags flew outside the West Riding Police headquarters.

In the suburbs the decorations were mainly organised by street groups where there were various activities, notably street parties. Many of these were based on the large housing estates: Lupset, Eastmoor and Portobello. The Rufford Street organisation had indicated that a 'reight good do' was planned for Saturday, 13 June, with a 'Bumper tea for all and each of the 37 children to have ¼ lb of sweets and ice-cream.' Such overt gluttony made me feel quite deprived, especially since Regent Street did not have a coronation street party at all. Although there were coronation celebrations involving the church and school, the nearest street parties to us were in the rival territories of Denmark Street and Clarion Street, where tea was planned for 200(!).

I didn't know at the time that large street parties required a critical mass of like-minded women, ideally of the same class, to organise and manage. Their menfolk might be roped in to carry out menial tasks such as lifting heavy tea urns onto wooden trestle tables, but the organisation and running of anything to do with food was largely the domain of women, who did

Flags fly outside the headquarters of the West Riding Constabulary during the Coronation, 1953. R. H. BARRACLOUGH.

The men look on as the women organise a street party. THE WAKEFIELD TIMES IN THE CITY OF WAKEFIELD CORONATION SOUVENIR BROCHURE.

this sort of thing routinely, albeit on a smaller scale at home, every day of their lives.

Regent Street did not have the necessary critical mass of like-minded women. There were many disparate groups and cliques in the area but they were not necessarily focused within the street itself; neither were the groups strictly class-based. In Mum's case her friends and kindred spirits were centred on the activities of St Catherine's Church, within groups such as the Mothers' Union and Young Wives' Association. One or two of these friends lived in Regent Street but most lived elsewhere in the district, from Belle Isle to Agbrigg and also 'back o' t'Alec'. Their class and location did not come into it: these ladies were wives of miners, railway men, shop workers, engineers, managers, and teachers, as well as policemen. Dad's close friends also originated from his main external activities, work and the Camera Club. He was on nodding terms with many men in the street but they were not his close friends. It seemed that coronation street parties were hatched wherever there was a strong sense of community, and that wasn't Regent Street.

Many halls throughout the city had been made available for viewing the Coronation, including the nearest one to us at Doncaster Road Methodists (with priority for people aged over sixty-five). Television sets were provided and manned by the television members of the Wakefield and District Chamber of Trade who, no doubt, had half an eye on the burgeoning market for their wares. Projection TV was also made available in Pinderfields and Clayton hospitals. Next door to us, Mary Lockwood had a television set but they were still quite rare in Belle Vue. I regularly scanned the rooftops for TV aerials and was usually disappointed that any new installations were for people I did not know and, more importantly, for people who did not want to know me. Throughout the country there were now some two and a half million sets which 'displayed' the Coronation to an audience estimated at more than twenty million people but I wasn't one of them – listening to it on the wireless instead. My reflections at the end of Coronation Day were that the best bit had probably been a day off school. It had rained for most of the time and, according to the 6 June edition of the *Wakefield Express,* the local area had experienced one of the coldest June days on record, with a maximum temperature of 48·9 °F. Of much greater fascination for me was the exciting news that the tallest mountain in the world, Mount Everest, had been climbed by members of a British expedition, Edmund Hillary and Sherpa Tenzing.

Coronation 'fever' had started months earlier at school. We spent many lessons being instructed on the fine details of the great event and the historical significance of the orb, the sceptre and other coronation trappings which, rather tediously, we also had to draw and paint. Weeks were spent on rehearsals at our own school for the mass display of dancing and singing by the city's junior and secondary school pupils at the Trinity rugby ground, two days after Coronation Day. In this regard they were somewhat of an anticlimax, but the very idea of performing at Belle Vue rugby ground was for me one of the more exciting aspects of the whole Coronation! By now I had convinced myself that I would one day play for Wakefield Trinity and here was an early opportunity to tread on the sacred Belle Vue turf. However, a Yorkshire Square Eight and a series of other cissy English country dances, concluding with a grand Circassian Circle with girl partners, were not really what I had in mind. Once on the field, I was overawed by its sheer size, compared with the pitches on the school field, and I soon realised that I had a lot of growing up to do before I could even contemplate playing rugby on a full-sized pitch.

The massed choir was particularly memorable for its one rehearsal, when a frustrated conductor made numerous attempts to co-ordinate the output of over a thousand disparate voices on the open terraces of Belle Vue, in rather difficult conditions. I suppose the minimum requirement was to produce something that didn't sound like a rabble at a rugby match, but perhaps the conductor should have taken lessons from Arthur Caiger in how to engage with a massed choir. It is not the Last Night of the Proms at the Royal Albert Hall that I am transported to whenever I hear *Jerusalem* and *Land of Hope and Glory;* it's the St Catherine's End of Belle Vue rugby ground in 1953, repeatedly belting out these and many other patriotic songs with 1,500 other kids who neither heard, nor eventually really cared, what was expected of them from the conductor. On the day itself a Miss M. Moseley had taken up the baton and we were herded into the 'Scrattin Shed' to deliver a more co-ordinated performance which, apparently, delighted the mayor, Frank West, and other city dignitaries. It was also noteworthy that for the first time during Coronation Week the weather behaved itself.

The excitement and palaver of the Coronation gradually faded away in the summer, until the autumn tree-planting ceremony at school. On 6 November 1953, during the first term of my final year at Sandal Magna County Junior School, each of the eight classes planted a commemorative tree below the playground, next to the school field. Each child took part in the ceremony which was attended by many officials, including Wakefield's director of education, Clarence Leo Berry.

Tree planting ceremony, Sandal Magna County Junior School, 6 November, 1953. In the foreground John Crowhurst does his bit for Class VA. Others visible in VA, clockwise from the left-hand foreground are: Doreen Denton, Hesse Payne, Keith Moore, George Lancaster, Michael McGee, Trevor Wise, Robert Austerberry, Donald Burkinshaw, Neville Rider, Derek Senior, John Rogerson, Ian Harrop, Keith Barraclough, Marianna Wagner, Paul Proctor (behind the tree), Jean Simcock, Kay Redfearn, Margaret Andrew, Mary Atack, Judith Lockwood, Anne Hewitt, Carole Lockey, Barbara Hawes, Brenda Cooper, Miss E. L. Hauton, Pat Bedford, Barbara Nicholson and Joyce Dennison. *Wakefield Express.*

Cricket was of huge interest in the summer of 1953, when the Australian team arrived to defend the Ashes. I had always dreamed of seeing a Test match but, as usual, the name of the game was patience, which made it even more special when it actually happened. Dad had taken a day's holiday for our trip to the cricket temple of Headingley, Leeds, to see the second day's play in the fourth Test match, which it was hoped would provide a breakthrough for Len Hutton's team after the first three Test matches had all ended in a draw. It was Friday, 24 July, and I had wanted to see my hero Len

A 'Len Hutton' cricket bat being treated with linseed oil. R. H. Barraclough.

Hutton thrash the Aussies around the ground with his local Horbury-made, Slazenger Gradidge cricket bat, the same make as mine, a size six imprinted with an autograph by the man himself. But I was already disappointed. The wily old Aussie captain, Lindsay Hassett (he was nearly forty) had again won the toss on Thursday, the opening day, and chosen to put England into bat on a difficult pitch. Ray Lindwall had torn into the English batsmen with his full repertoire of inswingers, outswingers and yorkers. Hutton had been 'yorked' middle stump for a duck by Lindwall's second ball of the opening day. Denis Compton soon followed, also without scoring, so by the start of our visit on the second day, only the English tail-enders remained.

There was a rather tense atmosphere in the long queues which, even by eight thirty in the morning, wound around some of the neighbouring Headingley streets outside the ground. Near the entrances there was a lot of pushing and shoving but the queue jumpers were soon told where to go, not least by Dad and other irate fathers. Gradually, this largely all-male army of about 30,000, mostly Yorkshire men with their young sons in tow, lumbered slowly into the ground to find a vacant seat, hampered by all the gear they were carrying, including various protective measures to combat the uncertain weather, and a range of provisions to sustain them over a long day. We came fully armed with cushions, rugs, rolled up plastic raincoats (Pakamacs), caps, pullovers and a range of bags, including the family shopping bag and Haversacks bulging with a whole day's 'snap': flasks of hot tea, separate little bottles of milk, large bottles of Dandelion and Burdock pop, hefty sandwiches hewn from solid white loaves, and slabs of home baked cake, prepared and packed by the women we had left behind in peace at home. A few young men had also arrived with cricket bats and balls so, whilst the hungry eagerly wolfed down their 'snap' long before the start of the morning's play, and hours before the official lunchtime, the keen ones passed the time in *ad hoc* games of cricket which always sprang up when a group of kindred spirits found themselves with a bit of spare time in the vicinity of an available bit of reasonably flat ground. These cricket fanatics had instigated similar games in all sorts of places, such as Heath Common and Scarborough Beach, but they had probably never played on such a perfect surface as the boundary edge at Headingley.

The most striking aspect of the Headingley outfield was how green and flat it looked; not a daisy, dandelion or undulation could be seen. At the centre of this beautifully mown and rolled swathe of green, a white strip, just over twenty-two yards in length and the focus for most of the day's action, was already receiving lots of attention from a few fussy groundsmen who brushed, poked and prodded the shaven turf, oblivious to the mounting buzz of excitement around them.

We waited for hours but, at last, the amateur cricket ceased, the outfield was cleared of bodies beyond the boundary and we all settled down to watch the real thing as the Aussies took the field to generous applause. I was immediately struck by how smart and athletic they all looked with their suntans – a rarity in this part of the world – beautifully creased cream flannels, cream shirts and cream sweaters, lined in the Aussie green and gold. Some wore the famous green cap. Their captain, Hassett, was a busy little chap, quite obviously the boss as he placed his field to the exact positions he had in mind. During these preliminaries, a tall, handsome floppy-haired fellow lolloped close to our part of the ground to retrieve a ball, and casually threw a sweet to a kid sitting on the boundary in exchange for the ball. Here, within touching distance, was the great Aussie all-rounder, Keith Miller. When the young boy gleefully gobbled the sweet straightaway, I can remember thinking that if I had received such a present from a cricket legend and heroic Second World War fighter pilot, I would have saved it. For how long I now wonder? Although sweets had, at last, come off ration a few months earlier in February, they were still a novelty in the summer of 1953.

We were seated on wooden benches near the front of a vast open terrace between the Kirkstall Lane End and the giant stand shared with the neighbouring rugby league ground of Trinity's intense rivals, Leeds. Dad was already complaining that the seats were uncomfortably hard but I hadn't noticed – I was too busy focusing on Ray Lindwall who was menacingly measuring out his run, looking the part: broad shoulders, strong arms, raring to go. I didn't know at the time that Australia's finest pace bowler had previously been a rugby league player for the St George's club in Sydney, and had reputedly run the 100 yards in 10·4 seconds – some athlete! Lindwall's bowling was so fast that I never actually saw his deliveries from our distant view and neither, apparently, did the England

A packed Friday crowd at the 1953 Headingley Test match against the Aussies.
K. G. BARRACLOUGH.

The Friday afternoon session of the 1953 Headingley Test match. At 51 for 1, the Aussies are making steady progress towards England's first innings total of 167, with captain Lindsay Hassett 26 not out and Neil Harvey 11 not out. K. G. BARRACLOUGH.

tail-enders, and they were much closer. Lindwall and Alan Davidson took less than an hour to dismiss the remaining three batsmen cheaply and England were all out for the modest total of 167, Lindwall having taken 5 wickets for 54 in a masterful display of fast bowling.

When Hutton led out the England team for the Aussie's first innings they appeared rather washed out compared with their counterparts from 'down under': paler faces and much whiter flannels and shirts. Hutton wore his blue England cap. The Aussies' colourful approach to the game was also quite a contrast to England's lacklustre, defensive display, and they soon gained a lead with impressive innings by Neil Harvey and Graham Hole.

By the end of the day's play they were bowled out 99 runs ahead of England, but this lead might have been more without the excellent bowling of the great Alec Bedser who that day became the world's leading wicket taker in all Test matches. I had not seen my hero Len Hutton bat, but had seen him directing play on the field. I had also witnessed some of the world's greatest bowlers in action – a memorable day.

The Headingley Test match eventually ended in yet another draw after breaks for bad weather and some defensive – some said negative – play by England, notably from Trevor Bailey. Thus the 1953 Test series was decided in the fifth and final match at the Oval which England won to regain the Ashes, despite Hutton losing the toss for an amazing fifth time in a row. The new Elizabethan age had got off to a good start.

Although I had finished going to t'Spit, I hadn't finished with the cinema and I was now a regular at the ABC (Associated British Cinemas) Minors Club held on Saturday mornings at the Regal cinema in Wakefield. This was a real adventure, made more exciting by the visit to the nearby Woolworth's store in Kirkgate where some kids pinched sweets, now temptingly displayed in huge volumes on an open counter. I think I would have liked to have followed suit but the fear of being caught and my parents finding out overcame the temptation.

The Regal was a more modern and up-market cinema than t'Spit. A grand entrance with curved façade at the corner of busy Kirkgate and Sun Lane was a direct contrast to the tiny, chamfered corner entrance of t'Spit, next to two unmade roads in Belle Vue. The Regal building was certainly not the best example of Art Deco cinema architecture, but there was a real 'modern' (1935) feel about the foyer, with its sweeping curves and fancy metal stair railings, down to the main stalls and upstairs to the Circle. The very idea of going to a cinema with an 'upstairs' made the event even more special. Soft concealed lighting in the auditorium emphasised the gentle, rounded corners of the decorative ceiling arches, which led the eye down to similarly curved shapes around the focal point of the screen and stage. Red tip-up seats, smelling of Dettol and occasionally stained with spilled drinks and ice cream, completed the picture.

I cannot recall the Regal filled to its capacity of over 1,500 on those Saturday mornings, but there were certainly more of us than at 't'Spit' and we certainly made more noise. However, the chaos at the Regal was much more organised, since the programme was carefully punctuated with regular items to give us a chance to let off steam. These included the singing of the ABC Minors song, when we would stamp our feet and shout the final line '… We're Minors of the A … B … C', emphasising the key letters. This dispelled any doubt of our allegiance to the ABC organisation,

'Upstairs' in the Regal Cinema – quite different from 't'Spit'. Copyright © phill.d.

also evident from our white metal Minors badge, embellished with the red and blue triangles of the ABC logo. With hindsight, the management of the ABC brand was very much on the ball! Other orchestrated items included the mass singing of 'Happy Birthday' to those brave Minors who had enough confidence to be seen on stage, on or around their birthday, to collect a free lollipop and a free pass for the following week's performance. These enticements were never enough for me to overcome my shyness and mount the steps of the stage around my own birthday, even though the presentations were done at the corner, not in the limelight of centre stage. Those ABC Minors who seemed to have several birthdays during the year more than made up for my absence.

The ABC Minors programme included regular features such as Roy Rogers, Abbott and Costello, and the Bowery Boys: by now some of the latest films were also in colour. I saw my first full-length Technicolor film, Disney's *Treasure Island* at the Regal, although I don't think this featured as an ABC Minors Club showing. ABC Minors cost about a shilling in the early to mid-fifties, much more than t'Spit, but well worth it given

Akela, Mr Peter Young, and the St Catherine's Church Wolf Cub Pack in the playground of St Catherine's Church School, *c.*1954. Left to right: Derek Senior, Trevor Wise, Chris Cowton, Ian Wise, John Crowhurst, David Morris, Keith Barraclough, Johnny Booth, Bruce Bolland, David Pick, Martin Wright, Barry Bolland, Tony Skenfield. R. H. BARRACLOUGH.

the comprehensive programme in which Three Stooges and any projector breakdowns were conspicuous by their absence.

It was around this time that I joined a different organisation which also combined various aspects of learning, entertainment and letting off steam, albeit in a different manner. This was the Wolf Cub pack of St Catherine's Church which met every Friday evening in a little hut, the 'Club', next to the main building of St Catherine's Church School. The 24th Wakefield Wolf Cub Pack was only a small group of two 'sixes', but I expect still quite a handful for the seemingly elderly Bagheera, Florence Young, in her navy-blue outfit, also worn on Monday evenings as Brown Owl of the Brownies, and on Wednesday evenings as Captain of the Girl Guides. Although Mrs Young was the registered leader, the traditional Wolf Cub Pack leader, Akela, was her son, Peter Young, who wore a beret and khaki uniform which included long trousers, rather than the traditional shorts normally worn by Cub and Scout leaders. Akela's general appearance, combined with the military way he barked out orders to his obedient pack, gave the impression of a soldier at work rather than a Cub master. The group had been revived in 1949 after a few years lapse following the end of the Second World War, but by 1951 had already been commended by Wakefield Group Headquarters on its smartness and general appearance. I am not so sure that the new recruits of 1952/53 maintained such high standards!

I never really understood all the strange associations between the Wolf Cubs and Kipling's *Jungle Book,* such as the 'Grand Howl' led by Akela at the beginning and end of every meeting, but the Wolf Cubs was a great means of relieving pent up energy at the end of the school week, as well as an opportunity to learn how to tie complicated knots in bits of rope. Our chants of 'dob, dob, dob' (doing our best) in response to Akela's command of 'dyb, dyb, dyb' (do your best!) and other commitments of loyalty and duty to God and the Queen were always present as the underlying culture of the Wolf Cubs. Some of this may have rubbed off on us, but the most significant aspect of our Wolf Cub Pack was the highly competitive atmosphere engendered by an intense rivalry between the two sixes in what were supposed to be friendly team games.

We found out that in wintertime the 'Club' was opened by the school caretaker well before the 6.30 p.m. Cub meeting so that he could stoke the smelly coke fire in the cast iron stove. By racing back from piano lessons I would join the other Cubs in a no-holds-barred game of indoor football before Akela and Bagheera would turn up and bring some order into the proceedings. By now, we were all trying to emulate the dribbling feats of our hero, thirty-eight-year-old Stanley Matthews, who had won his first FA Cup medal in the 1953 final, when he produced a brilliant individual performance to help his team, Blackpool, in a dramatic 4–3 win over Bolton Wanderers. This was another historic sporting occasion that I failed to witness on television, but it did not stop me from imitating Matthews's every dribble, including an outside swerve into the middle of the stacked wooden chairs in the 'Club'. I never thought that my written request for Stanley Matthews's autograph would be met but, even better, my hero sent a signed photograph through the post.

A highlight of being a Wolf Cub was the 'Bob-a-Job' week, when we had to solicit friends and neighbours to find us a job to do, in return for payment of a 'bob' or more. Despite being rather shy, I was not averse to cold-calling in the neighbourhood, because I was driven by the competitive urge to earn more money than the other Cubs. By now, I seemed to turn everything into a competition. I even sneaked into the Trinity ground and marched up to the office where the club secretary, Eddie Thomas, gave me a bob for sweeping part of the terrace at the St Catherine's End. There had to be no cheating, with each job recorded on a card

An autographed photo of Stanley Matthews, the football hero of 1953. Saidman Bros.

by the person paying the money. I was quite worried when Arthur Winter gave me a bob for seemingly nothing, having written on the card 'Services Rendered', the meaning of which was not clear to me at all. Mum explained that he was paying me for having previously helped him deliver the milk in the street, and that it would be perfectly in order to include this as a genuine job. I have often mused how this innocent exchange between a ten-year-old boy and a middle aged man would nowadays be readily misconstrued! My 'Bob-a-Job' earnings were 21 shillings in 1953; the following year it was noted in my diary that 'I beat my record' by earning 40 shillings and nine pence. The Wolf Cub Pack nominated me to represent them at the presentation of our record earnings to the mayor, Frank West, during one of his last official duties, a Cub and Scout function on 6 May 1954, the very same evening that a young Roger Bannister achieved a rather more impressive record of running a mile in less than four minutes.

The Wolf Cub's promise of doing 'a good turn' may not have been achieved 'every day' but I did try. Quite often I would run errands, chop firewood, and in winter I would enthusiastically shovel snow from the footpath. I would also ensure that the fire hydrant at the bottom of Regent Street on the junction with Doncaster Road would be readily accessible to the fire brigade, by scraping away any snow and ice and putting down salt to prevent re-icing. I regarded this as an important civic duty which was carried out with the utmost pride, and I was rather disappointed at not being recognised as a local hero since, as far as I know, the fire brigade never needed to access the hydrant at that time.

Next to the fire hydrant was the red public telephone box in which I made my first call to Bagheera for my telephone proficiency badge. Fortunately, it was a pre-arranged call, so I did not have to go through the business of pressing Button B to retrieve my pennies in the event of there being no reply. However, as most first time users of the public telephone system in those days will testify, even a pre-arranged call was not an easy procedure. There was that heart-stopping moment when, with the heavy weight of the huge Bakelite telephone in one hand, the other free hand had to wrestle with a stiff Button A, which always put up a strong resistance to the establishing of a connection to the person who was patiently waiting at the other end. Once the obstinate Button A was eventually overcome, it then seemed to take an absolute age for the pennies to drop into the Post Office coffers, with a loud clunking noise, before one could speak!

Mum and other mothers, including Constance Senior and Margaret Morris of Belle Isle Avenue, also played their part on the Wolf Cubs parents' committee, organising parties, fund raising (jumble sales) and day trips, including one to Hull where, at last, I could marvel at big ships for the first time. I had fully bought into the concept of the Wolf Cubs and the Scouting movement but, regrettably, there was no Scout Group in the immediate neighbourhood when I reached the age of twelve.

Meanwhile, I was preoccupied with the piano, choir, Sunday School, rugby, football, cricket, trainspotting, ABC Minors, reading, Meccano and model making. I spent a lot of time in the school field, the perfect playground

Model boats in Peasholme Park, Scarborough, July, 1953. R. H. BARRACLOUGH.

for many local Agbrigg lads with whom I became acquainted: Peter and John Cunningham and John ('Spud') Speight from Ashdown Road; Keith and Kevin Oldroyd, (the 'Oddies') from Station Street; and Billy Marshall from Agbrigg Road. Dads were always very supportive. When the stud nails pierced the sole of my football boots, John Speight's dad, Don, was on hand to hammer them down on his iron last at 17 Ashdown Road. The 'Oddies' dad, Eric Oldroyd, would shout himself hoarse when encouraging us from the touchline during competitive school matches and even during friendly *ad hoc* games of 'touch and pass'. Everybody had to 'Get stuck in'.

Our 1953 summer holiday in Scarborough had inspired me to move up a gear in model making. I had already made a static wooden model of the ancient ship, the Golden Hind, from a kit, but having seen model motor boats on a lake in Peasholme Park that summer I became obsessed with the idea of building one myself.

By now I was a member of the local library close to school in Sparable Lane, Sandal, where I borrowed a book containing drawings and instructions on how to build a two-foot long model motor boat. The only problem was that the hull required a huge solid block of wood which had to be tediously hollowed out and shaped according to templates. Even Fred Jackson didn't have a single piece of wood of the appropriate size, but Dad's network of mates came to the rescue when a carpenter friend of Uncle Harry, Frank Crabtree, glued planks of wood together in the form of a composite. After a few lessons from Dad in hand chiselling, I hacked out the hull and, gradually, the boat took shape. By Christmas 1953, I had acquired a small electric motor and propeller to power the boat which was eventually launched on a local pond near Heath Common, on a cold winter's day in early 1954. My pride and joy slowly purred away, slightly underpowered and rather bow-heavy from inaccuracies in weight distribution but, to my relief, it reached the other side. The battery soon ran flat when the propeller became entangled in weeds but, after months of endeavour, I had achieved my goal and had been rewarded by a savoured moment when I was captain of my own little boat. I didn't know at the time that perhaps it was a good thing not having a television set.

References and Further Reading

Coronation Souvenir Brochure and Programme of Events, City of Wakefield, 2 June 1953, Wakefield Library, Balne Lane, Wakefield.

CHAPTER SIX

Testing Time: Sandal Magna County Junior School, 1953/1954

S andal Magna Board School had been established in 1890 following
the great 1870 Education Act, which made elementary education
compulsory, eventually, for children aged five to twelve. The Act required
locally elected Boards of a particular district to build new elementary
schools, paid out of the local rates in areas where there was a clear need for
additional schools, beyond those provided on a voluntary basis by religious
denominations. The growing population of South Wakefield in Belle Vue,
Agbrigg and the town side of Sandal, needed a new school to supplement
the church school, St Catherine's in Belle Vue, and the Endowed School
in Sandal. After delays in the formation of a Sandal Board, Sandal Magna
Belle Vue Road Board School was eventually established in the west of
Agbrigg, along Belle Vue Road, well positioned between the two established
schools. As a result of various changes in local government administration,
the school changed its name several times, and by the early 1950s locals
still knew Sandal Magna County Junior School as 'Sandal Council'.

The main brick building of Sandal Council School, with its Huddersfield
stone dressing and blue slate roof, had been designed by the Wakefield
architect William Watson and had changed little in the sixty years since
its opening. It consisted of a long single storey building with a second
storey of one room under a central bell turret. There were limited facilities

Sandal Magna County Junior School (centre) on Belle Vue Road, Agbrigg, linked to the north by Sugar Lane (top, centre). This 1960s aerial photo shows neighbouring Ashdown Road (centre), the school playing field (bottom left) and Wakefield Cemetery (top right). The commemorative trees we planted in 1953 have disappeared but Fred Jackson's hut is still in the lower playground.
COPYRIGHT © ENGLISH HERITAGE, NATIONAL MONUMENTS RECORD AEROFILMS COLLECTION.

beyond the standard arrangement of cloakrooms, a school hall and a number of high-ceilinged classrooms, some still with an old fireplace from the Victorian days.

Hubert B. Cummins had been the headmaster of Sandal Council since about 1950. He was a Victorian gentleman and, like most headmasters in those days, was a devout Christian; by 1953 he was also president of the

Only a modern entrance porch disfigures the Victorian building of Sandal Magna County Junior School, more than a hundred years after it was built in 1890. ALWYNE GILL.

Wakefield and District Free Church Council. A neat, blue-suited gentleman with thin greying hair and a commanding, well spoken voice, Mr Cummins was supported by nine teachers: six women (three married and three single) and three men, one of whom was Mr A. N. Colley, who had replaced Mr G. A. Patterson as games teacher.

By the autumn of 1953 I had started my final year at Sandal Council, preparing for the eleven plus scholarship. We had been separated into two classes according to perceived ability, and I had been placed in the top class, VA, in which learning was a highly competitive and serious business. School was an extension of home and the Church; it was the third pillar of a solid, stable framework based on the consistent teaching of right from wrong, discipline, order and an expectation of 'getting stuck in' to both work and play. From an early age I considered myself smart enough to know where I ought to be placed in the pecking order at school: I fancied myself to be close to the top in sports and also in schoolwork. However, whereas I would stretch myself to the limit on the sports field, I would do just enough to ensure my 'rightful position' in the classroom, because I felt it was hopeless competing against brighter kids such as my friends Derek Senior and John Hannon. Conversely, I didn't like it if I was suddenly overtaken by someone whom I perceived to be not as bright as me. At that time I and many educationalists, apparently, didn't understand that the different rate of individuals' development transformed a static pecking order into an unpredictably dynamic one. My competitive instinct would usually only kick in if I thought I was in a reasonable position of winning, when I would pull out all the stops. Since this was usually only on the sports field, it didn't meet the expectations of my fourth form teacher, Edward Gloyne, who informed me that if I put as much effort into class-work as I did on the sports field I might have a chance of passing my eleven plus. Old 'Gluepot' often made such sardonic comments and, although this one hardly changed my lifestyle, with hindsight it was an accurate assessment which became indelibly imprinted on my memory for the rest of my life.

Our form teacher in VA was Miss Ethel Lilian Hauton, a strong, determined character, but also a kind, fifty-nine-year-old Victorian lady, approaching the end of her teaching career. Miss Hauton had taught at the school since the First World War period and had nearly forty years' experience, some of them as the teacher of the scholarship class. She had a leathery complexion with a few wrinkles around her eyes – perhaps a result of years of effort in trying to distinguish spidery handwriting from ink smudges on thousands of manuscripts. We sat in rows of wooden desks, facing Miss Hauton's large desk within the southwest corner classroom, with its huge, round-arched Victorian windows. Many of our desks also looked as if they had been there since the Victorian days: their shiny wooden bench seats had been polished by at least two generations of 'rutching' and wriggling bottoms. The wandering thoughts and fantasies of countless boys had resulted in years of doodling and, in some cases, the engraving of initials on the ink-stained desk lids. It was very tempting to do the same, but Miss Hauton had a keen eye for spotting those in fantasy land.

Miss Hauton's main teaching aid was a large wooden blackboard and easel, with sticks of chalk neatly placed on a grooved piece of wood, alongside a blackboard rubber. A blackboard monitor was appointed to clean the board at the end of the lesson before break time and to ensure the availability of chalk; an ink monitor was responsible for preparing large volumes of ink and filling the ink pots, designed to drop into a little hole in each desk.

A rigid timetable of events was controlled by the ringing of a brass hand-bell throughout the school. At the end of the lesson before a break period, the noise of the bell gave way to a crescendo of excited voices as around 250 children disgorged from the main building into the playground, relieved that they could now make as much noise as they liked. Break time was also the opportunity to gulp down the free third of a pint of milk that had been prescribed for each child by the School Milk Act of 1946; it was also the main opportunity to visit the outdoor 'Boys' and 'Girls' lavatories, on the north edge of the playground, bordering the back gardens of houses in Ashdown Road.

A hard, tarmacked playground surrounded the whole school building. During the break some boys might play touch-and-pass rugby, or soccer, whilst the girls skipped on huge ropes to the rhythm of various weird chants, handed down by several generations. Games of conkers, gathered from trees around Sandal and in Wakefield Park, were popular boys' games in the autumn and, during icy conditions in winter, the main playground was transformed into a number of long slides, generally encouraged, albeit carefully supervised, by teachers on playground duty. In the summer, games of cricket were played against the school building, and marbles ('taws') in the dirt of the lower playground, with strict orders to avoid damaging the recently planted saplings. Between the main playground and the lower level play area was a wooden hut with metal mesh covering its windows to protect them from the impact of balls being kicked and thrown around. My friend, the Belle Vue joiner Fred Jackson, had built the hut in the 1940s to house facilities for a youth club; it was now a school kitchen.

I usually went home for 'dinner' (i.e. lunch) but would race back down Sugar Lane to play in the school field. This was separated from the lower level playground by a brick wall and was accessed from the school grounds by an old iron gate. Sometimes in the summer, the kitchen ladies would bring out huge metal trays laden with slabs of pudding left over from the school dinner. The trays would be placed at one end of the field whilst we were assembled some distance away to race and grab a piece. I am not sure that Mr Cummins was made aware of this 'first come, first served' initiative. Surely, he would have recommended a more equitable means of distribution, along the lines of 'Feeding the Five Thousand'?

A regular feature of school life was the visit of the 'nit nurse', a most serious, expressionless lady in full nurse's outfit, including fancy hat which I suppose was quite useful, given the task in hand. She would scrabble around our hair at great speed to look for nits and lice. I cannot recall any being discovered, although it was always a very tense occasion, since her unannounced arrival meant that there was no possibility for checking hair at home beforehand. We were all lined up in an orderly queue, and the very thought of being singled out as someone having nits was enough to guarantee a fearful silence throughout the whole inspection procedure. What would Mum say? Only a one word instruction would be heard – 'Next!' I was always grateful for the existence of Robert Austerberry in my class since, at least amongst the boys, he was always first in any queue before me. Everything from the morning register to nit picking was always carried out in strictly alphabetical order; by being the second boy in line I had a moment or two to prepare for whatever was being asked, even if it just meant clearing the throat to speak my name or watching what Robert had to do.

The general school curriculum was based around the three Rs, interspersed with a few novel activities such as Schools Broadcasts for which a huge 'Open Baffle' speaker mounted in plywood, measuring at least three feet square, would be manoeuvred with some difficulty into the classroom and connected to some sort of wireless receiver – it may actually have been a wired relay system, commonly used in those days.

The programmes were usually based on rather feeble songs and stories for younger kids, nowhere near as exciting as *Journey into Space,* which was enthralling me on the wireless at home in the evenings.

Our own music-making was restricted to singing and playing the recorder. I can recall playing certain tunes and 'rounds' such as 'London's Burning,' but the most memorable part of recorder lessons was the strict 'health and safety procedure' (it wasn't called that then, of course) at the beginning and end of each lesson. Most of us didn't have our own instrument and we would line up in yet another silent orderly queue to take a recorder from a cardboard box on a table at the front of the classroom, dip the mouthpiece into a bowl of dilute, milky Dettol, followed by a second immersion in a bowl of clean water. A similar procedure was carried out at the end of the lesson. I may be imagining it but I have a strong suspicion that the school recorders were made of Bakelite.

Playing the recorder, Sandal Magna County Junior School, 1953. Those visible (from left to right) front row: Ian Harrop, David Pick; second row: John Hannon, Barbara Hawes, John Crowhurst; third row: Margaret Andrew, Barbara Nicholson, Judith Lockwood, Jimmy Stephenson; fourth row: Keith Barraclough, Derek Senior, Doreen Denton, Kay Redfearn. Neville Rider is at the very back.
Wakefield Express.

In the final two years of junior school we were writing with pen and ink, having graduated from crayons and pencils in the lower school. Judging the correct amount of ink to put on the standard issue nib, mounted on the end of a bare wooden shaft, was always difficult for me because I was probably in too much of a hurry, and the flow properties of the ink varied with the condition of the nib, not to mention the particular mix of powder and water that the ink monitor had concocted. Hence my exercise book became strewn with dark blue blobs amongst the blue-grey hieroglyphics purporting to be joined-up handwriting. There was a brief improvement when I used my new fountain pen, which delivered a constant stream of beautiful royal blue ink until I trod on it.

In scholarship year there was regular homework to be carried out for the first time and a reading list to be compiled, including comments on the books we had read. The list was kept at the back of our diaries, which we had to complete every morning to record the events of the previous day. I did not have a problem with reading and homework but creative writing was not my strong point. It was rather tedious thinking of something new to write in the diary once I had exhausted the regular updates on the Cubs, choir, church, sport and, in particular, the weather. Miss Hauton explained that we also needed to take note of the general news and current affairs. Thus, my diary tracked the Queen's tour of the Commonwealth from November 1953 until she returned six months later on the new Royal Yacht Britannia. I tried to identify the countries the Queen and the Duke of Edinburgh were visiting on a huge map of the world which had the Commonwealth (Empire) countries prominently coloured in red. It was quite difficult relating to such travels when the furthest I had been was London. I am quite sure that no irony was intended with the diary entry for 17 December, 1953, which had noted that 'the Queen has arrived in Fiji Islands', whereas 'it was a terrible wet day in Wakefield' and that 'at night I had my hair cut'.

We were also encouraged to write about politics, and I was immensely pleased with my entry for 25 January 1954, which had stated that 'Tomorrow the Forfar Conference starts'. I had gleaned this from listening to the BBC news on the wireless and had no idea what it was about, although I was aware of the existence of Forfar from its regular mention on the football results of *Sports Report* (viz Forfar Athletic). However, by Tuesday, 26 January, the diary entry for a misunderstood Forfar Conference had been corrected to: 'The Four Power Conference that had started in Berlin with Anthony Eden and other foreign ministers.' On 4 March 1954, the complex situation that was developing in post-war Egypt was summarily dismissed in a one-liner that 'Neguib went out of Egypt's government', alongside the more important piece of information that 'England won the third Test match' (against the West Indies). Sport was never far from my mind.

Like his predecessor, Mr Colley was keen on maintaining a good rugby team, and bestowed on me the great honour of captaining the school's rugby XIII. I immediately sat down with my friend and vice captain, 'Little Tish' to try and pick a team which would make us competitive in the forthcoming matches against other schools in the district. Needless to say, this was a serious business as far as I was concerned. Matches against local rivals such as the Roman Catholic school, St Austin's, and Snapethorpe Juniors on the huge Lupset housing estate, had always been intensely competitive, not least amongst the teaching staff. Team selection was not easy: each school year contained less than sixty children, around half of whom were girls, so we introduced younger boys from the lower years. One such boy was 'Little Oddie', Kevin Oldroyd, whose elder brother, Keith, 'Big Oddie', was a star of the team when I had made my debut two years earlier.

In that final year we played several matches against various schools in the district, with some success, beating Flanshaw (twice), Heath View and the old rival, St Austin's. We also lost against Crigglestone and twice against Snapethorpe, a well known nursery for good rugby league players in the district. Our closest games were two matches against Lawefield Lane Junior School. The first game at home was memorable for the pre-match preliminaries. The Lawefield Lane School captain was a sturdy blond-haired lad, who offered his right hand to shake before we tossed the coin to decide who should kick-off. As a Wolf Cub I had been taught to shake hands with my left hand, so I had to explain this ritual to my opponent who thought it highly amusing and probably thought I was indulging in some form of

Rugby rivals, 1953/54: Sandal Council School (top) and Lawefield Lane School (bottom). I was later re-acquainted with some of these opponents, including the Lawefield Lane Captain (chapter 7). R. H. Barraclough (top) and R. M. Walker (bottom).

gamesmanship. The match itself was played in a downpour, and ended in a 3–3 draw. In the second match at Lawefield Lane, they won 5–3, an unusual score corresponding to a converted try against our try. In most matches the scores were multiples of three, since few individuals of that age had the size

Wakefield's triangular-shaped Greyhound Stadium ('dog track', lower right), bounded by the '99 arches' and two other railway lines, south of the city. At the very bottom of this aerial photo is Avondale Street where we lived from 1957. WAKEFIELD COUNCIL MUSEUM COLLECTION.

and strength to kick a heavy, wet rugby ball over the bar between the uprights to score the two points for either a penalty or a converted try. The big blond-haired lad had converted their try and we had lost.

One of the sporting highlights of the year was the Inter-Schools Athletic Championships, held at Wakefield's Greyhound Stadium. The term, 'stadium' was somewhat of a misnomer, since it consisted of a piece of land trapped between three curved railway lines of similar length, giving it a triangular shape. One of these lines formed part of the old West Riding & Grimsby Railway running southeast of Westgate Station, connecting Wakefield with London via the old Great Northern Railway. In the mid nineteenth century a 1,200 feet, 95-arch viaduct had been built over the southwest outskirts of the city. The viaduct was now known as the '99 arches', some of which had been partly enclosed to form the main boundary and entrance to the 'dog track'. The other two railway lines bounding the 'dog track' were the old Northeast–

Bryan Heeley (extreme right) of Lawefield Lane Junior School shows great determination in a hurdles race at the Inter School's Athletic Championships, Wakefield Greyhound Stadium, 11 May 1954. *WAKEFIELD EXPRESS.*

Southwest Lancashire & Yorkshire Railway line and a line connecting Westgate and Kirkgate Stations, which looped around the elevated city centre. Inevitably, the 'dog track' inside was basically a triangular shape with rounded corners, so that both an artificial hare and the chasing greyhounds could readily negotiate them at speed. On race night the track would be lit up from numerous lights overhanging the track. There were no lights, hares or dogs on view in the sunny afternoon of 11 May 1954, only hordes of highly competitive juniors 'haring' around the 'dog track' in various races. I managed to reach the final of the boys' (over ten) flat race, but was beaten by a boy from QEGS juniors and two boys I would later come to know, Brian Mann and Alan Beck, both from Lawefield Lane School. Malcolm Stokoe, Kevin Oldroyd and Jill Matthews did much better for Sandal Council School in their flat races and lanky George Lancaster came third in the high jump. Hours of practice in baton changing had paid off for us: Sandal Council School won three of the four relay races.

In the final year at junior school we visited 't'owd' Victorian baths in Almshouse Lane every Tuesday morning. Only a few of the class could swim, though the average age was around eleven years. Dad had enrolled me in an abortive swimming lesson on our holiday in Scarborough the previous summer, during which I had failed to learn anything other than kicking out the legs whilst the hands were firmly clenched to the safety rail on the edge of the pool. Those lessons had been conducted in Scarborough's vast South Bay pool, an unheated, open-air, pre-war lido on the sea front. Despite its huge circular concrete sea wall, the pool seemed to consist solely of sea water which was 'refreshed' every full tide. This was the North Sea, of course, and to a skinny child in typical 1950s summer weather it felt very cold indeed, exacerbated by the lack of any upper body movement. My goose flesh and uncontrolled shivering became too much for Mum to bear so, reluctantly, Dad hauled me out of the water, and that was that until the lessons in Wakefield's 'owd' baths started the following autumn.

'T'owd' baths in Almshouse Lane had been built in 1874, following public pressure initiated by that sporting group of young men, the Trinity Church Young Men's Society, and a public meeting in the Corn Exchange in 1873. By 1954, the Victorian public baths was a small, intimate enclosure compared with the larger new baths in Sun Lane and the open-air South Bay pool in Scarborough. I recall 't'owd' baths as a symphony in green, with dark green wooden changing cubicles, accessed by short 'half doors', surrounding the pool which had a pea greenish hue from the various reflections and colour of the tiles. By coincidence, my enamelled metal mug which accompanied me on every trip, rolled up in a towel with my woollen swimming trunks for a very welcome, albeit very weak, cup of hot Bovril at the end of the session, was also coloured pale green with a contrasting dark green handle and rim. Shakily daubed initials in enamel green paint had met the school's specific instruction that each mug should be readily identifiable. At least the mug blended in with the surroundings, even if I didn't.

Swimming lessons at 't'owd' baths were not dissimilar to those in Scarborough but, mercifully, the water was not as cold, and at least we non-swimmers managed to last the full lesson without perishing. Sometimes we played around the shallow end before being told to move to the deep end, where we would hold tightly onto the side and 'kick out'. The main instruction to keep kicking was shouted from the side and echoed, frighteningly, around the pool. Occasionally we would look enviously over our shoulders to admire the performance of the proper swimmers. I was not only extremely jealous but also rather annoyed. Here was I involved in an athletic activity in which I should be excelling, but instead had to watch the performance of the good swimmers who were generally not athletic types at all. Some were actually quite fat, and hopeless at every other athletic event such as running, cricket, football and rugby, so why were they brilliant swimmers, I mused? They ploughed through the water at a great rate of knots, like motorised seals, their bodies generating so much heat that when they hauled themselves out of the water their pink torsos would be barely visible through the rising steam. Our 'lesson' would temporarily cease when we had to stagger out of the water, taking care that the weight of water pulling down on our heavy woollen trunks did not reveal too much (not that there was much to reveal). This little interlude was designed for us to watch the seals attempt yet another swimming award. These took the form of small rectangular pieces of coloured cloth, which were awarded for reaching a certain swimming/diving standard, starting with a blue one for swimming one length of the pool, followed by various colours for increasingly difficult feats such as backstroke and diving off the boards. Colours were sewn onto the costumes as proficiency badges. The seals' costumes were a multicoloured patchwork of badges long before most of us could even swim. It just wasn't fair!

I cannot recall the specific circumstances that led me to suspend myself horizontally in the deep end and instinctively kick and move my arms in a frog-like movement. It was at the end of the lesson on Tuesday 25 May 1954, when I had built up enough confidence to release the rail, before having to wait yet another week to tackle this wretched swimming business. And I swam; it was only a few yards, but I was moving and there was nothing to it, other than the not so trivial matter of confidence. On the following Friday and Saturday I secretly went to 't'new' baths on my own to practise swimming a length, since I had worked out that if I could swim a length of the much larger new baths without stopping, then I could easily swim a length at 't'owd' baths. During the lesson on Tuesday, 1 June 1954, I registered my interest to attempt my 'blue', and with the encouragement of my classmates lining the edge of the pool, I swam a length of 't'owd' baths non-stop, all 70 feet of it. Even the weak Bovril drink tasted rather special that day. Mum sewed the piece of light blue cloth onto my navy blue trunks, which I promptly lost, but I didn't care. I was no longer interested in progressing through the swimming colours, because I had no intention of competing with the seals. The main thing was that I could swim and I had overcome the obstacles that were created by my lack of confidence.

I was fortunate in being able to read from a reasonably early age, and had a good memory for spelling. However, I am not sure that Miss Hauton would have approved of my complete reading list, which was only partly disclosed at the back of my diary. At that time I was very much into comics, and I managed to persuade Mum to order the *Dandy,* which was delivered every Tuesday morning. Actually, it wasn't long before I declared a preference for the *Beano,* but Mum drew the line at the *Dandy* and, for some inexplicable reason, was not even prepared to swap it for the *Beano.* My only opportunity to read the *Beano* and other comics was at the barber's. There were several barbers in the area: Shaw's, located quite close to two ladies' hairdressers, (Marion's and Holmes's) on Doncaster Road was the closest, but Dad had always taken me to Gordon Winter's on Agbrigg Road. By 1954 I went there on my own. I had usually been an unwilling visitor to the barber's but I now leapt at the chance when Mum and Dad declared it was time for me to 'have some wool off' – a most appropriate expression.

Customers at Gordon Winter's sat waiting their turn, perched on flimsy wooden chairs similar to those in the Club at St Catherine's and most church halls at that time. There was a lot of smoking and reading but virtually no conversation. Gordon Winter was not the effusive type, offering little chit-chat as he went about his business. Only the gentle buzz of the electric shears and the snip of the scissors broke the silence. Catching up with the latest exploits of Dennis the Menace in the *Beano* was just about worth the embarrassment of intruding into Gordon's world, but it was marginal.

At change-over time customers were seated in front of a mirror and had a large cloth wrapped around their shoulders, before the clipping and shearing process began. The silence was reciprocated by the customers, as if any sort of conversation broke the rules of attendance. There were no instructions issued on preferred hairstyle or amount to be taken off, just as sheep had no say in the way they were sheared. 'Short back and sides' was the only offering from the supplier, and the customer would have been surprised if an alternative had been mooted, so there was nothing to discuss. Gordon used a mirror to show his handiwork to parts not visible to the sheep, but this hasty, notional gesture formalised the end of the operation, rather than providing an opportunity for customers to suggest slight adjustments in the form of, say, 'a bit more off'. Before Gordon triumphantly whisked away the cloth, like a magician revealing the result of some clever trick, the silence would be broken by his rather deferential query, at least to the grown-up customers, 'Owt on, sir?' It was the sort of comic routine that appealed to Dad's sense of humour, and Gordon soon became affectionately known within our family by his unique catchphrase. The offering of 'owt' was actually limited to either Brilliantine or Brylcreem haircream, the latter advertised by the famous Middlesex and England cricketer, Denis Compton, who with perfectly parted, shining hair looked down rather smugly on proceedings from a picture hanging on the wall. I am not sure that there would have been many takers of Brylcreem, though. Denis Compton had two things working against him in this part of the world. Firstly, he was a southerner and, secondly, he was far too smooth an operator – indeed a bit of a ladies' man – to rank as a favourite with the men in Wakefield, despite having hit the winning run against the Australians to regain the Ashes. I rather fancied trying out some sort of hair oil but it was rarely offered to children and, in any case, was discouraged by Mum who opined that it 'mucked up' the pillowcases. I would wend my way home from Agbrigg Road, past Willans's bike shop and up St Catherine's Street, past the painful noises coming from Maggie Ramsden's front room, feeling cold and slightly naked, wondering at what age one qualified for 'Owt on, sir?'

The *Children's Newspaper* was recommended as a source of good reading material by Miss Hauton, maybe as a countermeasure to the proliferation of comics being read at that time. A recommendation from a professional schoolteacher was enough for Mum to order the paper on a regular basis, since she probably thought it would enhance my chances of getting into grammar school, based on the same logic that two comics a week, such as the *Dandy* and the *Beano,* would be a passport to Manygates Secondary Modern School.

For taking part! COPYRIGHT © LOOK AND LEARN.

The *Children's Newspaper* was something I looked forward to, since I enjoyed the factual nature of many of its articles. Around this time, stories of Jennings, the famous Anthony Buckeridge character, were also being serialised, and I was captivated by the various scrapes Jennings and his cohorts got themselves into, although I did sometimes wonder why life at Sandal Council was so mundane compared with the Linbury Court Preparatory School.

I was convinced that I was going to win the 1954 National Handwriting Test in the *Children's Newspaper,* although that was not the view of my sister, who had beautiful handwriting and, therefore, a more realistic view of my chances. Entry into the competition had to be made on a specific *pro forma,* issued on request from the newspaper. The first effort ended in tears when I messed up the entry with a misplaced blob of ink, resulting in writing off for another blank *pro forma.* My best attempt was eventually submitted, but I was hugely disappointed when I was not on the prizewinners' list, especially when my entry was damned with faint praise in the form of an Award of Merit certificate, which Elaine pointed out was probably issued to all those who had entered. At that time my competitive streak found it difficult to come to terms with the Olympic ideal that it was the taking part that was important, not the winning.

I had already discovered the local library on Sparable Lane where I had made a few visits to borrow practical books on boat modelling but, once I discovered Enid Blyton and Captain W. E. Johns, I became a regular visitor in order to seek out a new story about the Famous Five and Biggles. As with the Jennings books, I became fascinated by the adventures of Enid Blyton's characters, rather than their strange world of governesses, vacations and boarding schools. I was absorbed by the different characters and their behaviour rather than the trappings of their class, although I wished my Uncle Harry was an aircraft pilot or a Secret Service agent rather than a mill worker in Shelley. I suppose I read more fiction in the early fifties than at any time in my life. Homework tended to be rushed at the expense of dipping into my latest book, and my battery torch was secreted in my little 'tent' to extend reading time. The lack of a new Enid Blyton or Captain W. E. John's book on the shelves of Sparable Lane Library was regarded as a complete disaster, but the time did arrive when I had read all those available.

It is a popular misconception that the future of children's secondary education in the 1950s was determined by the result of a one-off examination that gave a grammar school education to those few kids who passed, confining the rest as failures within secondary modern schools. It was much more complicated than that in Wakefield and, I suspect, within many other education authorities at that time. Certainly, by 1954, the local eleven plus examination was a two-legged affair, plus an oral examination for borderline cases. For those who didn't pass their eleven plus from junior school, there was also the opportunity after two years to be examined at thirteen plus for transfer from a secondary modern school to either Wakefield Secondary Technical School or the city grammar school, Thornes House. The Technical School provided the opportunity to develop skills such as typing and shorthand (usually girls) and engineering skills such as technical drawing and machine tool work (boys). In September 1952 my sister, Elaine, transferred successfully to the Wakefield Technical School from Manygates Secondary Modern School, to develop secretarial skills. At Thornes House, thirteen plus transfers had four school years to prepare for their General Certificate of Education Ordinary (O-level) examinations by dropping down a year. Later, there was also the possibility for some pupils to be transferred to Thornes House Grammar School at twelve plus, without losing a year. Wakefield was rightly proud of its flexible tripartite secondary education system in the early fifties. The proportion of children entering grammar school education in the city was over 20 per cent which, according to the Director of Education, Clarence Leo Berry, was 'unusually high'. Of course, there were flaws in the system, but it deserved more credit than it received, and was probably much better than many that replaced it in the great ongoing experiment of the British education system.

Trying to solve those wretched problems about men digging trenches. R. H. BARRACLOUGH.

I cannot recall much about my involvement in the first round of eleven plus intelligence tests, but they were much easier than the second examination, held on 31 March, 1954. My diary entry gave little away but was hardly upbeat: 'I hope I did well'. This lack of optimism was founded on long-standing weaknesses that had been thoroughly tested in the second examination: composition (creative writing) and problems (Applied Maths). At that time I simply could not get my head around the issue of transferring a mathematical problem written in plain English into a simple arithmetical calculation. The prototype of such problems usually involved men digging trenches of a certain length in a certain time, requiring a calculation of how many men it would take to dig trenches of a different length in a different time. It was the mixture of words and numbers that simply threw my confused brain into panic mode. Despite his lack of formal education, Dad could readily solve these problems but, persevere as he might, he was unable to help me 'see the light'. At this time, boys at Manygates School were given lessons in gardening, and I started to believe that I would end up as one of the men digging trenches for the rest of my life, rather than the smart-arse grammar school boy who worked out how many men would be needed for the task!

So it was no surprise that I ended up as an eleven plus borderline case and was called for an interview. As preparation for this daunting task I was asked to bring with me an example of one of my hobbies. Of course, I had a huge range of interests but didn't consider any of them worthy of a budding grammar school boy, whom I perceived would have more intellectual pursuits. I thought that many of my regular activities such as reading, singing, piano playing, trainspotting, Cubs and sports could be done by anyone with half a brain, and that my Meccano and model boats were glorified toys, better matched to a technical school pupil than a grammar school boy. So, without much guidance from school or home, I decided not to take examples of any of these hobbies and instead borrowed my sister's stamp album, containing many foreign stamps, beautifully arranged according to their country of origin. I had also started a stamp album of sorts but it was nowhere near as neat and extensive as Elaine's, which would show me off in a good 'intellectual' light or so I thought.

My interview in the afternoon of 17 June 1954 was held at the Education Department's offices in King Street, Wakefield. The room was tiny and three interviewers, a man and two women, huddled over a small desk, smiling and trying to put me at ease. The man was probably the headmaster of Thornes House Grammar School, Clifford Coates Bracewell who, apparently, chaired many of these interviews. I was interrogated on my general knowledge and I thought I had made a decent fist of my first ever interview until it came to the hobbies bit. The interview panel had barely finished nodding its approval of the stamp album before one of the ladies cunningly produced a number of foreign stamps for me to identify. I failed to identify a single stamp.

To my utter surprise I learned a week later that I had passed for Thornes House Grammar School, although my brief diary entry was hardly bubbling over with excitement: 'I passed. I was pleased'. I don't know what they saw in me, because I found out much later that some good candidates had failed their interview under the most bizarre circumstances. When asked to describe an orange, a later school friend, Derek Chappel, had described it in geometric terms, rather than as a

Sandal Magna County Junior School playground, summer 1954. The cast of a school play, in one of their 'last acts' before moving on to secondary school. Back row, left to right: Ian Harrop, Derek Senior, Keith Barraclough, Neville Rider, Margaret Andrew, John Hannon; front row, left to right: Robert Austerberry, Rita Burroughs, Marianna Wagner, Kay Redfearn. *WAKEFIELD EXPRESS.*

fruit, the answer sought by the panel! Fortunately, Derek passed the thirteen plus examination to Thornes House where his mathematical brain could flourish. The eleven plus interview system clearly had its flaws, but some of them could be corrected by the transfer system.

Nine of us from a total of around fifty-five in the final year at Sandal Council School had passed to enter the three local grammar schools at eleven plus. Significantly, many others who had not passed at eleven plus would transfer to Thornes House at twelve and thirteen, including my Regent Street friends, John Crowhurst and Judith Lockwood. About 30 per cent of pupils in my school year at Sandal Council eventually ended up at one of the three grammar schools in Wakefield. My friends Derek Senior and John Hannon had been awarded Storie Scholarships to QEGS. John Storie was a local seventeenth century philanthropist, whose will had provided for money to be made available to Green Coat School for Wakefield's poor. When this school closed in 1875, the income from the Storie gift was transferred to provide twenty-four scholarships at QEGS and, after it opened in 1878, twelve at the Girls'

High School. By the 1950s the Storie endowment had broadened to include awards to the top pupils in Wakefield taking the eleven plus.

In 1954, 143 children, (seventy-three boys and seventy girls) within the administration of the Wakefield Education Authority passed the eleven plus scholarship examination. Of these, 70 entered Thornes House; 36 entered QEGS; and 37 entered Wakefield Girls' High School. Eight pupils (five boys and three girls), i.e. around 1 per cent of the total number of eleven plus candidates, had been recommended for a Storie Scholarship. Generally, QEGS and the Girls' High School creamed off the Storie scholars, but there was the odd exception. A year earlier in 1953, John ('Bud') Briggs, a future schoolmate, was awarded a Storie Scholarship from Lawefield Lane Junior School, having waited two years after passing the eleven plus at nine years of age. John wanted to go to QEGS but his parents couldn't afford the cost of uniform and sports gear; his dad, Francis, earned very little as a car park attendant next to the Regal cinema. The Storie Scholarship only funded a place in the school, not the extras needed to take up the place. Instead, John kept up an amazing family tradition by following in the footsteps of his four elder brothers and three elder sisters who had been educated at Thornes House, where the start-up costs were not as high as those at the other two grammar schools. An additional Briggs family link with Thornes House Grammar School was the Parent–Teacher Committee on which John's mother Evelyn had served since its start in 1945. My entry into Thornes House Grammar School was under somewhat different circumstances; I had scraped in by the skin of my teeth.

References and Further Reading

Education at Sandal Magna, 1890–1960, P.I. Wood, a Local History publication.

Chalking Up Progress, 1833–1993, Diane Exley, a Local History publication.

The Making of Wakefield, 1801–1900, Kate Taylor, ISBN 978-1-845630-78-2, Wharncliffe Books, 2008.

CHAPTER SEVEN

Thornes House Grammar School, 1954/1955

The formation of Thornes House Secondary (Grammar) School, Wakefield, in 1921 was the result of a forward-looking local education authority grasping the opportunity presented by the Education Act of 1918. Local authorities were required to provide continuing education which could be interpreted as secondary schools with a grammar school curriculum, entered by a scholarship process. Suitable premises came on the market at the right time in 1919, enabling conversion to a school and eventual occupation by 1923.

The wealthy cloth merchant James Milnes had chosen an excellent location for his pile in circa 1779. High ground around Lowe Hill was the site of the earlier of the two medieval castles in Wakefield, where a beacon was supposedly lit to warn of the Spanish Armada in 1588. From here Milnes looked down on the village of Thornes to the south, and had a panoramic view of Wakefield a mile or so to the northeast, within easy reach of his business activities. Milnes employed Horbury-born architect John Carr to design and build a grand three storey mansion befitting the merchant's status, eventually becoming known as Thornes House. The exterior was in brick – Milnes had relatives who owned a local brickworks on nearby Westgate Common; the interior was handsomely decorated in the Adams style, including fine fireplaces of that period. With sweeping drives to its elevated position, an imposing 200-foot façade, an enchanting terrace with fountain, beautiful walled gardens, extensive lawns and a library, Thornes House soon became recognised as one of the finest Georgian houses in Yorkshire on completion in 1781; it was acclaimed the best of Carr's 'smaller houses'. This was praise indeed, considering that Carr had developed a high reputation for his involvement in extremely grand projects, such as Harewood House near Leeds. Further recognition came when Carr's plan and elevation of Thornes House was one of only twenty-seven buildings from the British Isles to be included in the 1802 edition of *Vitruvius Britannicus,* a periodic publication of the most important buildings of the previous decades.

James Milnes did not have any children, and on his death in 1805 Thornes House passed to his father's sister's grandson, Benjamin Gaskell, as part of his estate. The trustees of Milnes's will also bought Lupset Hall for Benjamin's brother, Daniel, who eventually became the first MP for Wakefield. As members of a cloth-merchanting family, the Gaskells were, of course, Liberals with strong beliefs in education and public service.

Thornes House before it was converted to a Grammar School. WAKEFIELD COUNCIL MUSEUM COLLECTION.

Benjamin Gaskell christened his son James Milnes Gaskell, thereby retaining the name of the founder of Thornes House in the family.

On the death of James Milnes Gaskell in 1873, his son Charles George Milnes Gaskell inherited Thornes House. In 1885 this Liberal progressive became MP for Morley, and in 1889 he became Chairman of the newly formed West Riding County Council, which had to deal with many difficult educational issues arising at that time. When Charles George Milnes Gaskell died in 1919, it is tempting to speculate that the social commitment and concern for education across the social spectrum demonstrated by him during his lifetime, made his family reasonably open to negotiation with the city of Wakefield for the sale of Thornes House, to accommodate a new secondary school. There is no direct evidence of this, but it is very clear that the widowed Lady Catherine Milnes Gaskell wished to return to the family seat in Much Wenlock, so Thornes House and its 112-acre estate were put up for sale. Wakefield County Borough Council bought Thornes House and surrounding land for £18,500 with the intention of using the building and 20 acres of land as the basis for the new secondary school. As described earlier, the original plan for a huge housing estate on the remaining 92 acres came to nothing, and, like its previous occupants, the new school's staff and pupils would continue to enjoy the surroundings of beautiful greenery.

Alterations were made to accommodate separate boys' and girls' departments of the same school, which opened in 1923 as Thornes House Secondary (Grammar) School, each department with its own head: Winifred Grace Chinneck for the girls' and George Ernest Liddle for the boys'. It appears that the city fathers had some leanings towards a secondary school with a technical orientation at that time, and there appears to have been some debate on its overall mission, but a grammar school it was, populated by pupils from a wide catchment area who had passed an entrance examination and had been awarded a 'minor scholarship'.

There were no problems in appointing good quality staff. By 1921/22, teachers were suffering from the effects of swingeing cuts to the education budget in this difficult period ('Geddes Axe') and the general unemployment

A recent photograph of the rear of the block constructed in 1932 shows little change to the exterior. In 1954/55, the wing on the extreme left housed the workshops; the wing on the extreme right housed the dining hall. The gymnasium (centre) was adjoined by changing rooms – boys' (left) and girls' (right). K. G. BARRACLOUGH.

situation made alternative careers unattractive at that time. The new school soon took root, establishing its own ambience and character, with emphasis on scholarship, social awareness and good manners: the school motto was 'In Fellowship'. Enhancements were made to its facilities in 1932, with the construction in matching brick of a gymnasium, dining room and kitchens to the north of the main building.

When the headmistress of the girls' department and the headmaster of the boys' department both resigned in 1940, Wakefield Education Committee decided to merge the two departments under a single head. In 1941 Northleigh Aneurin York Yorke-Lodge was appointed as headmaster of the new mixed grammar school, now Thornes House Grammar School, Wakefield. Mr Yorke-Lodge steered the new school through the war years until 1945 when a new headmaster was appointed, Clifford Coates Bracewell, an inspired choice to lead the school in the post-war era, but no-one foretold that six years later he would quite literally be in the hot seat.

The fire in the early hours of Sunday 15 July 1951 was a major tragedy for the school and for the area's heritage. Thirteen of the fifteen classrooms were completely gutted and valuable records were lost. Temporary classrooms were made available in nearby Holmfield House, which at that time was owned by the council and was the site of Wakefield's Museum.

Holmfield, later known as Holmfield House. WAKEFIELD MUSEUM COLLECTION.

This makeshift situation continued for years, and by Tuesday, 7 September 1954, had remained almost unchanged for the new entrants who wended their way past the old horse chestnut trees to the disrupted school at the top of the park. At least one of these new pupils was oblivious to the school's history, and to the sacrifices and endeavour made over a period of 170 years by countless people to provide an educational opportunity for many first generation grammar school kids like him. I was scared stiff.

There had been rumours circulating that the public school ritual of first year boys becoming slaves, 'fags', to older boys, was also practised at Thornes House. Failing to comply with fagging would result in a ducking in a school lavatory, I was led to believe. I had fully intended to implement my proven strategy of not standing out from the crowd but it wasn't to be, and it was all Mum's fault. During the summer, parents had been issued with a very comprehensive list of the required clothing and items needed for Thornes House Grammar School, from the regulation school uniform to the various items of sports kit, and even an apron for woodwork and metalwork, which Mum and Dad thought highly amusing. We also joked

Thornes House Grammar
School uniform.
R. H. Barraclough.

about the requirement for 'plimsolls' to be worn for PT (physical training) because we never used the word at home. Dad reassured me that they were just 'pumps', and nothing to do with ships, so that was all right. It was the uniform that caused the anxiety.

The school badge was based on the crest of the Gaskell family, consisting of a yellow stork holding in one of its claws a large scallop shell, a symbol of pilgrimage and of the apostle St James the Great. A stork on each pillar of the main entrance gate on Thornes Road gave it the name, the Stork Gate. A small stork badge adorned the boys' navy blue caps and the girls' navy blue berets. A larger badge decorated the breast pocket of everyone's navy blue blazer; the girls' blazers were also edged in bright yellow braid. I wanted one of the snazzy navy blazers sold by Southcotts in town ('Tailors for Ladies and Gentlemen/School Outfitters') with its elegant, graceful stork woven into the breast pocket as part of the complete outfit. However, Mum felt this was far too expensive and opted for a cheaper solution which involved sewing a separate badge onto a cheaper navy blue blazer. I don't know where she acquired the badge but it was a very old version of the stork: a rather fat, squat, monster that looked more like a vulture. This out of date version was referred to as an 'old bird' by experienced Thornesians and I had learned that one should not be seen dead wearing such a badge. But that wasn't all.

Mum was quite good at running up, repairing and modifying items of clothing, on her hand driven Singer sewing machine, but a new pair of trousers for the grammar school merited a visit to a proper tailor. So off we went to Marian Lord in Agbrigg, armed with our own length of grey cloth that Auntie Flo' had donated to the cause; she had probably woven it herself. Mrs Lord was undoubtedly a good seamstress but, unfortunately, she and her husband Harry, also a very good tailor, were both deaf and had severely impaired speech (commonly, but unkindly, termed 'deaf and dumb' in those days). Our arrival at the door of 10 Warwick Street was signalled by an electric light in the kitchen of the Lords, who welcomed us like long-lost family, with some rather strange noises. I found the excursions to Mrs Lord's extremely embarrassing, but Mum seemed to relish combining a charitable act of providing work for a disabled person with the opportunity to exercise her skills at lip-reading and her unique version of semaphore. There was a lot of exaggerated, but totally silent, mouthing of words and vigorous hand signals, combined with even more emphatic nodding and shaking of heads for the affirmative and negative. Occasionally, Mum's technique would lapse and she would shout a word to try and emphasise a point, usually to no avail. Mrs Lord responded with her strange noises, as I just stood there to be measured. My first voluntary contribution to proceedings came during about the third visit when the trousers were taking shape. 'They're too big,' I whispered, amazed that I was summoning up the courage to speak at all in this strange world of non-communication. 'You'll grow into them,' declared Mum, immediately revealing the reason for some of the frantic 'discussions' during the previous visits. Poor old Mrs Lord might have expected to have been commissioned to make a pair of bespoke trousers that actually fitted me, rather than a version of me in two years' time. These supposedly short trousers were designed to last.

There was never a problem with footwear. Mum always ensured new shoes fitted perfectly, even if it meant a visit to a quality shoe shop and several investigations under the x-ray machine. This wonderful new device was located at the base of a tall wooden box into which one stepped whilst wearing the new shoes. The feet, shoes (and certainly other parts of the body) were appropriately irradiated with a heavy dose of short wavelength x-rays, to reveal a superb image of the foot bones on a fluorescent screen near the top of the box. It was marvellous seeing your toes wriggling round, but nobody cared about health and safety!

So, my shoes were fine as I alighted from the number 20 bus at the Horbury Road entrance to Wakefield Park, but I felt distinctly sheepish and self-conscious in my cheap blazer and elephant trousers. I trudged past the Lodge House at the drive entrance, with my left arm and new leather satchel carefully hiding the 'old bird' badge, past the sloping football pitch on the right and the empty children's playground on the left. As I climbed the steep drive to Thornes House I started to worry that perhaps I wouldn't last here anyway. I had just scraped in, so I might easily be booted out. Perhaps I would be on trial? I would have to be extremely studious and well behaved if I were to make the grade. My strategy was to keep my head down and my nose clean in order to minimise the possibility of being kicked out.

And so, with this rather negative outlook, life began in Class III W (White) in room fifteen, upstairs in Holmfield House; the specialist facilities for art, science, woodwork, metalwork, PT and games were in and around the main school, five to ten minutes walk away, depending how keen we were to cross the park. The art department was based in an old Victorian stable block that had escaped the ravages of the fire. Also untouched by the fire was the block constructed twenty-two years previously, containing the dining hall, kitchen, gymnasium and workshops. The dining hall was the largest assembly room, but not quite large enough to cater for major events involving the whole school – more than 500 pupils. Speech Days for the seniors were held in Unity Hall in the city. A new hall was starting to take shape as part of a new school building next to the old remains, but it was at least a year away from completion. Meanwhile, we became used to tramping through the mud next to a noisy building site.

Our form teacher was 'Katie' Bulmer, a new member of staff who taught Geography. Form IIIW had a total of thirty pupils; III B (Blue) and III R (Red) were about the same size, giving a total first year intake of about ninety pupils, of whom seventy-three of us had been awarded scholarships by the City of Wakefield Education Authority; the rest had gained entrance via the auspices of the West Riding Authority from districts as far afield as Darton and Wombwell on the outskirts of Barnsley. We were largely

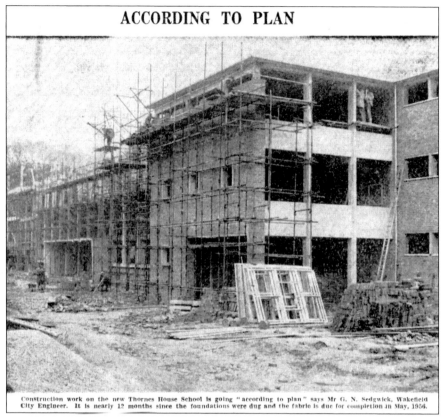

ACCORDING TO PLAN

Construction work on the new Thornes House School is going "according to plan" says Mr G. N. Sedgwick, Wakefield City Engineer. It is nearly 12 months since the foundations were dug and the fabric is due for completion in May, 1956.

This February 1955 *Wakefield Express* cutting shows a photo of the construction work on the new school building, with its main entrance in the distance – on schedule to complete in May 1956. *WAKEFIELD EXPRESS.*

working-class pupils from a wide catchment area, examples of what nearly sixty years later became known as 'social mobility'.

I started to get to know my new classmates, particularly the boys; the girls sat together and kept themselves to themselves. The other new entrants from Sandal Council, Neville Rider, Mary Atack, Brenda Cooper and Marianna Wagner, were in different forms. The only face I recognised in IIIW was the blond-haired lad who had captained Lawefield Lane's rugby team. His name was Rodney Walker who became known as 'Wacker'.

Eric Abbiss had been assigned to IIIW, so one fear was overcome when I discovered that I was not first on the alphabetical register. Eric was a chirpy lad from Eastmoor who shared my interest in boats and loved playing in goal for the football team. Also from Eastmoor there was a tall lad with quiffed hair, Terry Morrell, who was a good runner, but the best runner was the smallest lad in the class, Bryan Heeley from Lawefield Lane School. Colin Bridge was also very sporty and was often in trouble for being caught doing the wrong thing at the wrong time – he was readily picked out by his straight blond hair. Swarthy skinned Richard Pitts with his infectious laughter and straight black hair was also very distinguishable. Stephen Fox from Snapethorpe stood out from the crowd with his pale, freckled face and deep ginger coloured hair. I immediately found a kindred spirit in little Jack Larkin, bless him. Like me, Jack had a 'hybrid' blazer, and his trousers also appeared quite large, especially in relation to his skinny legs. Jack had facial features that looked older than his years, and he had a largish head containing a huge memory, which he had programmed to recall in a flash the name of every capital city in the world. His party piece would be regularly tested by the rest of the lads gathered around him during break time, but we could never catch him out. That such a genius should wear an odd uniform like mine made me feel much better.

The bespectacled Michael Siswick had a more obnoxious party piece. He often brought from home a number of tablets, supposedly medicine of some sort, which when crushed underfoot released a terrible sulphurous smell. These novel stink bombs would be released just before the start of lessons taught by the most vulnerable, female members of staff such as the new French teacher, Jean Holden, and our form teacher 'Katie' Bulmer, who both pretended that nothing had happened by ignoring the giggles and snorts from the boys' half of the classroom.

Then there were the quiet ones: John Parr from Newmillerdam, bespectacled Brian Crowther from nearby Thornes and little John Spencer. I suspected they were perhaps like me, borderline entrants who were keeping their heads down. I didn't know at the time that many members of the first year had gone through the interview selection process. Similarly, no one really cared about my uniform except me. There was no fagging or significant bullying, although a scuffle with a boy from the Lower Fourths, anxious for a fight, was unavoidable as we crossed paths between the main school and Holmfield House. Nothing much came of it, apart from a torn blazer and a lost button. There was nothing to fear but fear itself.

After that first daunting day we didn't see much of the headmaster, Mr Bracewell, apart from one occasion when he swept into our classroom for an urgent word with 'Katie' Bulmer, who told us in no uncertain terms to stand to attention. As soon as we were on our feet, he instructed us to be seated with a gentle wave of the hand. It was obvious from the outset that the headmaster commanded respect across the whole school. Clifford Coates Bracewell had many traits and mannerisms which in a lesser man may have found their way into disparaging nicknames, but to everyone in the school the headmaster was fondly known as Cliff or 'the Boss'.

Cliff was a tall gangly fellow with a smallish, egg-shaped head atop a longish neck, giving him an uncanny likeness to that well-known actor, Alistair Sim. He had the endearing mannerism of clasping the back of his head and neck with a cupped hand when in deep thought or when delivering an important speech – as if his head might become unstable and topple from its perch when the contents were working overtime. Cliff had an angular gait and his long legs would drive him around the school at high speed, head thrust forward, shoulders hunched, with gown flowing behind in a black wake. A bald pate emerged from tufts of greying hair, and a pair of large spectacles nestled on the bridge of a crooked nose that looked as if it might have suffered a fracture in the past. Powerful lenses magnified bright, intelligent, twinkling eyes that communicated warmth and a sense of humour.

Cliff had been born in Rochdale, Lancashire, in 1899. He had been educated at the famous Manchester Grammar School and at the University of Manchester, and still retained a slight Lancashire accent in 1954. During the Great War, Cliff had served in the Lancashire Fusiliers, and in 1918, at the tender age of nineteen, had been awarded the Military Cross for gallantry and leadership of his platoon when he was wounded during a successful attack on an enemy position. Of course, very few of the new entrants knew about this in 1954, although they may have noticed 'MC'

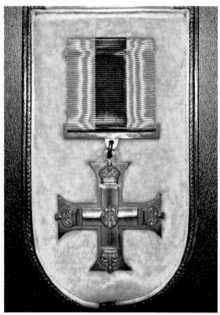

Headmaster, Thornes House Grammar School, Clifford Coates Bracewell MC and the Military Cross medal awarded for bravery in 1918. PICTURE COURTESY OF THE YORKSHIRE POST NEWSPAPERS (LEFT) AND MRS J. GELDART (RIGHT).

after Cliff's name in the school's formal prospectus. In those self-effacing days such brave acts of leadership were not widely broadcast, least of all by Cliff himself. Very few would have related such a feat to this peaceful, gentle man who led his school by example and coercion, not by bawling out commands and the application of brute force.

Cliff was a great believer in the power of argument and persuasion: he always thought carefully before he spoke, then the words came quietly but were delivered in a firm and convincing manner. In the 1950s he still had corporal punishment at his disposal but rarely used it, apart from the occasional use of the 'slipper'. To be sent to 'the Boss' was usually the last resort on a sliding scale of various punishments. If Friday afternoon detentions (a 'ditto' or a 'double ditto' for more serious misdemeanours) did not have the desired effect then the perpetrator would most likely end up in 'the Boss's' study, and that would probably be the best thing that could have happened to him. Cliff had probably seen enough physical brutality in the Great War to last a lifetime so, rather than wield the cane and administer 'six of the best', which was the usual punishment from headmasters in those days, Cliff preferred to hold a counselling session, with the aim of discussing how the error of the boy's ways impacted on others and on the school. Sometimes these sessions would, nevertheless, end in tears but they were tears of regret and shame, shed by a boy who had never experienced a punishment quite like it. Cliff was a fine man who provided continuity to the progressive liberalism of the school's founders, by placing the welfare and happiness of all his charges at the very core of his job, as well as providing a well-rounded education. He was a people person who had reminded all staff and pupils after the fire in 1951 that, 'the school is not the building. You are the school!' His legacy to the thousands of Thornes House pupils who were in his charge during a sixteen-year tenure was aptly summarised by a former member of staff, Roland Hill, on the occasion of Cliff's retirement in 1961: 'His teaching and example have been woven into the very stuff of their lives.' And so say all of us.

Cliff's Christian values pervaded the whole school: some of his staff were Methodist local preachers and many more were members of local churches. Like all successful leaders, Cliff had the full support and backing of his seconds in command, senior master, Mr John (Jack) Rhagfyr Davies and senior mistress, Miss Marjorie ('Ma') Waring. By 1954 both had accumulated vast amounts of teaching experience. Jack Davies had an honours degree in science from Aberystwyth University, with special qualifications in physical education. He started his career at Thornes House in 1925 as the boys' physical training and games teacher, switched later to teaching Chemistry, then Physics, and eventually became head of sciences. Jack Davies was a small, craggy Welshman, strict but fair. 'Ma' Waring had been at the school since 1938 and her subject was History. She also taught Scripture and was the main piano accompanist to the school choir. In her senior mistress role she seemed to spend a lot of time lecturing girls on their uniform and general behaviour. Many girls complained that she was too strict, but they would always confess later that she was also very fair and quite kind-hearted.

The longest serving male member of staff was Roland Henry ('Pop')

Hill who had been there since the school started in 1923. He had served in various capacities, from his initial appointment as senior master to temporary headteacher twice, until permanent appointments were made. 'Pop' Hill taught French and Scripture, and was the glue that held the school together during its many difficult times. He was from Sheffield, where he obtained a bachelor of arts at the local university. As a good footballer in his youth, he may have influenced the decision that Thornes House boys should play soccer as their primary winter school sport. A Methodist local preacher in Sandal, Roland Hill was a mercurial little chap, very eccentric and a passionate teacher whose lessons were an unforgettable experience. At first I thought he was stark raving bonkers when he ended up on the classroom floor kicking his legs in the air. Although he taught us Scripture in the first year, it wasn't until he became our form master and French teacher in the following year that he came into his own. Everyone had to become engaged in these theatrical performances. Inhibitions were lost and it was almost a pleasure to make a mistake, in order to witness his antics. He cleverly avoided exposing the mistakes of individuals, preferring to castigate groups, who were given all sorts of names – 'Sharlston muckheaps' and 'blockheads' were his favourites. It was impossible for us to forget that the French plural should be silent because he would draw a huge letter 'S' on the blackboard as a constant reminder. Similarly, when using the French word for 'nothing' – he drilled it into us that 'pas' is followed by 'de', so we renamed John Parr, Pas de. 'Pop' Hill made learning French fun and we couldn't wait for his next lesson. He took an interest in every child and had an encyclopaedic memory for personal details. One day, out of the blue, he asked how my father was getting on in the police force. Dad had just moved from the Driving School to Wireless Operations, and it seemed that 'Pop' Hill knew about everything and everyone in Wakefield, not just within Thornes House! Some may have construed his attitude as nosey, but to me it felt good that he should take such a personal interest. School reports from 'Pop' Hill contained the most detail, often as complete sentences, not just a word or two. I hated being 'Satisfactory', 'Fair' or even 'Very Good'.

A few other teachers had joined the staff in the early days of the school, and were close to retirement by the mid-fifties. Beatrice Dillistone had taught Art since 1923 as one of the first members of the girls' department. She was a gentle, sensitive lady from the south of England who had turned her talents to designing and selling Christmas cards in order to buy pictures for the school. George Frederick ('Tom') Pearce, the Chemistry teacher, was a great believer in using the natural senses to identify complex chemicals, rather than more esoteric tests. If we didn't know the result of our experiments 'Tom' would tell us in no uncertain terms, and with complete disregard for health and safety, to –'Smell it boy, smell it!' Tom had a twinkle in his eye, as did Mr Edward ('Twink') Swinden, the retiring metalwork teacher.

Another long-standing member of staff, Edward ('Chunk') Hepworth taught us Geography in the second year but I came across him earlier through the school's house system, the basis for all internal competitions across many activities, notably: music, the arts, cookery, elocution, chess, photography, engineering, woodwork, gymnastics, athletics, including cross-country, and games. Hardly a week went by without some sort of house competition, which would be fiercely contested at all levels. On entry to the school we were assigned to one of four houses: Bargate, Kirkgate, Outgate and North Westgate. Each house was led by members of staff as house masters/mistresses. I had been assigned to Bargate, led by 'Chunk' and Harry Dixon, a Chemistry teacher who had been one of the first on the spot during the 1951 fire and, heroically, rescued the school's grand piano.

Shortly after arriving at the school I had my first and most memorable Bargate House meeting, which set the tone for grammar school life beyond the classroom. 'Chunk' was a stern, imposing figure in his blue suit, complete with waistcoat. His greying hair was always neatly parted and his facial features gave the impression of an oriental gentleman, especially as he often seemed to be sun-tanned after returning from the holidays. 'Chunk' gave a well-rehearsed Churchillian speech about Bargate House being the best, how important it was to uphold the tradition of winning everything, and that there was to be no shirking by anyone if the good name of the house was to continue. We all swallowed this hook, line and sinker, and from that day on, I was prepared to die for Bargate House. I did wonder how a borderline entrant had ended up in the best house but I was determined to do my best for Bargate which could only mean doing well for myself. I bought into the system.

I always wondered how 'Chunk' had acquired his strange name. Many nicknames had obvious roots and, in the absence of particular traits, were quite often based on Christian names or their derivatives, e.g. 'Lil' Howard, our first year Maths teacher, and 'Joe' de Decker who taught Art. 'Ma' was used either in the absence of known Christian names ('Ma' Richardson, our relatively new English teacher) or as a short form of Marjorie or Margaret. Miss Margaret ('Ma') Markland, our revered Music teacher, was also known as 'Markie'. Appearances were a dead giveaway in the case of 'Grannie' Gornall, a tiny white-haired Maths teacher. It was Stuart Burnet in our year who came up with the splendid name, 'Hibou' for the new French teacher, Miss Jean Holden, a tall young lady with a blushing round face and big round eyes, made even bigger by a pair of huge spectacles. A few years later the French department acquired another member of staff, Geoff Boocock. Much to everyone's delight, 'Hibou' eventually became Mrs Boocock. The Boococks lived in Sandal and were members of the local Methodist church.

'Trog' was a Maths teacher by the name of Jack Ripley whose scruffy, hang-dog looks and ungainly gait had been likened to that of a troglodyte by someone in the dim and distant past. 'Trog' wore a rather creased, green-checked double breasted suit, day in, day out, but Mr Ripley was too brilliant a mathematician and teacher to worry about appearances and, since most pupils appreciated that fact, 'Trog' was a term of endearment.

Compared with Trog's attire, that of art master, Joe de Decker was 'cool', at least for the mid-fifties. He wore modern shoes, flashy ties, different coloured pullovers and checked sports jackets, some with leather patches on the elbows. Joe had style which he carried off with an air of arty nonchalance as he ambled slowly to his den in the old stables. On Speech Day, Joe's gown was the flashiest on view, full of fancy fur and bright colours, quite a contrast to the dull colours of gowns representing most universities. Someone did point out that if an art college couldn't design a fancy gown, who could? Joe had a rather pungent wit but, if pushed too far, was not averse to launching a wood-backed blackboard rubber as a missile which quite often turned into a hittile.

The boys' PT department consisted of Bill 'Spike' Rennie, who would patiently try to teach us various gymnastic manoeuvres, but we soon tired of repetitive forward rolls on black rubber mats, forward and backward rolls on the horizontal wooden beams and shinning up those thick smelly ropes which, to my mind, had rubbed against far too many sweaty crotches in the past. Our patience was rewarded at the end of term when 'Spike' allowed us to play 'Pirates', a version of tag in which 'pirates' chased 'sailors' on a 'ship', consisting of most of the apparatus in the gym: the wall bars, beams, and ropes. The gym floor fulfilled the role of the 'water', apart from small islands created by the rubber mats. Stepping on the 'water' ended participation in the game. This was more like it! Unlike the boringly formal gymnastics, we were now in our element as our imagination and competitive instinct ran riot. The gym was suddenly transformed into something more like a madhouse than a ship, with boys leaping around at breakneck speed, taking outrageous risks to avoid being tagged or forced onto the 'water', as if their very lives depended on it. Needless to say, exuberance got the better of certain 'pirates' who would ignore the basic rules of tag and haul the weaker sailors onto the 'water', sometimes from the top of the wall bars, requiring 'Spike' to whistle a halt to proceedings whilst he fetched the first aid box.

Although 'Spike' had a lithe, elastic frame, ideally suited to the contortions of formal gymnastics, he was by no means the prototype Adonis-like sports master. His lean frame was propelled by a pair of rather splayed feet; on the move he tended to lean slightly forward, as if he were anticipating yet another forward roll. 'Spike' had a pale complexion and sometimes wore glasses with powerful lenses, which some kids unkindly likened to jam jar bottoms. When not in the gym wearing regulation black 'plimsolls', 'Spike' wore black lace-up shoes, a poor match to a maroon tracksuit. A

Thornes House School Staff, 1957. From left to right, back row: Mrs P. Keenan (school secretary), Miss C. Cook, Mr D. Bowen, Mr W. Rennie, Mr G. Boocock, Mr D. Watson, Mr F. Bottomley, Mr V. Prooth, Mr K. Stewart, Miss S. Thomas, Mrs Atkinson(?); middle row: Miss L. Cowling (head of school kitchen), Mrs K. Bulmer, Miss A. Chrispin, Mr S. Leak, Mr J. de Decker, Mr B. Chambers, Mr R. Day, Mr J. Ripley, Miss J. Holden, Mrs E. Richardson, Miss M. Gornall; front row: Mrs L. Howard, Mr D. Smith, Miss E. Denton, Mr E. Hepworth, Miss M. Waring, Mr C. C. Bracewell (headmaster), Mr R. H. Hill, Mrs K. Coutts, Mr J. R. Davies, Miss M. Markland, Mr H. Dixon. GEO HOLDSWORTH & SON.

1940s short back and sides hairstyle was topped by a spiky quiff that was not in fashion until about fifty years later. In typical PT instructor fashion 'Spike' would precede every command with a loud 'OK', in order to quell any background chatter and attract everyone's attention. Bill Rennie had a spiky frame, spiky hairdo and was quite spiky by nature. 'Spike' was quite versatile, and also taught Maths and History to some classes in the lower school. He also had the dubious honour of a second nickname. In the 1950s German was not a regular foreign language option at Thornes House, but was compulsory for A-level science students, since an ability to understand scientific German was deemed essential for those continuing their education, particularly at university. 'Walter' Rennie was the main teacher of the German language, and I had that pleasure to come.

I ran my heart out for Bargate House in the winter Cross-Country Competition and the School Sports in the summer. Much to my surprise Bargate House won the 1955 School Sports overall, despite not having many of the star athletes such as Clive Thewlis in the juniors and Alan Kenworthy in the seniors, both of Outgate House. Collective efforts in events such as the junior relays had made the difference, and 'Chunk's' call to arms had actually worked! However, for me, the only purpose of running was in pursuit of a ball, and I was particularly keen to learn more about soccer, for which most of us in the first year had never received any proper coaching. Our soccer skills were pretty inept and it was an uphill struggle for the school to convert rugby league players into footballers. Being a mixed grammar school limited the choice of participants in many activities at Thornes House, particularly sports, yet in 1954/55 the school's first soccer XI was enjoying reasonable success and had many good players at the top end of the school, such as Geoff Flood, John Oxley and my hero, Kenworthy, who had gone further than Dad by signing as a part-time professional for Huddersfield Town AFC.

Our school dining hall stank of cabbage and was very utilitarian but most pupils ate lunch there since the school was relatively isolated. The presence of staff seated at tables on a slightly elevated stage at the front imparted both a sense of formality and theatre to the proceedings. A member of staff prowled the hall on duty, whilst sixth form prefects sat at the head of the rectangular tables to maintain order and ensure hungry juniors didn't race to the serving hatch before their turn. The offerings from Lucy Cowling's adjacent kitchen were quickly gobbled up by the boys and picked at by the girls, who complained about everything, especially the overdone cabbage, the soapy spuds and lumpy gravy. There was usually a choice of 'sweet', either a milk-based dish or one of a variety of quite tasty sponges served with thin, pale custard from large white jugs plonked onto each table by the monitor. The teacher on duty would ring a hand-bell to silence the background chatter before announcing the choice of 'sweet'. Loud retching noises from the boys and turned up noses from the girls always greeted the announcement of tapioca pudding as one of the choices, sometimes the only 'choice'. Universally known as 'frog spawn', the very name made tapioca pudding disliked across the board, yet it appeared regularly on school dinner menus throughout the whole country in the 1950s. The main complaint related to its very smooth texture but I never knew what the fuss was about. At least tapioca pudding could be readily swallowed, unlike raw tripe.

At the end of school dinner there was usually at least three quarters of an hour to devote to a huge range of activities. The smokers lurked furtively around the bike sheds in search of 'a light', whilst others busied themselves in more healthy pursuits: rehearsals for plays and the choir; indoor games of chess; outdoor games of cricket and football; and clubs for woodwork, metalwork, art and photography. Staff gave their free time willingly and enthusiastically to these extracurricular activities which would be packed into lunchtimes and the end of the school day, especially if a house competition was looming. There was much to do, and the reputation of the house often depended on it, so I soon became used to having a go at many new activities. 'Mucking in' was 'Chunk's' ethos as well as my mother's, so who was I to argue with that? School was quite often more than an eight-hour day, excluding the time it took to travel there and back, and then there was the formality of homework.

Homework was routinely set for every weekday evening and weekend. I did this religiously as part of a disciplined work ethic without any persuasion from my parents, and I became a 'swot', fearful of what might happen if I did not work hard. Gradually, this started to pay off. I started to like most subjects because I could do them. A small success resulted in a little boost of confidence, which bred more success and eventually a love of learning. Suddenly, instead of Applied Maths being an ogre it became a doddle, and I have 'Lil' Howard to thank for that. I loved the logic and precision of algebra and geometry, the fun of learning a foreign language, learning about foreign countries in History and Geography and unravelling the mysteries of Physics and Chemistry. To my utter surprise I came top of IIIW in the summer exams and was awarded a form prize, a book of my own choosing, *The Observers Book of Ships.* This success was repeated at the end of the second year in Lower IV W and earned accolades from 'Pop' Hill and even Cliff at the bottom of my school report. Hard graft was starting to pay off.

References and Further Reading

Thornes House, The Story of a School, Nora J. George, 1993 Wakefield Library, Balne Lane, Wakefield, WF2 0DQ.

Thornes House Grammar School, website, http://www.thorneshouse.org.uk/

Wakefield District Heritage, compiled by Kate Taylor, published by Wakefield European Architectural Heritage Year (EAHY) Committee, October 1976, p.140.

Thornes Park, Richard Bell ISBN 1-902467-03-5, Willow Island Editions, 1999.

CHAPTER EIGHT

Watershed, circa 1956

In December 1955 I joined that group of crazy mixed up kids known as 'teenagers', with their own youth culture sandwiched between childhood and adulthood, in search of their own direction and identity, rather than those chosen for them by their parents. It was a period of conflict, frustration and, for the first time in my life, failure. Adolescence brought sexual awareness and an increased resistance to the old-fashioned ways of my parents. I became a constant source of aggravation to them by identifying with many of the cultural changes emerging at this time. For once, older folks like my parents who had lived through two world wars, a depression and the dour, austere period of the post-war forties and early fifties, had good reason to shake their heads in 1956 and mutter that 'things would never be the same again'. Change was everywhere and a lot of it was driven by the younger generation, to whom they found it difficult to relate at all.

After several years of full employment, people had more money to spend; they demanded a change in lifestyle and got it. Home ownership was on the increase and the young were spending more money on fashionable clothes as well as holidays, cars and television sets, often on the 'never-never'. The grey years of austerity were gradually transitioning to a colourful age of consumerism. Chancellor of the Exchequer, the Right Honourable Harold Macmillan, was probably thinking that we had never had it so good, but he would refrain from telling us until he became Prime Minister the following year. In the meantime he kept his counsel: his policy of wage restraint was being strongly opposed by the trade unions.

In music a revolutionary 'rock and roll' style was firmly established by new young artists who would become iconic figures in decades to come, and a source of continuing annoyance to the older generation. It was a watershed year for the theatre when the old order, portraying the comfortable middle and upper classes in their posh drawing rooms, was challenged for the first time by a twenty-six-year-old playwright, John Osborne, in a new style of 'kitchen sink' drama, focusing on the plight of the working class and their everyday life. In the field of sport young stars of the future emerged, whilst established players created records that would stand for all time.

1956 also marked a watershed for the old imperial attitudes of the British government, when a misjudged adventure into the Middle East ended in embarrassing failure, following the nationalisation of the Suez Canal by the Egyptian government, precipitating the downfall of Prime Minister Anthony Eden. Elsewhere, old political ideals were also challenged, in some cases by uprisings and revolutionary action. In Hungary an uprising against Soviet occupation was brutally quashed by Moscow, whilst in Cuba communist revolutionaries led by a young Fidel Castro landed on the island to start their struggle to overthrow the dictator, Fulgencio Batista. Less controversial, some four years after the Great Smog, was the UK government's environmental legislation in the form of the Clean Air Act, which for the first time attempted to control smoke emissions from all those old coal fires.

It was an exciting period for technological and engineering development, including the laying of the first underwater transatlantic telephone cable and the widespread availability of products incorporating the transistor, perhaps the greatest invention of the twentieth century, for which its US inventors were awarded the 1956 Nobel Prize for Physics. Britain led the way in the peaceful use of atomic energy as the Queen opened the world's first full-scale nuclear power station at Calder Hall in Cumberland. Closer to home, major building projects were nearing completion after years of planning, including

The power station looms over the Belle Vue Engine sheds. Steve Armitage.

Baitings Dam near Ripponden, improving the supply of water to Wakefield, and a new local power station to secure its future electricity supply. Although the official opening of this supposedly low polluting, coal-fired power station was still a year away, the near-white concrete structures of its two gigantic hyperboloid cooling towers, and the huge 350-foot chimney south of the city on the river Calder, were already dominating the skyline and the low, grimy buildings in the surrounding neighbourhood of Belle Vue and Agbrigg.

Further west in the green of Wakefield Park, a new school building had risen from the ashes of the old Georgian mansion, symbolic of major changes taking place in secondary education.

The new school building was virtually complete by the summer of 1956 and was being made ready for occupation in the following autumn. It had been a long time coming, this new school. Cliff had made several patient appeals for key decisions and acceleration of the building programme, especially during his reports at annual Speech Days in the years following the fire, but there were several delays and budgetary issues to contend with. There was also the overriding political matter concerning the purpose of

The new Thornes House School building at the top of Wakefield Park, *c.*1956.
R. H. BARRACLOUGH.

this new school, which became caught up in the ongoing national debate about the future of secondary school education. The requirement of the 1944 Butler Education Act for a tripartite system of secondary modern, grammar, and technical schools was perceived to be failing in many local authorities by the early fifties, and there was a move nationally to fix this by combining the grammar and technical elements into a new type of school, grammar-technical schools ('grammar techs.'). Even though Wakefield had a relatively successful tripartite education system, the early to mid-fifties was not a good time to be spending a quarter of a million pounds on a new grammar school building. In fact, a bilateral grammar tech. was already in the long term plan of the Wakefield Education Committee at the time of the fire in 1951. Thornes House Grammar School became Thornes House School, a grammar tech., located in a new building with facilities for increased activity in technical subjects. This occurred some thirty-five years after the school's foundation when the city fathers had held a similar debate about the role of Thornes House in technical education. 'What goes around, comes around ...'

Having rid themselves of a grammar school, the Wakefield Education Authority was at pains to point out that Thornes House School would still retain its selection processes and, whilst the scope of the curriculum would be widened and its annual intake increased to four forms, the traditions and academic standards of a grammar school would be maintained. However, the curriculum already had a technical emphasis at the expense of the classics such as Latin, which was not compulsory and was generally only an option higher up the school. In the lower school, subjects such as woodwork and metalwork were part of the standard course for boys; domestic science was taught to the girls. A further broadening of the curriculum meant that the authorities had taken a big step towards a comprehensive education system, already being trialled elsewhere in the country. For those of us part way into our grammar school education, there was little change, apart from the welcome move from the cramped classrooms of Holmfield House into a spacious new building.

At the end of my second year in the summer of 1956 I was commanded by a bossy teacher to write an article about the new school building for the school magazine, the *Stork*. Writing was still not my strong point and I was relieved that it merely involved gathering information from the architects, engineers and builders, whilst older boys David Hammond and Rodney Murton wordsmithed the facts and figures into readable bullet points. This one-page article appeared in the 1956 edition of the *Stork,* and I was convinced that it would label me a teacher's pet, rather than 'one of the lads' in the Lower IVs, which is what I wanted to be.

The new building was opened officially by the Countess of Harewood on 9 November 1956, some two months after we had moved in but well before it started to have a 'used' appearance. The City Engineer and Surveyor, J. Norman Sedgwick, had designed a modern glass and concrete structure with just enough brick to remind the traditionalists of the good old days, although its orange appearance did not match the deep red-coloured remains of the old school. Huge areas of glass (a total of 13,473 square feet) in vast rectangular frames caused some concern to those with an eye on health and safety, whilst those with conservative tastes baulked at the rather gaudy colours everywhere. Old-fashioned it certainly wasn't!

All thirty-two classrooms were painted in bright colours, of which there were twenty-six different shades, aptly described by the Countess as 'gay'. It was the era of thermoplastic floor tiles in eye-catching colours, marketed with the most unlikely descriptors such as Chateau Grey, Mermaid Green and Sienna Gold. The new facilities included up-to-date Physics, Chemistry and Biology laboratories, facilities for domestic science, commerce and crafts as well as a library and special rooms for music and art. A state-of-the art fire detector system had been installed and connected directly to Wakefield Fire Station at great expense (£800), which caused mutterings from the cynics about 'closing stable doors after the horse has bolted'. But the *pièce de résistance* was the new assembly hall.

Main entrance, Thornes House School, *c.*1956. R. H. BARRACLOUGH.

With steps down to a grand entrance, large side windows, polished wood-block flooring and a proper stage equipped with a vast curtain and modern lighting, the new hall was now the hub of the school. Here, at last, the whole school could gather as a single entity for regular assemblies, school plays, dances and concerts. In a hushed morning assembly we would gaze towards the stage at the beautifully crafted wooden furniture, presented by Old Thornesians in memory of the many former pupils who had made the ultimate sacrifice in the Second World War. We would observe Cliff's

The new assembly hall juts out from the new Thornes House School building, *c.*1956. Some trees were preserved; many were uprooted to make room for the new building. WAKEFIELD COUNCIL MUSEUM COLLECTION.

sweeping entrance down a central aisle and listen attentively to his words of wisdom, delivered like a true oracle in the setting of a modern forum. We would let rip with hearty renderings from our *Songs of Praise* hymnbooks and listen to the beautiful four-part harmonies of Margaret Markland's prize winning choir. At the end of each term we would loyally bawl out the school song, 'O Brother Man,' an anthem based on a poem by John Greenleaf Whittier, set to music by Geoffrey Shaw, an appropriate choice since it encouraged brotherhood and the translation of worship into care and concern for our fellow human beings. Whittier had been an American Quaker and abolitionist.

The first school play in the new hall celebrated G. B. Shaw's centenary with a production of *Arms and the Man.* Whilst it was highly commended by senior master Jack Davies, he noted in his critique in the 1957 edition of the *Stork* magazine that, although we had the largest and finest stage in the city, school productions needed to learn how to use it. Moving shadows of people in the wings falling across the set on stage were distracting to the audience, and it was recommended that stage crews should avoid parting the curtains before the performance to see how the hall is filling. Jack also reminded stage crews that if they needed to buy ice creams during the interval, they now had a stage door to access the front of house, rather than using the stage itself!

The school hall was also where older pupils would gather tentatively for their first school dance, when shy boys would rather coyly ask their latest sweetheart to stumble around the floor in a clumsy quickstep, a wooden waltz or, perhaps, even a jive to live music provided by the Ace Sextet. In the summer term the hall would be filled with rows of desks where, with even greater trepidation, candidates would be seated to attempt the Northern Universities Joint Matriculation Board's (NUJMB) Ordinary, Advanced and Scholarship level examinations for their General Certificate of Education, GCE.

Teenagers: Class Upper IVA (1956/57). Back row, left to right: Bryan Heeley, John Spencer, Stephen Fox, Michael Paterson, Richard Pitts, John Parr, Neville Rider, Stuart Burnet, Trevor Smith, David Royle; middle row, left to right: Rosemary Jones, John Rhodes, Melvyn Lynes, Ann Summerscales, Brian Crowther, Craig Palmer, Margaret Scaife, Melvyn King, Stuart Robinson, Keith Barraclough; front row, left to right: Agnes Drysdale, Pamela Eccles, Janet Collings, Penelope Robinson, Sheila Spence, Barry Chambers, Elizabeth Jewson, Anne Frank, Betty Roberts, Ann Davis, Joan Naylor. GEO HOLDSWORTH & SON.

It wasn't dancing or exams that were causing me anguish in the Upper Fourths; it was round two in the battle of the trousers, one of many teenage battles fought with my parents at this time when I was one of the few remaining boys in the class wearing short trousers. I managed to dissuade Mum from another visit to Mrs Lord for my first pair of long trousers in favour of an 'off-the-peg' pair from outfitters John Manners Ltd. ('Good Value in Good Clothes'). I don't suppose these trousers fitted me any better than the 'short' elephant trousers, but that didn't matter; the Upper Fourths were full of rapidly growing adolescent boys clad in ill-fitting long trousers, either so long that the turn-ups lodged under the heels of their shoes, or so short that they displayed an ample length of sock in the large gap between turn-ups and shoes.

Although the rules for school uniform were quite strict, there were a few lads who stretched them as far as possible in order to accommodate the latest fashion. Thus, narrow rather than baggy trousers (grey/black), thick crepe soled shoes (black), navy blue blazers as long as possible and yellow and blue-striped school ties as thin as possible started to be worn in the third, fourth and fifth years. Any attempts for sixth form boys to look 'with it' were severely compromised by the requirement for them to wear caps with a bright yellow ring. It was even worse for prefects whose caps also consisted of an outrageous yellow and blue tassel!

Hairstyle was the most significant aspect of fashion which allowed the most degrees of freedom within school rules. Longish oiled hair, slicked back into a quiff at the top and combed along the sides to a 'DA' (Duck's Arse) at the back, became fashionable, replacing the regular short back and sides of conventional youth. The trend was set by American pop stars and the few Teddy Boys who could now be seen around Wakefield at this time. One or two girls followed suit as Teddy Girls but there were not enough of them to make any significant impression on schoolgirls' fashion at that time – certainly not under the watchful eye of Miss Marjorie Waring.

For Teddy Boys there were no school rules, although their outfits had more than a touch of uniformity about them. They were usually lads who had left school and were earning money, i.e. typically the sixteen-to-twenty age group. Their long drape jackets came in various striking colours such as blues, greens and even shades of purple, with black velvet lapels and pocket flaps. High-waisted black drainpipe trousers, brightly coloured pink or green socks, crepe-soled shoes, Slim Jim ties and masses of oiled hair completed the typical outfit. It is an irony that the style was adapted from the Edwardian period (King Edward VII, 1901–1910) as marketed by expensive Savile Row tailors to the middle and upper classes in London shortly after

Teddy Boys. British Pathé Ltd.

the Second World War. It is also a complete misconception that these costumes came cheap; some were very expensive and paid for by weekly instalments. They were a statement of independence by a group who were not prepared to follow the tradition of their fathers who, almost to a man, wore working clothes on Monday to Saturday and a best dark grey suit on Sunday. Teddy Boys earned their own money and they were not going to be told how to spend it.

It was initially the outrageous costumes of these young peacocks that incensed the older generation – the same generation that controlled the media. The extremely adverse reaction to Teddy Boys by the BBC and newspaper columnists was meat and drink to folks like my parents, who were outraged at Teddy Boys for being so 'brussen' by 'cocking a snook' at normality and tradition. Attitudes towards Teddy Boys hardened even further when they were accused of having a gang culture and involvement in violence, especially after the riots and vandalism following *Blackboard*

Jungle, a film about antisocial behaviour. But it was their association with the latest rock and roll music that my parents despised the most.

Dad thought that all popular music was rubbish. In the early 1950s the only source of music at home was the wireless, but it was quite difficult for my sister and me to hear any popular music at all. We had no opportunity to tune in to *Radio Luxembourg* in the evening; the only other possibility in those days was *Two Way Family Favourites.* However, the mere announcement of a request for a song by Frankie Laine, Anne Shelton, Dickie Valentine, Al Martino or Tony Bennett would result in Dad turning down the volume to inaudible levels. The likes of Johnnie Ray, Mario Lanza and David Whitfield would make his hackles rise so much that the wireless would be switched off instantly. Dad would just about tolerate the quieter, dulcet tones of Bing Crosby and Nat King Cole, but most crooners and popular singers were dismissed in one word, 'tripe' – that's how bad he felt they were! Mum's feelings were summed up in yet another derivative of her favourite word: 'muckment'.

When I first heard Bill Hayley and the Comets in 1955, and Elvis Presley's 'Hound Dog' in 1956, I was as excited as Dad was apoplectic. Here was a new noise that wasn't music as either of us knew it; sounds that could not be simply played on the piano from sheet music and sung by any Tom, Dick or Harry. The act of switching off the wireless was now accompanied by Dad pulling the trigger of an imaginary gun, but even such extraordinary measures could not stop this encroaching culture. Dad had to retreat into the safety of brass bands, classical music and light classical music on the *BBC Light Programme,* such as *Semprini Serenade.* Mum and Dad would religiously settle down in front of the fire and join in with Semprini's reassuring little ditty at the start of every programme: 'Old ones, new ones, loved ones, neglected ones.' They may have been slightly suspicious of the 'new ones' but Semprini provided a nice, predictable comfort zone in this unpredictable world.

Since listening to programmes of my choice on the wireless was proving so difficult, I decided that the only way forward was to acquire a set of my own. The ideal choice would have been one of the new portable transistor radios that came to the UK market around this time, but I was unaware of their existence and would not have had the money to buy one anyway. The only alternative was to make my own crystal set, by following instructions in a library book. After much fiddling around with the crystal and electrical contacts I managed to receive the odd squawk on a set of cheap headphones, a major triumph but a far cry from the dream of having my own source of audible pop music.

In 1956 I was still scrounging viewing time on other people's televisions; in fact, I had developed my scrounging skills into quite an art! The Tattersalls had moved away from number 11 Wesley Street in about 1953 and a young family had moved in, Marian and Arthur Pearson and their toddler son, Martin. I befriended Arthur, a giant of a man who, as a very good professional cricketer in the Heavy Woollen District of the Yorkshire League, became my cricket mentor and coach. Marian was a kind, gentle young woman and I immediately fell in love with her when I discovered that 11 Wesley Street was home to a television set. I would often loiter outside their back gate until Marian invited me in to watch sports and popular music shows.

Neither I nor any of my friends had a record player, but there was one available at the Crusaders 1956 Annual Dance in St Catherine's School hall, where my sixteen-year-old sister tried patiently to teach me to jive to a scratchy 78 r.p.m. recording of Little Richard singing 'Tutti Frutti'. I was still far too young for the dancehalls in town, so the only other possibility to hear the latest pop music was at one of the occasional fairs in Wakefield. It was usually the music blaring out on the big rides which attracted me and many teenagers. Without worrying about paying or safety instructions, the Teddy Boys would leap onto the moving waltzer and 'show off' by gyrating to its pulsating rock music and the rolling mechanical movement, their fags glowing in the dim light, not a hair out of place. I envied the Teddy Boys' confidence but most of all, I envied their independence; I had neither.

I had wanted independent transport in the form of a proper 'grown-up bike', displayed in shops such as Moorhouse's at the bottom of Kirkgate and the local bike shops: Willans's on Agbrigg Road, Amy Gill's on the corner of Ashdown Road and Belle Vue Road, near Sandal Council school, and Harold Whone's on Doncaster Road at the bottom of Denmark Street. I would spend hours peering through these shop windows, nose squashed against the glass, imagining riding one of these bikes, but too shy to go in and actually touch them. Hercules, Dawes, Humber, Triumph, BSA, Raleigh – they were all so near and yet so far away. I first saw my ultimate dream machine in Whone's. The prime attraction of the Raleigh Lenton Sports was its striking silver-green frame in the proprietary Raleigh colour, Special Super Chromatic Lenton Green. I loved its racing drop handlebars, steel racing pedals, caliper brakes and that triumph of British engineering, the smooth four-speed Sturmey Archer F.M. hub gears, although I eventually preferred the racier option of the Benelux four-speed derailleur gears offered on the 1957 Mark III model. The 21-inch frame was not too big for me and, anyway, I was used to growing into things. The clincher was the endorsement by the world cycling sprint champion, Reg Harris, who trained on a Lenton Sports. It was perfect, apart from the little matter of price. In 1956 the Raleigh Lenton Sports, including purchase tax, came with little change from £20, about three years' pocket money. I had to get a job.

Having thought I could just walk into a paper round, I was disappointed to discover that there was not a single job available in Belle Vue at that time. The Raleigh Lenton had to remain a dream, and the reality was a bike assembled by Dad from second-hand parts. He acquired a frame from somewhere, painted it a bright gloss green and stuck a few transfers on it. Even worse, this mongrel bike had straight handlebars, a saddlebag and a large bell, designed for practicality and safety, rather than racing. Much to the annoyance of his ungrateful teenage son, the road safety guru didn't do 'racing'.

As a teenager, piano lessons suddenly became very low down on my list of priorities. My lack of enthusiasm hadn't gone unnoticed by Maggie Ramsden, who informed me that she would have no time for me once the next set of London College of Music examinations were over. Dad was outraged that his abject son should waste such an opportunity, especially since he had had to wait for music lessons until he could afford to pay for them himself. This rollicking did spur me to practise before the examination, in the hope that Maggie Ramsden would reinstate me, but she didn't, and to add insult to injury I never received the prize that had been promised to the pupil with the best marks in the exams. And so, with some degree of bitterness combined with relief, piano lessons ended.

My next teenage failure was cricket. I had honed a decent batting technique through hours of practice in Back Regent Street, and in the nets in Dewsbury where Arthur Pearson often took me. At the end of my first year at Thornes House, I had already played one game for the first XI, alongside sixth formers such as Kenworthy, who at that time was also playing in league cricket for Ossett. I had also been selected for a Yorkshire under fifteens trial, and that is when it all went wrong. Cricket is a game of confidence which, if undermined by the opposition or oneself, will wipe out any technical ability in the most unforgiving manner. During the trial game at Castleford, I had been asked to open the innings, became petrified and psyched myself out first ball, and then again when the selectors had given me a second chance. In a word, I had 'bottled' it and this humiliation played on my mind so much that I was never able to play a decent innings of cricket again. Although I was eventually made captain of the school's first XI, I came to loathe cricket as a participatory sport, but would continue to be intrigued by those players who were able to overcome their fears and show 'bottle', especially at the top level of Test cricket.

I went with Arthur to Headingley for the second day's play in the third Test match against the Australians on Friday, 13 July 1956. Many of the old guard from the pre- and immediate post-war era had disappeared from Test cricket, including my hero, Len Hutton. However, Hutton's opening partner for many pre-war Test matches, Cyril Washbrook, was making an amazing return to the England team at the grand old age of forty-one. There were lots of mutterings from the corners of Yorkshire mouths about this strange selection, not least because Washbrook was a Lancastrian as well as an England selector! The old stalwarts, Ray Lindwall and Keith Miller were still in the Australian line-up, but it was their third and probably last

Ashes tour to England. The fast bowler to watch was the ebullient Yorkshire favourite, Freddie Trueman, who was making his first appearance against the Aussies in a Test at Headingley. Allegedly, Fred was one of those Yorkshire bowlers who would systematically undermine the confidence of opposing batsmen by any means available, including going into their dressing room before the match and telling them he could already see several wickets for himself. Fiery Fred was building quite a reputation.

Those in the Yorkshire crowd who had criticised Washbrook's selection were now secretly hoping for his demise, but they were soon downcast when he played a dogged innings and was unlucky to be out just two runs short of a memorable century. As usual, Lindwall made light work of the tail-enders and had Arthur purring with appreciation at his rhythmic run up, mechanically smooth action and perfect side-on delivery that many purists described as poetry in motion. But the crowd was saving itself for Freddie Trueman, for whom the vocal support during his first over that July afternoon was the best example of the meaning of 'crescendo' I have ever heard. The noise would start with a few individual shouts of encouragement as Fred strode back purposefully from the bowling crease to the start of his very long run up, busily rubbing the new ball on his scruffy flannels and constantly flicking that mop of jet black hair from his eyes. By the time the start of the run up was reached, many more voices had joined the chorus of support, but they could still be picked out as individual shouts. Once Fred had started running in, the individual shouts became a unified roar that became louder and louder with each of Fred's long strides, until that critical moment when the ball was released.

Trueman's action was not dissimilar to Lindwall's: it was a smooth, classic, side-on delivery, but Fred's overall attitude was much more venomous and full of histrionics. He expected a wicket with every ball and threw up his hands in despair as the 'lucky' batsman deprived him of a wicket, but he didn't have to wait long for success. After the first five balls of Fred's first over, the roar of the crowd died away into a disappointing, 'Ooh' when the opening batsmen dealt with the hostile deliveries, but the sixth and last ball of the over was edged by Colin McDonald and he was out, caught behind by wicketkeeper, Godfrey Evans. Instead of an 'Ooh', suddenly there was a joyous 'Yes!' shouted by everyone in the ground as they leapt to their feet and cheered long after poor old McDonald had disconsolately trooped off the field into the distant pavilion. I felt very sorry for him, but didn't say anything.

Fiery Fred had made the critical breakthrough in front of his home crowd, but the match was won by the Surrey spinners, Jim Laker and Tony Lock. Off-spinner Laker was unplayable in the next Test match at Old Trafford,

Thornes House School's under fifteens football team, 1956/57. Back row, left to right: Jeff Golding, Alan Beck, Brian Mann, Stuart Robinson; front row, left to right: Roger Whincup, Barrie Snowden, Colin Green, Keith Barraclough, Michael Branford, Bryan Heeley, John Crowhurst. GEO HOLDSWORTH & SON.

where he skittled out the Aussies by taking 19 wickets for only 90 runs, a feat that not only retained the Ashes but established a world bowling record, predicted to stand for all time. I witnessed this event unfold on television at 11 Wesley Street, where Arthur Pearson casually informed me that Jim Laker was actually a Yorkshireman who had been overlooked by his county and had chosen to play for Surrey instead. Fancy that, I mused.

We all fancied ourselves as the next Stanley Matthews but the skills of the school's under fifteens football team were woeful, resulting in some feeble performances against local schools. In a match against Ackworth

Quaker School the score against us had even reached double figures. Having humiliated us on the field, our opponents then politely hosted us in their posh dining room where they courteously served tea and cakes, using proper cups and saucers and matching plates, beautifully arranged on a polished wood dining table. There was further humiliation when Cliff announced the results to next morning's assembly. With neck firmly clasped, Cliff tried to put a positive spin on our dismal performances whilst the rest of the school gasped in disbelief; the merciless even guffawed at our incompetence.

'Spike's' solution to our problems was certainly not part of any 1950s football coaching manual, but he was never short of an innovative idea or two. We would be instructed to lie on our backs on the cold gym floor and, with eyes closed, had to imagine being a famous footballer in the act of accomplishing a major feat – such as a centre forward scoring a sensational goal or a goalkeeper miraculously saving a penalty. We then had to focus on our mental picture and make it come alive with as much detail as possible, presumably as part of some magic process that would embed it in the subconscious so that it would trigger similar feats when our own bodies were performing! Unfortunately, 'Spike's' psychological approach was not taken very seriously by teenage boys in 1956. When a certain individual was asked to name the person held in his imagination, 'Marilyn Monroe, sir' was not the answer 'Spike' was looking for. 'Spike's' approach had little effect on our performances: it was our feet not our heads that were in need of creative therapy. At the time the irony never dawned on me that sports psychology may well have helped my cricket, but 'Spike' didn't do cricket.

My friend John Hannon, now at QEGS, was much more interested in soccer than rugby, and occasionally I would accompany him to watch Huddersfield Town AFC, known locally as t'Town, in the hope I might learn something to improve my own game. It was such an easy journey on the train from Wakefield Kirkgate Station to Huddersfield, followed by a simple stroll to the ground on Leeds Road. We would wander past the huge blackened Corinthian pillars of the station's impressive Victorian-built portico, down the steps into George Square and past the famous George Hotel, the birthplace of rugby league where twenty-two northern rugby

GROUND:
LEEDS ROAD.   TELEPHONE No. 35.

CLUB COLOURS:
BLUE & WHITE VERTICAL STRIPE.

HUDDERSFIELD TOWN ASSOCIATION FOOTBALL CLUB, LTD.

(Winners of the English Cup, Association Charity Shield, and West Riding Senior Cup, Season 1921-22).
(Football League Champions, Division I, Seasons 1923-24, 1924-25 and 1925-26).
(Central League Champions, Seasons 1914-15, 1924-25 and 1925-26).

H. BEEVER, SECRETARY.
JOHN F. CHAPLIN,
MANAGER.

REGISTERED OFFICE:
LEEDS ROAD, HUDDERSFIELD.

MEMBERS OF
The Football League.
The Central League.
Yorkshire Mid-Week League.

Dear Sir,   Jan 31/28.

In reply to your letter respecting arrangements for Thursday next, February 2nd.
I shall be glad if you will join our team at Lunch at 12-0 at the George Hotel, Huddersfield, and also bring your boots along with you.
Kindly drop me a post card confirming that this will be quite in order.

Yours Faithfully,

Manager.

Dad's postcard invitation to a trial for the illustrious Huddersfield Town AFC in 1928. K. G. Barraclough.

clubs had met in 1895 and decided to break away from the Rugby Football Union to form the Northern Union. It was also where at twelve noon on 2 February 1928 a nervous Reg Barraclough had been summoned by John Chaplin, the manager of the mighty Huddersfield Town AFC to bring his boots and join the team for lunch before the trial game.

Dad had been overawed and didn't play well enough to be considered further for this level of football. At that time Huddersfield Town AFC was a top class team, already with an illustrious history, established within twenty years of its formation in 1908 (the year Dad was born). By the start of the 1956/57 season, however, t'Town had been relegated to the second division and, as is often the case in such circumstances, there had been changes in personnel, including the appointment of a new manager, a tough dour Scot, Mr Bill Shankly.

It felt very safe standing on the huge terraces of the Leeds Road ground in much larger crowds than at Belle Vue. Visiting supporters usually intermingled freely with the home crowd and exchanged humorous banter.

When a tall, bald-headed centre half from an opposing team mis-headed the ball, he was advised by a Town supporter to 'put some chalk on thy cue' to which a visiting supporter jovially retorted that 'he also needs a bloody rest'. It was more akin to camaraderie amongst long suffering supporters than intense rivalry. As usual, there was plenty of advice directed at Mr Shankly and his team. We saw a skinny, blond-haired sixteen-year-old Scot make his debut for t'Town in the 1956/57 season, but many supporters doubted the wisdom of this selection and expressed the view that his puny frame and poor eyesight were not up to scratch. However, this lad obviously had ability and a fearless approach to the game, which eventually changed our opinion. Bill Shankly certainly knew a thing or two when he introduced Denis Law to the football stage.

Back in Wakefield, the Trinity had experienced a lean period since winning the Yorkshire Cup in 1951. One notable event of a difficult 1952/53 season was a thrashing by the Australian touring team, when Trinity forward Jack Booth had also been sent off for fighting. In 1954 Dennis Boocker had broken the club's try scoring record in his last match, after which he had also signed my autograph book before club secretary, Eddie Thomas, hastily whisked him away to the office at the top of the St Catherine's terracing for a little presentation 'do' with the committee and, presumably, to 'settle up' before he returned to Australia. Also in 1954, Trinity forward, Don Robinson, was a member of the Great Britain team that won the first Rugby League World Cup in France. However, the Trinity team had not won anything for nearly five years until their fortunes changed in 1956, a watershed year when new young signings started to make their mark.

The most notable of these signings was the result of a stealthy operation in October 1955, when Neil Fox, a sixteen-year-old, centre three-quarter from nearby Sharlston, was captured from under the nose of Featherstone Rovers, for whom he was already playing as an amateur in their under eighteens junior team. Neil Fox had a fine rugby pedigree. His dad, Tommy, had played professional rugby league for Featherstone Rovers in the 1930s and his older brothers Peter and Don had followed in their dad's footsteps. All three had natural ability and each had a fine rugby brain, which the

Trinity staff had also spotted in young Neil. By 7 January 1956, Neil was due to play his first match in the Trinity A-team against Hull K.R., but he nearly didn't make it. There was such an interest in this home fixture that all the buses from his home in Sharlston were full with supporters, so our debutant had to cycle to the ground, arriving with only twenty minutes to spare! I was one of the many keen supporters who gathered near the players' entrance in the 'Paddock' beneath the main stand to appraise this new signing at close quarters. Neil Fox modestly lumbered out from the changing rooms looking quite apologetic and embarrassed that such a fuss should be made of him. He was a big lad for a sixteen-year-old, already about six feet tall, around thirteen stone in weight with a solid frame and legs like tree trunks. He scored a try, kicked a goal and gave a scoring pass in an easy 40–0 victory for Trinity, but as we all shuffled out into the gloomy streets of Belle Vue, few spectators were raving about the start of Neil Fox's professional rugby league career; and certainly no-one was aware that they had seen the start of something very special indeed.

In the 1955/56 season the A-team was beating most opponents, and its youngsters were playing scintillating rugby. Neil Fox, 't'Big Fella', as he was soon to be known, had plenty of opportunities to demonstrate his natural skills and goal kicking ability. Jack Booth was the ideal captain of the A-team. After long service in the first team, this huge forward was the epitome of Trinity's old guard, nearing the end of his playing days. With over ten years' experience he could still look after himself and, most importantly, he also protected his young charges. Like most hardened rugby league forwards Jack Booth was not a handsome specimen. After years of toil in all those contested scrums, his large head appeared to have been scrunched into his shoulders, depriving him the benefit of a neck and pivotal joint. Jack appeared particularly ponderous alongside his sharp youngsters, but he was a very popular captain. It was therefore very fitting when, at the end of the season, he lifted the Yorkshire Senior Competition Championship Shield and the Yorkshire Senior Competition Challenge Cup, made particularly memorable by a hat-trick of thrilling tries in the Cup Final by another of the young signings, right wing Fred Smith.

Wakefield Trinity 'A' (reserve) team, winners of the 1955/56 Yorkshire Senior Competition Cup and League 'double'. Back row, left to right: Ted Wilkins, Francis Sweeney, Mick Lumb, David Lamming, Norman Ashall, Neil Fox, Albert Firth; front row, left to right: Aubrey Houlden, Keith Bridges, Roy Evans, Jack Booth, Johnny Bullock, Fred Smith, Stan Moorhouse. *WAKEFIELD EXPRESS.*

In January 1956, twenty-year-old Fred Smith had signed for Trinity in circumstances which initially outraged me and many other supporters, because he came as part of a transfer deal which took our international star forward, Don Robinson, to Leeds in return for Smith and £3,000 much needed cash. Not many of us had really heard of local lad Smith, and we grumbled that Trinity was becoming a 'selling club'. However, it was soon clear from his star performances in the A-team that Fred Smith was a real bargain. Although he was slightly built, in the Dennis Boocker mould, Smith had searing pace, a devastating outside swerve and he could deftly chip the ball at top speed over opponents and outpace them to the touchdown. Fred Smith alone was worth watching A-team matches for in the 1955/56 season.

By the end of the 1955/56 season both Fox and Smith had made their first team debuts. In October 1956, Trinity won the Yorkshire Cup to end their five year barren run without a trophy. But the seminal watershed moment of 1956 was the emergence of Trinity's triumphant young backs in the first team's 17–12 defeat of the Australian touring team on 10 December, a hastily arranged fixture on a Monday afternoon, when the small attendance seemed to consist of a lot of boys who had bunked off school. Centre Keith Holliday was just over twenty years old; the rest were twenty or younger: right wing, Fred Smith (twenty), scrum half, Johnny Bullock (nineteen), full back, Ted Wilkins (eighteen), stand-off half, Ken Rollin (eighteen), centre, Neil Fox (seventeen) and left wing debutant, Ken Hirst (sixteen), who scored a memorable try from inside his own half within two minutes of the kick-off! Suddenly the future looked bright at Belle Vue.

To cap it all, round the corner at number 52 Regent Street, things also took a turn for the better. After years of waiting, it became home to a brand new television set.

References and Further Reading

Thornes House, The Story of a School, Nora J. George, 1993 Wakefield Library, Balne Lane, Wakefield, WF2 0DQ.

Family Britain, 1951–57, David Kynaston, Bloomsbury Publishing plc 2009, ISBN 978-07475-8385-1.

Neil Fox, Rugby League's Greatest Points Scorer, Robert Gate, London League Publications Ltd., November, 2005 ISBN 1-903659-24-8.

CHAPTER NINE

We Have Never Had It So Good, circa 1957

As with all major decisions on expenditure, it was the director of the household who had taken complete charge of buying the new television set: the rest of us were not consulted, even though I considered myself to be an expert. I expect Dad consulted his mates at work but the decision on the best make of television was really a 'no-brainer' for him. Loyal to the brand and the faithful dog, Nipper, of its famous trademark, Dad had decided on a 14-inch HMV model. It was like having a new baby in the family as it was gently unwrapped and carefully positioned in the living room. We all hovered over it, rather apprehensive at first, but its beaming chubby face indicated it was happy in its new home. Meanwhile its elder brother, the wireless, sat alongside looking rather rejected, perhaps even jealous and certainly old-fashioned. Mum was probably grateful that at least the new addition to the family only needed cleaning and was not another mouth to feed.

Suddenly, we had different routines. Chairs were now rotated away from the fire towards the box, and the curtains were drawn even in daylight, much against Mum's better judgement: 'What will the neighbours think?' For years the neighbours had been doing the same, and in wintertime they were also switching off their electric lights, transforming their living rooms from peaceful, cosy havens of soothing yellow light into centres of violent electric storms, flickering and flashing with light of a bluish hue. By now there were many televisions in the street, and I no longer needed to inflict myself on the Pearsons. I had never had it so good.

There were now conflicts between old favourites on the wireless and new TV programmes, the final decision inevitably leaving someone disappointed. We knew the schedule of the wireless programmes off by heart, but now had to consult the *Radio Times* for the schedule of the new medium. Tea remained fixed at the same time before the start of the evening performance, but the evening snack ('supper') was often rescheduled from the precise stroke of nine o'clock to catch a new TV programme. Much to my irritation, Mum introduced a strict house rule of forbidding eating and watching television at the same time – there were enough disruptions for her to cope with. Activities that might block the line of sight of the television were rescheduled: washing up was fitted in, as and when, rather than immediately at the end of tea and supper; coal had to be brought up from the cellar and the fire fettled in advance of an important programme, not during it. Mum probably struggled with this change to hitherto rigid routines, but she gradually became used to the new regime. I also had to juggle with my routines, especially the increasing amounts of homework being set in the Upper IVs, an important school year when options for O-levels had to be weighed up and chosen. Characteristically, Dad had a different perspective on television from the rest of us.

A good amateur photographer knows all about the contribution of contrast, brightness, resolution and grain to the quality of a picture; a competitive one spends hours tweaking these parameters to deliver that perfect print. Dad would spend a whole evening in the attic, fiddling with different blends of photographic papers, exposure times, shading and chemicals to produce just a single print, before he was satisfied that it was suitable for a forthcoming exhibition. The dim, filtered light of the dark room couldn't conceal his excitement as an image he had composed days ago would gradually emerge in the developer dish, from a faint, ghost-like sketch to a stunningly sharp black and white print capturing the finest detail. It was hardly surprising then that he should bring this expertise and artistic interpretation to the television set in the quest for the perfect picture. For Dad the best part of the whole television experience was tuning his set to the test card, optimising the appearance of the myriad lines and shapes. He was in his element, although he would grumble about the limited resolution offered by only 405 lines. The number of tuning options on a 1956 TV set was also rather limited, but there were enough for a pedant to take quite some time before being satisfied that the correct combination had been found, especially as he would frequently pause to appraise the effect of his fine adjustments from the appropriate viewing distance. Fortunately, this tuning operation could usually be done outside peak viewing times but occasionally, during a proper programme, Dad would leap up from his chair to make an adjustment when his critical eye detected that, 'there's something not right with that picture'. Mum might shake her head and voice her disapproval but Elaine and I kept quiet – we were just grateful that, at last, Dad had moved into the second half of the twentieth century.

We had acquired our TV set towards the end of 1956, just before ITA started broadcasting commercial television programmes to viewers in Yorkshire from the new Emley Moor transmitter that had been built only a mile or so from Dad's birthplace. However, without any sentiment, Dad pronounced that, compared with the BBC, the commercial programmes were of an inferior quality ('tripe'), whilst Mum felt that many of them were vulgar and common ('muckment'), so ITV's Granada Television franchise did not stand much of a chance at number 52 Regent Street. Mum and Dad also disapproved of the American-style advertisements, which they felt were 'conning' the general public into spending their hard-earned money on products whose claimed superiority over other brands was at best dubious and at worst dishonest. They were totally resistant to this new seductive face of consumerism ('they must think we were born yesterday').

I didn't really care about the limited opportunities to watch ITV: at that time two flies crawling up the screen would have held my attention and I was enthralled even by the news and current affairs programmes on the BBC channel. Around this time the *Tonight* programme was broadcast every weekday in the early evening from six to six forty-five, anchored by Cliff Michelmore, with support from top-quality journalists such as Brian Redhead, Geoffrey Johnson Smith and that wiry, bearded Scot, Fyfe Robertson. The more serious stuff was handled by Richard Dimbleby in *Panorama,* and perhaps it was his familiar gravitas that enabled him to narrate so convincingly to us all the famous April Fool hoax about the spaghetti harvest in Switzerland. Real documentaries on foreign countries and wildlife were very popular, notably *On Safari* with Armand and Michaela Denis. I rather fancied the lovely Michaela.

Hancock's Half Hour always went down well in our house, presumably because its message, veiled in light-hearted comedy, reinforced our more serious understanding that pompous attempts to be posh and impress people always ended in catastrophic failure, but we all reserved a soft spot for the lovable loser that was Anthony Aloysius St John Hancock. However, light-hearted entertainment, in the form of 'shows', was quite often branded as unsuitable by my parents. Despite its ground-breaking use of the new television medium, Mum and Dad censored the *Benny Hill Show* on the grounds that his slapstick routines were far too 'simple' (i.e. stupid) and his jokes far too smutty, not to mention the banal theme tune, 'Yackety Sax'.

We all looked forward to sports programmes, especially the occasional live outside broadcast and the weekly magazine programme, *Sportsview,* anchored by the smooth-talking Peter Dimmock. The Rugby League Cup Final was still not being shown live on television but I saw in the comfort of home the only live televised football match in 1957, the FA Cup Final between Aston Villa and the much fancied Busby Babes of Manchester United. It turned out to be a dramatic affair with Manchester United suffering an early loss to injury of their goalkeeper, Ray Wood, who was unceremoniously shoulder-charged into his own goal as Aston Villa scored a very doubtful goal. Against weakened opponents, Aston Villa went on to win the Cup, but I always thought it was an unsatisfactory result for such a

Dad is presented with the Samuel Pickles Cup, at a mid-fifties awards ceremony of the Wakefield Camera Club. R. H. BARRACLOUGH.

glamorous occasion. From that day on I had a soft spot for Manchester United, and nine months later this turned to deep sorrow when many of these Busby Babes lost their lives in a dreadful air crash at the end of an icy runway in Munich, West Germany. The result of a football match was suddenly put into perspective.

It was the televised Wimbledon Championships of 1957 that introduced me to tennis, which enchanted me with its grace and fair outcomes, never blighted by either the physical violence of soccer and rugby or the mind games of cricket. I think the time I completely lost interest in cricket was when I eagerly joined many others on the tennis courts in Wakefield Park attempting to emulate Lew Hoad, the 1957 Wimbledon Men's Champion.

Dad's photography was reaching its zenith. Despite the arrival of the television set, he was spending more time in the attic and was regularly submitting entries for photographic competitions and exhibitions at the Wakefield Camera Club and across the globe. In 1957 he exhibited at the Tenth New Zealand International Exhibition of Photography in Wellington, for example. In 1955 and 1957 Dad was a proud exhibitor at the respective 46th and 48th International Exhibitions of the prestigious London Salon of Photography, in London's gallery of the Royal Society of Painters in Water Colours. These were by invitation-only from the London Salon, whose declared aim was to exhibit only that class of work in pictorial photography in which there is distinct evidence of personal artistic feeling and execution. Membership of the London Salon of Photography was the pinnacle of pictorial photography and was an exclusive club with only thirty members chosen by the members themselves. In the mid-fifties members included society photographers Hugh Cecil, Marcus Adams and

Walter Bird. The famous teacher and photogravure, Adolf Fassbender of New York, was also a member. By exhibiting at the London Salon, Dad was on a par with the top photographers of the day. I have often wondered what the celebrity photographer, Cecil Beaton of 8 Pelham Place, SW7, thought of the exhibit, *From Time Immemorial* from the self-taught chap of 52 Regent Street, Wakefield, listed next but one to him in the 1955 catalogue. Other exhibitors that year included society photographer Dorothy Wilding, the official Royal Photographer for the 1937 Coronation, and also Russell Gay, a London glamour photographer whose contribution was simply entitled, *Nude.* In the 1950s many voluptuous young women had modelled for Gay in his London studio, none more prominent than a Miss Norma Sykes from Stockport, commonly known as Sabrina, his major 'discovery'.

Dad became quite well known in photographic circles. He gave talks to local groups, including Thornes House Photographic Society, and had a network of contacts with whom he would regularly correspond on technicalities, sometimes on his own little process secrets. George Mallett, ARPS, (Associate of the Royal Photographic Society) of the Stratford-upon-Avon Photographic Society wrote on the 4 September 1957: 'First of all I would like to let you know how much your two pictures have been admired. Secondly, I wonder if you would be kind enough to let me know your paper negative process, step by step ... I have searched our local library but can find nothing on paper negatives.' Of course in the spirit of true amateurism, Dad's reply explained everything, step by step.

In 1957 Dad received an invitation from the editor of A*mateur Photographer* to write a 750-word article for the magazine's series, 'How I Make My Exhibition Pictures'. The article described his paper negative process and also extolled the virtues of hard work, (no surprise there!), learning by mistakes and joining a camera club. It also included two examples of his prize winning exhibits *Youth at the Helm* and *Winter.* When the article appeared in the 16 October 1957 edition of *Amateur Photographer* Dad received an honorarium of 10 guineas. His hard graft to the top had been followed by reward and recognition but, apart from

From Time Immemorial, rather worse for fifty-seven years of wear after its exhibition at the London Salon in 1955. The rear states 'Paper Negative Process'.
R. H. BARRACLOUGH.

handling the ensuing flow of correspondence, it was his last major act on the serious photographic stage.

I am not sure that the term 'mid-life crisis' was invented by 1957 but, with hindsight, Dad was having one, I am sure. By now he was determined to leave the police force after twenty-five years' service and couldn't wait to do something different. He was only forty-nine years old and would still be only fifty-one on completion of twenty-five years' service. However, that meant he needed to plan for a new job and somewhere new to live. By 1957 owner occupation had surged to about 38 per cent of the total housing market, demand for private housing stock was on the increase and so were the prices. Average house prices in the UK had increased from £2,000 in 1955 to £2,300 in

Article in *Amateur Photographer* magazine, 16 October 1957. AMATEUR PHOTOGRAPHER.

1957. The option of renting was out of the question for him, a sound judgement bearing in mind that the Conservative government's 1957 Rent Act allowed some relaxation of rent controls, which paved the way for unscrupulous landlords, such as Peter Rachman, to pressurise many tenants to vacate their rented accommodation so that new tenants could be charged higher rents. Dad started planning to buy his own house ...

In 1957 the salary of a police sergeant with more than three years' experience was £755 p.a. compared with the national average income of about £600. By now, my sister Elaine was also earning her keep as a shorthand typist at the National Coal Board Area 7 offices in Newton Hill, where her first earnings were less than £3 per week. We were not poor but, if a house were to be bought with a mortgage, there was the little matter of finding the money for a deposit. Buying a television set and running an expensive hobby meant that there was not a lot of capital saved up for a house, so something had to give. It was the photography.

Dad's photographic equipment had usually been acquired in various deals with his mates from the Wakefield Camera Club. One particular 'wheeler--dealer' was John Lockwood, who worked at Duffin & Greaves Ltd. of 24 Wood Street ('Wakefield's Leading Photographic Shop') where Dad could often be found in his spare time. In about 1955 Dad's pride and joy was a Franke & Heidecke, German-made Rolleicord, a twin-lens reflex camera worth around £80. He would have preferred the Rolleiflex, a more refined camera, but that was beyond his budget. By 1957 the Rolleicord had been traded and he now owned three cameras: a 35mm Leica IIIa rangefinder camera, a Voiglander Bessa II folding camera and a Thornton Pickard reflex camera. Import restrictions on the highly acclaimed, German-made Leica cameras made them difficult to come by in the 1950s and this is where having a network of mates in the business seems to have come in handy, especially those who might travel to Germany. The second-hand value of the Leica IIIa camera was around £65 in 1957; the total value of all three cameras, including their state of the art lenses, was estimated to be around £150. When the second-hand value of all the other 'gear' was taken into consideration, Dad's complete photographic equipment was probably worth over £200, equivalent to a 10 per cent deposit on the price of an average house.

It is not absolutely clear that he needed to raise so much additional capital for a deposit on a house, but he probably felt that he had achieved everything possible as an amateur photographer and that it was going to be extremely difficult, if not impossible, to move up to the next level. Dad had mastered the whole process of black and white photography but the art was moving on. By 1957 significant advances were being made in colour photography, requiring the investment of more time and money, which Dad didn't have. Without any trace of sentiment, Dad put all his beloved equipment up for sale. Within a month of his *Amateur Photographer* article being published, everything had gone.

The chosen house was within a budget of about £2,000 and was located in Avondale Street, off Denby Dale Road, south of the city on the edge of Thornes. Mum had been involved in this major decision but, yet again, there had been no consultation with Elaine and me. So, in the early morning

The view of the railway arches and the Greyhound Stadium from the back garden of 21 Avondale Street, *c*.1958. R. H. BARRACLOUGH.

of Friday, 1 November 1957, we both left 52 Regent Street for the last time and in the early evening turned up at our new home for the first time to find local removal contractor, Fred Hoyle of Park Street, Wakefield, still unloading our worldly goods in the dark. Their hard day's work had cost the grand sum of £7-2s-6d.

Number 21 Avondale Street was a detached house, but only a few feet separated us on one side from the wall of a neighbouring semi. On the other side of the house, a piece of unmade spare ground, ripe for development of some sort, separated us from the next group of semis. Opposite us were terraced houses with doors opening directly onto the street. Some 50 yards away the street ended in a dirt footpath under a bridge of the old Lancashire & Yorkshire railway. We soon found out that the piece of spare ground next to us was the only place for cars and wagons to turn and drive back down the street onto Denby Dale Road, so it was quite noisy during the day. At the back of our house a short garden separated us from ground owned by Comberhill Motors, who parked rusty old wagons up against their boundary which had barbed wire strung across concrete posts to deter thieves and vandals. In the distance, some 120 yards to the northeast, it was possible to see some of the 99 arches of the old railway viaduct and the familiar Wakefield Greyhound Stadium, which announced itself in gigantic white lettering painted on the wall of the bricked-in arches.

By now I had lost interest in trainspotting, so living next to three railway lines was not the bonus it would have been in the past. Ironically, we were constantly reminded of the busy railways, especially in the middle of the night when engine drivers took great delight in blowing off steam through the whistles of their stationary locomotives. We all thought we would never get a decent night's sleep again.

Our new home was hardly the best location in Wakefield but it was a convenient one: the city centre was now much less than a mile away and I could walk to school through the nearby park. The number 85 bus travelled along Denby Dale Road, so the journey time to Mum's family in Shepley was reduced by at least ten minutes, compared with the journey from Belle Vue on the same bus.

Our house had been built in about 1925. Its red brick walls had not yet been completely blackened by smoke to blend in with its dark-grey pitched, slate roof. The upper section of all the front windows and the upper panel of the front door contained ornately coloured leaded lights, exquisite forerunners of the acclaimed Art Deco style of the 1930s. However, there was a limit to such extravagant embellishments; out of public view at the back of the house all windows were plain glass. The floor plan was similar to the Victorian terraced house in Belle Vue, with a living room at the rear and a separate front room, both accessed from a small front entrance hall. However, we now had a separate scullery, accessed from the end of the hall, not as an annex to the living room. The same layout was continued upstairs, with two normal-sized bedrooms and a small bedroom (box room) over the hall. We now had a complete bathroom suite in white porcelain, including a lavatory (with a hinged lid) and a large open bath (without a hinged lid). The bathroom walls were half tiled in black and white; black and white chequered lino covered the floor. Our posh two-tone bathroom earned a big tick in the box as we all laughed about our past excursions down the back yard in Belle Vue. I pretended not to hear the barbed comments about 'no smoking'.

But there was more to this house than just a two and a half bedroom box with a bathroom. Built on to the far side of the house next to the spare ground was a brick annex, accessed from the scullery to what had been the rear of a shop; this was separated from a sizeable area, previously the shop itself, which had been latterly converted to a garage with large wooden doors opening onto the street. Here was the main reason why Dad had bought the property. We knew he could not afford to buy and run a car so this annex would not continue as a garage; it would be his den where he would get his teeth into the next hobby and master it by gnarling it into submission through sheer dogged persistence. But we didn't yet know what the next craze was going to be.

The scullery door opened onto a small rectangular back garden, with a circular rose bed set in the middle of a tiny lawn. Flowerbeds had also been cultivated along the borders, and a privet hedge running down both sides had been carefully trimmed in a wavy style by a previous occupant whose artistic ambitions had got the better of him (or her). Two large square-sectioned wooden clothes posts supported a line to dry washing, which on Mondays would obscure the view of the railway arches and the Greyhound Stadium. Coal was stored in a little brick building ('t'coyl oyl') outside the back door. About four feet of frontage separated the house from the pavement and, since the terraced houses opposite did not have any frontage at all, the neighbours seemed to be on top of us – much closer than in Belle Vue. The arrangement of furniture in t'front room and living room was more or less the same as in Belle Vue, except the piano had now been promoted to t'front room.

Naturally, I was assigned the small box room, slightly longer than my previous bedroom so a thin wardrobe could now be squeezed in at the foot of a single bed to house my school uniform and a charcoal grey, 'off-the-peg', £10 suit from Burton's. Later, I ventured into John Collier's for a 'made-to-measure' suit in a green checked cloth. Its narrow trousers were enhanced by a pair of bright brown, almost orange, suede shoes which I considered to be the last word in teenage sophistication. Dad thought otherwise and likened my appearance to that of a bookie. When I visited Shepley in this suit, Auntie Edie pulled one of her faces, so I guess she didn't like it either. This loud, tasteless outfit was probably as near as I could get to a Teddy Boy's suit without my parents throwing a fit.

Denby Dale Road had been built as a new turnpike following an Act of 1825, but there had been few residential developments in this area south of the city until the twentieth century. The 1893 map of Wakefield shows clusters of cottages and small terraced dwellings along Denby Dale Road, including Dale Terrace, close to the area where Avondale Street would be built, and a group of terraced houses nearer town, close to some of the arches of the railway viaduct. Further south, and east of the Lancashire & Yorkshire railway line, there were also groups of housing around Bethel Place, Saville Place and Queen's Place. Beyond the West Riding & Grimsby railway line to the east there were Victorian housing developments around Thornes Lane, close to the malt houses on the River Calder. Otherwise, the buildings in the vicinity during Victorian times were much grander affairs, enjoying spacious surroundings of what was later to become Wakefield Park, including Holmfield, and the vicarage of the local church, St James's, built in 1840 with support from Benjamin Gaskell, the owner of nearby Thornes House.

The foundation stone of St James's Church along Denby Dale Road had been laid by Benjamin Gaskell's son, James Milnes Gaskell, in 1829, and was one of many 'Million Act' churches built in the West Riding to meet the supposed needs of its growing population. One million pounds had been made available by Parliament, supplemented by a war indemnity from Austria. One thousand pounds of this central fund had been granted towards the building of St James's, but most of the cost was met by the Gaskells. Shortly after the church was built a school was founded, and by 1861 St James's School occupied a building southeast of the LYR railway bridge, close to the bottom of what is now Avondale Street.

St James's Church, Denby Dale Road, 2012, little changed in 180 years.
K. G. BARRACLOUGH.

The Cotton Horne almshouses in Horne Street, from an original 1970s photo.
WILLIAM PERRAUDIN.

The area was transformed during the hectic building period in the early part of the twentieth century. By 1957 the north–south A636 Denby Dale Road was flanked by housing on both sides apart from the eastern boundary of Wakefield Park, home only to the disconsolate Queen Victoria. Housing occupied the new streets feeding into Denby Dale Road from the west side of the LYR railway: Avondale Street, Cotton Street and Horne Street. Avondale Street had taken its name from Prince Albert Victor, Duke of Clarence and Avondale, who had visited the nearby site of the proposed Clarence Park in 1891 and planted a white horse chestnut tree at the foot of Lowe Hill. Cotton Street and Horne Street had been named after Cotton Horne (circa 1580–1656) who had provided for the building of almshouses for some of Wakefield's poor; his son William continued this generous philanthropy. By 1897 the almshouses in Almshouse Lane in the centre of Wakefield were declared to be no longer worth the cost of repair and a site for the construction of new accommodation was eventually chosen off Denby Dale Road. After considerable delays in the planning and specification of the new almshouses, the foundation stone for a two-storey terrace of some twenty houses was laid on May 15, 1901, along the north side of what became known as Horne Street. On the northern boundary of the park, housing had also been built along Park Avenue and streets feeding into Park Avenue: Wauchope Street and Symons Street.

Unlike Victorian Belle Vue, there were few shops in the area since we were really too close to the city centre for any major amenities. In that regard Avondale Street was fortunate in having a thriving grocery store run by Robert Buchanan and his wife Vera who lived at number 15, about 30 yards from our house. Mr Buchanan ran his shop in a very professional manner. Dressed appropriately in a brown smock, like a proper grocer, he was extremely courteous to his customers and tried his best to meet their needs. The shop was clean, well-organised and immediately met with Mum's approval, to the extent that she placed a weekly order which was delivered regularly to us in a cardboard box. Further down Avondale Street on the corner with Tew Street, about 50 yards from our house on the opposite side, was Lawton's fish and chip shop. For Mum this was

Terracing in Clarence Park *c*.1957. R. H. Barraclough.

far too close and convenient, but even she had to admit that the fare was 'not bad' – in Mum-speak that was quite a compliment. So, we now ate a fish and chip supper occasionally, rather than having to wait for an annual event such as a funfair. We also had the luxury of a nearby sweet shop and tobacconist, Robinson's, located on Denby Dale Road almost opposite Avondale Street. Confectionery was also obtainable at the tiny premises of the Bon Bon, about a quarter of a mile further south, near the junction with Thornes Lane. This was a favourite haunt for many kids walking to and from Thornes House School, and during summer weekends the Bon Bon did a roaring trade with the many visitors to the nearby park.

The immediate vicinity was largely a working-class area with a sprinkling of lower-middle-class professionals. Most occupants were established families, quite a few without children at home so, unlike Belle Vue, the area did not resonate with the lively sound of young children 'playing out'.

Next door to us at number 19a lived childless Eric and Ivy Morgan on whom Dad, with tongue in cheek, bestowed the collective name, 'urrican'. Eric was a small, thin railwayman who moved with an awkward gait at quite a slow pace and seemed to love his railway outfit so much that he was rarely seen in anything else. Our social interaction with Eric was limited to animated discussions about Wakefield Trinity, as his little head strained to make itself visible over the wavy privet hedge. 'Rubbish' was Eric's favourite word when summing up the latest woes of the Trinity team. This would be followed by an explanation of his solution, in a brief oration which would end with an unsuccessful attempt to draw smoke from a very thin, grey cigarette that barely glowed and was always having to be relit. Ivy was a kind, nervous lady who got on well with Mum and they often invited each other into their respective homes for a cup of tea and a proper cigarette.

Further down the street in another semi at number 27 lived Ken and Joan Lewis. Joan was very welcoming and, by immediately informing us that her husband was also a policeman, albeit in the Wakefield City Constabulary, she probably had hopes of promoting some sort of social interaction between the respective menfolk. In the event, Dad probably interacted as much with Ken as the West Riding Constabulary interacted with the Wakefield City Constabulary. Although rarely seen together, they must have provided the neighbours with some amusement from their contrasting appearance in the street: Ken was as plump as Dad was thin; Dad strode down Avondale Street at lightning pace, anxious to change out of his uniform and get stuck in to his latest project; Ken waddled slowly along, cape over his shoulder in classic PC Plod fashion, with all the time in the world.

A couple of blocks away in Horne Street, opposite the almshouses at number 36, we eventually got to know the Spence family. Sheila was a bright, quiet girl who was in the same class as me at school. Her mother Marian was very chatty and affable, and her father Harold had a wit as sharp as a tack. Harold was a painter and decorator by trade and I can only recall him in a pair of white overalls, daubed with every colour of paint under the sun.

Round the corner from us at number 63 Denby Dale Road lived Miss Edna Denton, a teacher of English and Scripture at Thornes House School, better known as the daughter of Wakefield-born cricketer, David Denton, who had died in 1950 and was buried in St James's churchyard. The family home on Denby Dale Road was now occupied by Edna who had reputedly inherited the huge sum of £10,000 and was also a lifelong member of the Yorkshire County Cricket Club.

Miss Denton was a stern, gaunt lady whose large horn-rimmed spectacles made her look especially fierce: the word dragon comes to mind. I would try to avoid her on the way to school for fear of her telling me off for wearing my cap at the wrong angle or some other trivial misdemeanour. Miss Denton never taught me but, apparently, she was quite strict and a pedant for the English language which, if abused by members of her class, would be received by looks of disdain and corrected by withering comments. I only found out later that there was more to Edna Denton than the fierce-looking daughter of a famous cricketer. She was yet another Thornes House Methodist local preacher who lived and practised her Christian faith and was a most kind-hearted soul. One of her friends was the Revd Kenneth Waights, who established youth clubs known as the Good Companions in places wherever he ministered, such as Liverpool and Scarborough. Edna Denton started a Good Companions group in Wakefield which met on Friday evenings in premises down Market Street, close to the General Post Office building on the opposite side. With help from young assistants, Edna Denton ran this club for years, and as many as forty Wakefield youths aged fourteen and upwards would attend these meetings in the 1950s.

I was probably a bit too young for the Good Companions when it was at its most popular, and by the time I reached the appropriate age my friends and I were attending youth clubs and dances at other places, such as St George's Church hall in Lupset. I was rebelling against most things overtly 'religious' and, since my voice had broken, it was a good excuse not to continue in a church choir, despite persuasion from the new vicar of St Catherine's, the Revd George Philip Williams. I never set foot in the local

St James's Church, and I suppose it was the covert, but constant background influence of Methodism at school and the Christian values at home that continued to provide some form of moral compass at a time when it would have been quite easy for me to wander down a more wayward path.

At home, Dad's direction was now clear, and he didn't need any sort of compass to point the way, moral or otherwise. Stage one of the plan, a new home, was complete and it didn't take long for the new hobby to emerge. The surge in house owner occupation in the mid-fifties meant that there was a dearth of skilled labour to undertake general building and home improvement work. Also, many owner occupiers could not afford to pay anyone to undertake such work, so the era of home improvement through 'Do it Yourself' (DIY) was born. For Dad it was the perfect pastime. He had all the necessary skills and tools, but in his case it was more than a casual pastime: it was yet another relentless pursuit of perfection, just like the photography.

It started off fairly low-key, with part of the annex being made into a sort of laundry room for Mum, now the proud owner of a twin-tub washing machine, her first kitchen appliance, which was ceremoniously wheeled out for its regular Monday morning performance. I was assigned a little partitioned area containing a small table to do my homework. Dad annexed a small area for a workshop where he built a new workbench with metal and woodworking vices and storage cupboards for his old tools and new ones, notably a very loud Wolf electric drill. In a short space of time brightly coloured Formica surfaces and plastic laminates started to appear. But refurbishing the annex was just a preliminary bout to the main event.

Dad set about improving practically every room like a man possessed. Woodwork, metalwork, plumbing, painting and decorating jobs were carried out as if he had done them all his life. Dad's DIY signature became the space-saving sliding door, often finished in strange modern colours such as 'Avocado' and 'Sandalwood'. Everything that opened on a conventional hinge such as kitchen cupboards, airing cupboards and medicine cabinets, was ripe for transformation into pairs of flush wooden panel doors with inset handles and plastic runners, which had to slide with so little friction that Dad would only have been really content if they had opened themselves on voice command. Later, in a gross act of modernisation, defying decades of convention, Dad opened up t'front room and the living room by knocking a hole in the separating wall to form a wide connecting archway. A neat compromise with modernity was struck when he installed a pair of glazed sliding doors to retain the option for t'front room to be shut off in the traditional manner.

The summer of 1958 was the first opportunity for Dad to get stuck in to the exterior of the house. He pointed the brickwork from top to bottom, and it now became a standing joke with many of my friends that they only knew my dad as the chap on the ladder in blue overalls. At the rear boundary a brick wall with matching pillars was built and the spaces filled in with wooden panels for cultivation of climbing plants, in an attempt to block out some of the adjacent eyesores. At the front the same theme was continued with brick gate pillars and a low brick wall matched to a new porch, which was inset with decorative glass bricks in the two side walls to let in the light.

We eventually became really 'with it' when central heating was plumbed in, but old habits die hard, and this mod con was only installed downstairs. Both Mum and Dad declared that they could not see the point of having radiators and warm rooms upstairs when the only purpose of spending any length of time up there was in a warm bed. So, in winter I still changed into my pyjamas at lightning speed before diving between the sheets into my tent. In the even colder mornings a sharp finger nail would scratch away the beautiful dendrites of ice on the inside of the windowpane, a constant reminder that, although we had never had it so good, any little pleasure in life had to be paid for with a little dose of pain elsewhere.

References and Further Reading

Amateur Photographer, 16 October, 1957.

Wakefield District Heritage, compiled by Kate Taylor, published by Wakefield European Architectural Heritage Year (EAHY) Committee, October 1976, p.44.

CHAPTER 10

Music, the Food of Love? circa 1958

Dad started to reconnect with his real passion, music, and had been persuaded to join the Wakefield Cathedral Choir as a bass-baritone. There was almost certainly a mismatch between his religious beliefs and those expected of the members of such a relatively high church, but he came through their approval process, despite also being a shift worker unable to attend regular practices and church services. Eventually, however, most of his music was enjoyed in the comfort of his own home.

The piano was now being regularly exercised; I should say it was regularly exercising him. This period was made even more remarkable by the fact that, for the first time in my life, t'front room was being used for something beyond the entertaining of relatives at Christmas. The Beethoven sonatas were Dad's favourites, and he would usually start with the impassioned and dreamy first movement of *Sonata No. 14 in C-sharp minor, Moonlight,* which would always sound pretty good, since Beethoven had been kind enough to open up his famous work with a movement that most amateurs could attempt without being too embarrassed. Dad also played the second movement, *Allegretto* (fairly quick) with calm authority and great control, but we all dreaded what was coming next: the third movement, *Presto Agitato* (very fast in a restless agitated style) is an understatement of what is required from the pianist in terms of technique, touch and sheer passion.

This is as difficult as the first two movements are straightforward. A range of very fast arpeggios requires the fingers of both hands to scuttle up and down the keyboard and produce an overall effect of frightening ferocity and unbridled beauty. Of course, Dad would make a good fist of the third movement but even if he did play the right notes in the right order, he would struggle with the required tempo, so difficult was the finger work. He would end up playing certain passages over and over again, trying his damnedest to do justice to this masterpiece, and would only finish the session when in his opinion he had made significant progress to justify the reward of a smoke from a fresh pipe of St Bruno flake tobacco. Even Dad didn't play the piano and smoke at the same time.

Dad derived great pleasure striving for perfection on the piano and, as with his photography, he ceased playing only when he knew that he had reached his absolute limit. The piano was eventually put up for sale at a time when they were rapidly going out of fashion, and it ended up being sold 'for next to nowt' to a pub which wanted it for a blind pianist to play sing-alongs. For twenty years, Mum had dusted and polished the piano, and was obviously saddened at its demise, but Dad didn't give two hoots: he had decided it was time for his music to move on.

Once Dad discovered vinyl records he became obsessed with classical music as it should be played. Choosing an appropriate record player was not a straightforward matter, of course. One or two were trialled and eventually a Magnavox radiogram was selected. This particular brand had its origins in the United States of America, although some of its technology was British. It was a floor-standing, rectangular box-shaped object, slightly bigger than a food trolley and about as attractive. The days of beautiful solid wood cabinets had long gone and we now looked at a box finished in wood-effect laminate, embellished with strips of gleaming brass, purporting to be gold. I can't imagine that it was the pair of smooth sliding covers on the top of the box that had persuaded Dad to choose this model, rather than the more important features of its sound system, but one never knows with an eccentric. The sliding covers revealed a deep storage compartment for records on one side and the controls for the radio and record turntable on the other. Most of the large cabinet underneath was empty, apart from space occupied by the electronics, a motor, a very complex set of gears under the turntable, and a set of loudspeakers at each end to give the effect of stereophonic sound. Dad had done his market research and assured me that Magnavox was renowned for its speakers.

The record changer was a work of art, based on British technology from a company called Collaro. Many automatic changers at the time would only play records of a certain size, such as the commonly used 7-inch (Extended Play, EP, 45 r.p.m.) and the 12-inch (Long Play, LP, 33⅓ r.p.m.) sizes. However, the Magnavox player could, in principle, play any size of record, (e.g. 10-inch LPs which were still quite common) stacked on the changer, provided the largest were stacked first. The detailed workings of this mechanical masterpiece were extremely intriguing to Dad and me, as we peered underneath at the complex mechanism, trying to understand how it worked.

There were three standard analogue controls: volume, treble and bass which, although pretty basic, still gave Dad far too many combinations to fiddle with. However, once he had determined the optimum settings for each record, the exact position of each knob was sketched on the rear of the record sleeve for future reference. Fiddling with the controls was now becoming systematic!

It is a pity there was no systematic way of eliminating 'noise' on vinyl records. For Dad this was a constant battle which he never really won and, sadly, was unwinnable. In the days before the sophistication of compact discs, digital recordings and fancy electronic noise cancellation techniques, music fanatics had to put up with various levels of what Dad called 'snap, crackle and pop'. The incidence of scratches on vinyl records and the related loud 'pops' they produced every revolution could be fairly readily minimised with careful handling, but the occurrence of dust, static and other sources of spurious noise were extremely difficult to control. Dad would optimistically try out the latest commercial gadget to remove such noise, ranging from magic cloths and sponges to devices such as Lencoclean, a sort of miniature mop made of a spongy material on the end of a plastic tube containing a proprietary fluid that was supposed to mop up the muck from the grooves during the playing of the record. It certainly ended up making the entire surface of the record extremely wet, and to continue reaping any benefits of this process, the record had to be played wet for evermore. Dad even tried out his own clever schemes, but none was completely satisfactory and he would grumble that, although man could now launch satellites into space, he still couldn't come up with a method of playing back music better than the vibration of a needle in a plastic groove. He included me in this hopeless group of mankind, now that I was showing a preference for science and technology at school rather than the arts, but I could offer no solution to his problem, and neither could anyone else at that time. The key component of the compact disc player that would eliminate the need for a mechanical stylus, the semiconductor laser, had not even been invented, and like many technologies would take years before its benefits would hit the streets in the form of reliable consumer products. Dad's relatively modern Magnavox radiogram still relied on valves in its amplifier, despite the invention of the transistor over a decade earlier.

So Dad had to put up with the limitations of the technology available at the time but, once he started listening to the music, rather than for the noise, he could now hear beautiful recordings of the Beethoven sonatas played by the top pianists of the day, such as Vladimir Horowitz on the RCA label, Yuri Boukoff on a Philips recording and Wilhelm Kempff on Deutsche Grammophon. The regular jaunts to Duffin and Greaves were now replaced by trips to record shops in Wakefield, such as Alwyn Isherwood Ltd. He also joined the World Record Club Ltd., a UK mail order company requiring its members to order a minimum number of records per year from an increasingly large selection, which worked out much cheaper than shop prices, especially since membership of the club was free. At that time it was possible to buy an LP from the World Record Club for little more than £1, compared with up to £2 in the shops. Many recordings were franchised from organisations such as Everest Records and Westminster Records, but the World Record Club also produced its own recordings using its own sound engineers. Dad bought one of their first major successes, a 1958 recording in Hammersmith Town Hall of Brahms's *Violin Concerto in D Major, Opus 77* played by Endre Wolf, accompanied by the Sinfonia of London, conducted by Anthony Collins.

Over a period of several years Dad accumulated a collection of around 200 records, spanning music from the romantic period up to modern works by composers such as Shostakovich, Copland and Vaughan Williams. A World Record Club recording of Vaughan Williams's *Symphony No. 9 in E Minor* had been issued only a few years after the work was completed in November 1957 – the same time we had moved to Avondale Street. Dad really was keeping pace with the second half of the twentieth century!

I would eventually be grateful that I had been introduced to the likes of Anton Bruckner and Gustav Mahler at home in the late 1950s/early sixties period, but my appreciation of Shostakovich remained as distant as Dad's appreciation of Elvis Presley and Buddy Holly. He still could not relate to 'pop' music, although he tolerated Mum's preference for light music on records by Jim Reeves and Mantovani. I was allowed to play my records on his radiogram, but usually preferred to avoid confrontations by listening to pop music on juke boxes in the many coffee bars that were springing up in Wakefield around this time.

Thornes House Grammar School had a very strong tradition in choral music; its mixed choir had developed an aura, and it was obviously 'the thing to be in'. The choir had achieved a very high reputation following the arrival at the girls' department of music teacher Margaret Markland, in September 1938. When the school became a mixed grammar school, Miss Markland soon established a mixed choir, which became one of the best in the whole of Yorkshire within the eleven-to-eighteen age group. Marjorie Waring, a gifted musician and pianist had arrived at Thornes House at the same time, and provided tireless support to Miss Markland and the whole choir as piano accompanist.

In 1947 the school choir had won first prize at the Harrogate Music Festival and had recorded Christmas music at the BBC studios in Leeds for subsequent broadcast on Christmas Eve. Then there was that famous command performance for HRH Princess Elizabeth and the Duke of

A 1950s jukebox, an electromechanical wonder. Bʀɪᴛɪsʜ Pᴀᴛʜé Lᴛᴅ.

Edinburgh outside the Town Hall in that memorable summer of 1949. In 1951 the choir reached the Yorkshire semi-finals of the Festival of Britain, National Competitive Music Festival in Hull and was placed third in its class despite competing against adult choirs. The fire in July 1951 was a major blow to the choir, which lost many valuable manuscripts and recordings, including a highly treasured one of the performance for Princess Elizabeth in 1949. A fire had also gutted St James's Church in Chapelthorpe a few weeks earlier, and it was to the school choir's great credit that it kept its promise to sing in the ruins of the church in aid of the restoration fund, on the evening of the very day that their own school had been burned down. Such spirit and determined leadership were key factors in the choir's continuing success, and by the mid 1950s it had established a very high reputation which we were constantly reminded of.

As many of the early members of the mixed choir left school in the early fifties, some continued to meet and sing together and they persuaded Miss Markland to provide them with leadership and direction. The Old Thornesians Choir was born and rapidly grew from a small madrigal group to a fully fledged choir. Subsequently, this choir attracted many singers who were not former pupils of Thornes House Grammar School and it became known as the Thornesian Guild of Singers, still retaining its original identity with Thornes. One of its early memorable performances was in 1952, when it had sung Brahms's 'How Lovely are Thy Dwellings Fair' and 'Blessed are They That Mourn' at a moving ceremony devoted to the dedication of the school's memorial furniture by the Bishop of Wakefield. The Guild established a fine tradition of singing Sargent's the 'Boar's Head Carol' in a procession with lanterns at the beginning of their annual carol concert.

It was hardly surprising that the leadership of Margaret Markland would inspire many pupils to follow a career in music, as well as the hundreds who would pursue singing as an amateur pastime in choirs throughout the land. 'Markie' was particularly proud of many of her 'Old Boys' who had been regular soloists at school concerts in the early 1950s, and who were now progressing with their music careers beyond school. Oliver Broome, an extremely talented bass singer, was one former pupil who had gained admission to the Royal Manchester College of Music, where he attained his diploma and won the Ricordi Prize for conducting. He continued to study conducting and singing in Italy; he sang at Glyndebourne and also with the BBC singers and the Ambrosian Singers. Oliver Broome conducted studio recordings of operas for BBC radio, as well as concerts with the BBC Orchestra, including events in the Royal Festival Hall.

Another talented 'Old Boy' was David Grundy, who had been a regular piano soloist at school concerts in the early 1950s. In the 1954 summer concert he had also arranged a quartet, 'Lone the Night Lay, Dark and Dreary'. After leaving school David studied at the Royal Academy of Music and by 1959 had been appointed organist and choir master at St Mary's Church in Islington, London.

But it was the extraordinary Darling brothers who were the most acclaimed of Miss Markland's 'Old Boys'. Both John and Edward Darling pursued singing careers as outstanding tenors. John was an operatic tenor, and by the time he had adopted the name John Wakefield he had won the prestigious Kathleen Ferrier Memorial Award in 1958 at his first attempt. John eventually became an established singer with the Sadler's Wells Opera chorus and sang leading tenor roles with them, many of which were recorded. John's brother, Edward Darling, sang tenor with the Linden Singers who recorded light operas such as Gilbert and Sullivan's *The Gondoliers* and *Pirates of Penzance*. Edward (Ted) Darling also became

Margaret Markland and the Thornes House School Choir in front of the stage of the new school hall in 1957. Geo Holdsworth & Son.

a 'Minstrel' in many episodes of the long running TV variety show, *The Black and White Minstrel Show,* and he sang in some of its recordings such as 'The Minstrel Stars'.

Whereas I had bemoaned being a member of St Catherine's Church choir, I rather liked the idea of becoming a member of the school choir as soon as I arrived at Thornes House in 1954. Here was an activity that just might keep me at the school, should my academic performance not be up to scratch. Later, I also rather fancied some of the girls in the choir. However, despite already having some credentials as a chorister, I was overlooked, as most boys were before their voices broke. Only the very best boy choristers were selected as sopranos, since Miss Markland had a huge choice from a large number of very able and keen girls. David Royle in my first year had made it into the choir, but he was an exceptional boy soprano from Sandal Endowed School and head chorister at St Helen's Church in Sandal.

Margaret Markland was always on the lookout for tenors and basses at the higher end of the school: the next 'Darlings' and Broome. We had to do lots of singing in music lessons as Margaret's sharp ears scanned for talent, trying to differentiate the serious singers from those who preferred to lark around. You could always tell when she had heard someone who met with her approval because they would be on the receiving end of one of the most delightful and captivating smiles in the whole school. Margaret Markland was certainly not an out and out beauty, but she had immense charm and was blessed with very strong, attractive features: high, wide cheekbones, dark hair and a pair of expressive eyes, the most striking part of that smile. 'Markie's' looks were similar to those of a Native American and this image was enhanced by her preferred footwear: a pair of open sandals in the summer and sensible flat shoes in the winter. Our revered music teacher was not a 'flashy' dresser.

In about 1958 I became the lucky recipient of that smile during one of Miss Markland's talent spotting sessions and I was persuaded to join David Wade and company in the tenor section of the school choir. There were lots of practices, concerts and competitions, as well as sports and preparation for O-levels, so the busy times continued. The main work performed at my first school concert was Coleridge-Taylor's *Hiawatha's Wedding Feast*. It was the intense rehearsals for *Hiawatha* that made me fully appreciate the magnetism of our leader. We would be drawn as if by magic along her radiating lines of force. Each of her requests would be indicated by the slightest body movement, to which we would all respond instantly. She always smiled during performances, even if we were not always singing as she would have liked; the most radiant smiles were kept for competitions when she recognised that we might be nervous and overcome by the occasion.

The full choir of over thirty voices usually performed at school functions and concerts, when we were often joined by members of staff such as Harry

Margaret Markland draws out the best from the choir of Thornes House Grammar School as they perform for HRH Princess Elizabeth and Prince Philip in Wood Street, Wakefield, July 1949. THORNES HOUSE SCHOOL WEBSITE.

Dixon and also Cliff's wife, Dora Bracewell. Competitions such as the ones at the Harrogate Festival, and recordings at the BBC studios, usually involved a smaller, elite group known as the Madrigal Choir, consisting of about a dozen voices, which I was eventually invited to join. Many of our Elizabethan madrigals were jolly four part harmonies, more often than not set to simple rhymes about merrymaking and chasing wenches ('Come, shepherds, follow me, run up apace the mountain'; 'Now is the month of May-ing, when merry lads are playing ...', etc). This was actually most appropriate as far as my aspirations were concerned, since chasing one particular 'wench' in the sopranos was the main purpose of my joining the madrigal choir, never mind its elitism. My mission was accomplished on the return journey from the BBC studios after we had recorded a contribution to the *Let the People Sing* series. But I am now quite sure that there was more action in the haystacks during Elizabeth I times than on the backseat of a 1950s motor coach in the reign of Elizabeth II, especially under the prying eyes of the rest of the choir. Miss Markland sat at the front and pretended not to look.

This sexual encounter was typical of the times: short, sweet and unfulfilled. We were beginners, feeling our way and testing the boundaries, never going anywhere near 'all the way' at this novice stage, even though we had a good idea of where and what it was. To me and most boys at this time, however, the whole complex issue of sexual intercourse was shrouded in ignorance, hearsay, gossip and fear. Although we knew, or thought we knew, about the basic physical mechanics, our knowledge had been gradually gleaned over a number of years and was subject to a considerable number of errors and misconceptions. Sex was the subject most discussed in the classroom, once we had given up trying to catch out Jack Larkin on his capital cities. However, it was always difficult to have a free and open discussion and volunteer a question, for fear of demonstrating one's own ignorance and being laughed out of court. Many lads claimed to know all there was to know about the jigsaw of sex, but quite often the pieces didn't fit. The vivid illustrations on the walls of school lavatories and elsewhere also contributed to the available sources of information, but were of uncertain provenance, and had a limited lifetime before they were scrubbed out. Such stories and their related crude drawings could not be confirmed by any authoritative source such as a textbook, manual or teacher. There was no instruction on the facts of life at home or in school. If anything approaching the subject of human reproduction had been taught by Sid Leak in Biology lessons then I certainly didn't make any connection with it, and by about 1957 I had dropped Biology as one of my science subjects anyway. It was said that the versatile 'Spike' was set to give a series of lessons on the facts of life to young first years at Thornes House in 1951, but these were curtailed by the July fire that year, thereby sparing embarrassment for 'Spike' and his pupils, seemingly forever.

Thus, we learned by fumbling around and from our inevitable mistakes. By the time we were about sixteen years old, the fictitious route map of this tortuous journey of discovery was still very coarse indeed. Its general guideline for the male participant was to start at the top and work down, but this multi-stage journey would often end abruptly with a slap on the face when short cuts were attempted. Sensitivity to the girl's feelings was virtually nonexistent, and they were usually treated as mere sex objects. Within male-dominated domains there were always lots of dirty jokes and metaphorical 'willy waving', which became very real when we had to strip to the bare essentials in the boys' changing rooms for a quick shower after PT and games! In the classroom, girls often had to put up with boys' obsessions with tits, bums and genitalia. Few of us knew what the meaning of male chauvinism was, but we were already practising it.

And if the destination of the long journey happened to appear somewhere on the horizon, the fear factor soon put paid to 'it' ever being reached. The fear of pregnancy usually terminated any serious hanky-panky, especially in the absence of contraception. Detailed knowledge of contraception was lacking and, in male domains, rarely went beyond jokes about condoms, or 'rubber johnnies' as they were commonly known. Contraception was mainly an issue for married couples and older youths, not pupils preparing for their O-levels. However, that did not stop enquiring minds trying to understand the subject, especially those with experience of the Boy Scout movement and its core requirement to be prepared!

I had gleaned from the classroom gossip that 'rubber johnnies' were obtainable at a barber's, which I always thought was a rather strange place to buy anything other than a haircut. Although I had now stopped going to Gordon Winter's in Agbrigg, qualifying for 'Owt on sir?' was one thing; being asked if I wanted 'Owt for t'weekend, sir?' was a different matter altogether. Actually, this prototypical expression was not commonly used in the establishments I visited, and the acquisition of condoms at the barber's was, yet again, a virtually silent exchange, spotted only if you were alert and not too engrossed in the exploits of Roy of the Rovers. Once the customer had been sheared, oiled and had the cloth whisked away from his shoulders, he would trigger the process by whispering his request in the barber's ear, normally as he was about to 'settle up'. The barber would then surreptitiously open a drawer, with as little movement as possible, to retrieve a small package which would be deftly passed to the customer by sleight of hand. The primary aim of this little game of pass-the-parcel was to keep it totally hidden, but if either party was careless, a quick glimpse might be visible to the prying eyes of alert youngsters peering above an opened comic. Such exchanges were so discreet that they bordered on the furtive, not dissimilar to an illicit purchase, akin, I imagined, to a major drugs deal, rather than the sale of something as ordinary and as legal as a packet of condoms at a cost of no more than half a crown. But in the fifties this was no ordinary matter, and anything to do with sex had to be furtive rather than fun. I had to wait years before drumming up enough courage to participate in this furtive procedure. The fear of being refused or, even worse, mocked at my presumption of being a qualified buyer was, yet again, accepted as part of the delayed gratification process that continued to be part of fifties life in one guise or another.

Once the talk of straightforward sex had run its course, it was the turn of homosexuals to be on the receiving end of classroom banter, jokes and ridicule. Homophobia only added to the confusion, since quite a few of us still did not understand all aspects of heterosexual behaviour. At first I found it difficult to fathom out what 'queers' and 'homos' got up to, not to mention lesbians, although the latter hadn't really appeared on our radar at that time. Of course, schoolboy behaviour merely reflected the typical attitude to homosexuals in the fifties, when they were seen as a threat to society for practising what was a criminal offence in those days. Lord Montagu of Beaulieu was often the butt of many jokes at school, on the basis that he was a well known southern toff who had been slung into the local Wakefield jail after being found guilty of homosexual offences in 1954. 'Backs to the wall!' was the usual cry that greeted the appearance of any boy deliberately displaying a limp hand or any effeminate behaviour. We didn't know at the time that there were some lads genuinely confused about their sexuality. Not only had they to put up with crude jokes and comments about homosexuality at school but, had they summoned up enough courage to talk to a doctor about their 'problem', they might have been told to pull themselves together or perhaps recommended for 'treatment'. In the 1950s a few male homosexuals, including some prisoners from the local jail, were being treated with electric shock aversion therapy or the female sex hormone, oestrogen, in an attempt to control the attraction to the male sex. By the mid-fifties, however, there was a growing feeling that homosexuality should no longer be regarded as a treatable illness. After three years of study, the Wolfenden Committee made its report in 1957 on *Homosexual Offences and Prostitution,* with the key recommendation that homosexual behaviour between consenting adults in private should no longer be a criminal offence. However, it would take a further ten years before this would be enshrined in law; no consolation at all for those who just happened to have been made that way.

Meanwhile homosexuals kept themselves to themselves in the big outside world, unlike the many heterosexual males who were more than willing to trumpet their vast knowledge on the subject of sex. By now I was experiencing the manly world of work in various vacation jobs, earning money at every opportunity, an education in itself and quite an eye-opener for a young virgin from the grammar school.

In about 1957 my first vacation job was at Rawson's mill in Portobello, where I joined many Pakistani labourers from nearby Dewsbury earning a pittance to make all sorts of shoddy goods. The foreman soon recognised an unsuspecting grammar school boy and pointed me in the direction of one of the brash young women, with an encouraging whisper in my ear that she would drop her knickers at the drop of a hat. The fear of the unknown and its possible repercussions overcame my trembling excitement and, with some regret, I chickened out with the lame quip that I didn't wear a hat. Although I eventually cursed myself for erring on the side of caution, I had managed to convince myself that such an open invitation was actually a red flag, signalling very dangerous territory indeed, certainly well within the boundaries that Mum would have classified as 'common as muck'. I was trying to break loose from the influence of my parents but they were always somewhere in the background, still affecting key decisions in my life.

The instruction to 'fetch the bucket of steam' for this wag of a foreman was also resisted but I did fall for the one 'to fetch the long stand from Fred'. After being told to wait awhile, Fred eventually asked me if I had been standing long enough. We grammar school boys thought we

Rawson's Mill, by the River Calder, Portobello. City of Wakefield MDC Libraries Photographic Collection.

were smart but we had a lot to learn about life, especially at a place like Rawson's. However, I didn't last long there. I had been assigned to the gang responsible for making coconut matting, absolutely foul stuff made of loose fibres which found their way everywhere, including the noses of members of the work force. Just like the effects of smog, the fibres instantly turned a white handkerchief black, so after drawing my first week's wage of a few quid, I took Mum's advice and packed the job in.

Equally educational was my next job at Lunn's bakery, a family firm located at the beginning of Doncaster Road. At first, the regular Monday morning inquisition was quite startling: 'Did yer get yer end away at t'weekend, then?' enquired the van driver to his new van boy assistant, an immediate indication of where his weekend priorities had lain. My 'end' had not ventured anywhere beyond the confines of its own trousers, but such an honest answer would not have been appropriate in the circumstances; neither was a boastful response, since I would probably have been readily ensnared in my own ignorance and dishonesty. After a microsecond's consideration, I hoped that the reply, 'Not this time' was sufficiently honest, yet upbeat enough about my 'end's' future prospects, for the driver to draw a line under this brief progress report on my sexual performance. Of course, he was not really interested in my feeble exploits anyway. The question had only been asked as an entrée for him to regale me with his own latest conquests, which regularly bordered on the outrageous. Wakefield's women in the Embassy dancehall and elsewhere were apparently falling over backwards to be 'shagged' by him before he returned home to attend to his wife as well. This particular van driver was also having an affair with a foreign girl who was sending passionate love letters to one of the shops on his round for him to collect on a regular basis. Doing 'it' was one thing; managing several at a time was another!

Lunn's bakery was not only host to sexual athletes; it also had to cope with fraudulent activity. One of the 'perks' of being a van driver loading up the morning's deliveries was the possibility of stealing an extra tray or two of bread and cakes for subsequent private sale on the round. This fraud was carried out on a regular basis by my driver, whose overall attitude was starting to make me feel very uncomfortable indeed. One early morning we were flashed down by a driver from another bakery who warned us that our supervisor was on the road looking for an extra tray of stolen cakes that had been traced to our van. The stolen tray was hastily transferred to the other van on a main road, only a few minutes before the supervisor flagged us down to check the contents of our van. Over a period of a few weeks I had been paid for sitting in a van, lifting the odd tray of bread and cakes, eating the odd free bun, whilst simultaneously learning about the sexual exploits of local women, how to conduct affairs with foreign women and being complicit in a cake fraud. I can't imagine what Mum and Dad would have made of such a disturbing combination of indolence, immorality and impropriety.

By comparison, most vacation work in the next few years was quite boring and repetitive. I delivered thousands of cards and letters in the Christmas Post, counted thousands of vehicles in a local traffic census, filed thousands of papers at the NCB offices in Newton Hill and planted out thousands of wall flowers in the nurseries of Wakefield Park. I also rolled thousands of Swiss Rolls at the factory of J. Lyons & Co. in Thornes, but this was far from dull. Most of this factory was a modern conveyor belt operation, working around the clock and requiring little human intervention. A continuous roll of baked sponge emerged from a huge oven and was automatically plastered with the appropriate amounts of jam and cream, before it was sliced into individual portions which were then hand rolled into Swiss Rolls, at that time the only step of the process that could not be automated. The 'rolling bench' was where I and my mates, John Speight and Jimmy Ferguson, acquired the sensitive touch needed to make a Swiss Roll. Our first ham-fisted efforts produced large numbers of rejects, which were eagerly gobbled up until we became sick at the sight of a Swiss Roll. Eventually, we developed the ability to make roll after roll, two at a time using both hands, without even looking at what we were doing, but listening intently to all the stories and jokes from the regular all-male workforce, who now had a captive audience. Here they described their sexual conquests in the most graphic detail and recounted dirty jokes and stories with such an acerbic wit that it is a wonder the cream fillings didn't turn sour on the spot.

In a few weeks' holiday work I had probably learned more about the real world than the whole of my school days put together, but it was still just talk; practical experience was still way behind the theory. Most of my interactions with girls were still centred on school. During Christmas 1958, a group of school friends from Upper VA started having parties, the first at Anne Frank's in Lawefield Lane, then at Sheila Spence's in Horne Street. We drank cider, nibbled tasty sandwiches and jived to the latest pop music. One of the lads, Bob Stock, played his guitar and sang the Buddy Holly songs, 'Peggy Sue', 'That'll Be the Day' and 'Everyday'. It was all good clean fun and romantic fantasy, part of the slow process of growing up and the long wait for sex to be 'invented'. But there would be no new Buddy Holly songs to look forward to: he and other prominent pop musicians, Ritchie Valens and J. P. 'the Big Bopper' Richardson, were killed in an air crash on 3 February 1959, which later became known as 'The Day the Music Died'.

References and Further Reading

Family Britain, 1951–57, David Kynaston, Bloomsbury Publishing plc 2009, ISBN 978-07475-8385-1.

CHAPTER ELEVEN

Reward and the Way Forward, 1959–1961

There were many key events in 1959 that had a significant bearing on the future. It was the year marking the opening of Britain's first motorway, part of a new road network that would eventually change the face of Britain and directly impact Wakefield and its people. The British Motor Corporation launched its revolutionary new car for the mass market, the Mini, as more and more drivers took to the open road in cars that were now becoming affordable. It was the year of a General Election, an opportunity for the Conservative government to test whether the electorate really felt they had never had it so good, rather than telling them so. Closer to home, Wakefield Trinity embarked on a quest for glory, I took my GCE O-level examinations, Dad retired from the police force and started a new job.

Although Dad still couldn't afford to buy and run a car, we all feared that he might join the throng by taking to the road as a driving instructor. He had already launched himself into some private coaching, as well as teaching lady drivers the subject of car maintenance in his spare time. However, we all knew that he didn't have the enduring patience to subject himself to the vagaries of learner drivers, day in, day out, and we were all relieved when he dropped cosily into a job at County Hall, as an assistant road traffic engineer in the Highways and Bridges department of the West Riding County Council, a rather pompous local government job

Dad's ladies-only car maintenance class. P<small>ICTURE COURTESY OF</small> Y<small>ORKSHIRE</small> P<small>OST</small> N<small>EWSPAPERS</small>.

title that Dad immediately ridiculed in typical self-deprecating fashion. Dad formally retired from the police force on 29 August 1959, when the chief constable of the West Riding Constabulary, Captain Henry Studdy, signed off the leaving certificate of Police Sergeant 106 with a one-word reference to his conduct in the past twenty-five years: 'Exemplary'.

At school my academic success had been largely achieved through hard graft but the top stream, Upper VA, contained one or two bright pupils who appeared not to do any work at all. One such lad was Melvyn Lynes, a natural linguist and scholar. Like many of my generation, Melvyn had the sort of interesting background which could have been penned by a novelist such as D. H. Lawrence. Melvyn's mother, Eveline, was a Welsh schoolteacher in the mining village of Crofton where she had met her man, Wilfred Lynes, a bluff, tough Yorkshireman who worked down the local pit. They had three boys: the eldest, David, was a school year above Melvyn and me at Thornes House; the third boy, Andrew, was twelve years younger than us. The Lynes family lived opposite Sandal Railway Station in a detached stone property, Springwell House, guarded by Tina, a large Alsatian which struck fear into most visitors, but was always kept under strict control.

Wilf was a typical miner, strong as an ox and called a spade a bloody shovel. As a pit deputy and shot-firer at Crofton – then later Walton – colliery, Wilf had responsibilities for the underground safety of a number of men. Coal mining remained a hazardous occupation and we were all starkly reminded of this fact when an underground explosion at Walton colliery on 22 April 1959 resulted in five deaths and one injured.

After completing his shift in the grimy atmosphere of the pit, Wilf would scrub up and change into his best sports jacket and tie. He wore a trilby hat cocked at a distinctively cheeky angle, made more noticeable by its frequent doffing to acknowledge the presence of a lady. Dad was also a regular hat doffer, a common trait amongst this generation, reminding us that the roughest of diamonds had acquired good manners and gentlemanly conduct from their Victorian parents.

The destination of the smartly clad Wilf Lynes was his 'local', the nearby Duke of York pub, where he would slake his thirst on a pint or two of draught bitter. T'Duke was a popular watering hole in Agbrigg, a centre for camaraderie, a forum to discuss Wakefield Trinity's latest prospects, and a place for friendly banter and gossip, to which Wilf was a prominent contributor. Wilf's Irish ancestry had, undoubtedly, served him well in his development as a master raconteur but, sometimes, the preliminaries were more dramatic than the tales themselves, especially those that might be associated with the latest gossip. An upward nod of the head, a half closed eye and a quick glance left and right were part of Wilf's special code, signalling that a revelation was about to be made to the chosen few. Satisfied that no infiltrator was within earshot, Wilf would then lean closer towards the privileged few to deliver 'the latest' from the down-turned corner of his Yorkshire mouth, glaring at his audience with closely spaced piercing eyes over a pair of spectacles perched precariously on the end of a large nose. If any secrecy was intended, the gaff was usually blown quite quickly as Wilf's deep, bold voice resonated around the tap room. As the beer flowed and tongues loosened, there was also a lot of sentimentality and nostalgia in t'Duke. Towards the end of the evening, the tap room would be urged to ''ave a bit of 'ush' for one of the finest pub singers in the district, who was persuaded to 'get up' and deliver his emotional renditions of 'Brother, can you Spare a Dime?', 'Sonny Boy' and 'Mammy!', with such an uncanny likeness to Al Jolson that Wilf and the rest of the hardy regulars would be brought close to tears.

Like most dads, Wilf wanted his boys to 'get on' and acquire an education so that they didn't end up 'down t'pit'. David was well on his way in meeting his dad's aspirations: he had passed for the city grammar school and was also good at athletics and most sports. By contrast, Melvyn was considered by Wilf to be somewhat of an odd ball, despite being exceptionally bright. 'Too bloody clever by half, yon lad' was Wilf's oft pronounced sentiment. Wise and knowledgeable way beyond his years, Melvyn was the apple of his mother's eye, but Wilf found it difficult to cope with his son's considerable intelligence. Wilf was undoubtedly proud of his son's academic prowess but, unlike David, Melvyn was hopeless at all sports, and was a highly sensitive individual, interested in the arts and classical music, hardly the sort of topics likely to be regularly discussed down t'pit or in t'Duke.

Unlike most boys in the A stream, Melvyn shone at English grammar and English literature. Parsing (six column analyses of sentences), poetry and analysing novels to the nth degree came naturally to Melvyn; the rest of us struggled. We had a very patient English teacher, Donald Watson, a thin, bespectacled, rather meek fellow whom we christened 'Willie' after the famous double international cricketer and footballer. However, unlike his namesake, our Willie Watson spoke with a very respectable 'received pronunciation', (RP), most appropriate for readings of Shakespeare, but not J. B. Priestley. For one of his early lessons Willie had selected that delightful essay, 'T'Match' in which J. B. Priestley describes a visit to a rugby league match in characteristically humorous style. Willie thought he had won over the boys to English literature as we all tittered throughout his reading, but it wasn't the story that we found so amusing, it was

Willie's RP of the Yorkshire glottal stop and the Yorkshire vowels; even the title, 'T'Match' was pronounced as, 'Ter Metch'.

The prescribed texts for our 1959 NUJMB Ordinary level examination in English literature were William Shakespeare's play, *Julius Caesar,* and Jane Austen's novel, *Pride and Prejudice.* Most of us struggled with the intricate details and foibles of Jane Austen's characters, especially that silly Mrs Bennett and the haughty Mr Darcy, but we eventually became captivated by *Julius Caesar* and its wonderful speeches and phrases. Just as the classroom banter was often interspersed with bits of French, or 'Franglais', quotations from *Julius Caesar* were now thrown around with gay abandon. Instead of telling a group of lads to 'get lost', they might be told, 'Hence! Home you idle creatures, get you home.' Any bad news in the classroom was prefaced by, 'If you have tears, prepare to shed them now.' The idea of throwing up one's sweaty nightcap to express disgust was also quite appealing. So, when Willie arranged a theatre trip to see the real thing on stage we looked forward to it with relish. Suddenly we were enjoying English literature, and many of us ended up knowing practically the whole of *Julius Caesar* off by heart. Well played, Willie Watson!

And then it was our turn to be seated at the orderly lines of desks in the school hall, armed with ample supplies of pens and pencils, checking that our Timex watches were set to the correct time and that our brains were in gear. O-level exams were serious stuff, made even more formal by the venue and the printed examination papers, instead of the blurred text on cyclostyled paper copies, typical of internal exams. With pass marks as high as 50 per cent, failure at O-level was quite common in the 1950s. The average number of subjects passed per pupil in the top stream, UVA, was six but, interestingly, the average number of passes in the transfer class, UVT, was the highest of the rest of the Upper Vth year, clearly demonstrating the value of the thirteen plus transfer system for the 'late developers'. Of more than a hundred pupils in the Upper Vth year about twenty of us stayed on in the sixth form; the rest readily found jobs.

I had chosen Maths, Physics and Chemistry, the combination best matched to my strengths and interests, as well as General Studies. Melvyn

Prizewinners, Thornes House School Speech Day, 25 November 1959. Picture
courtesy of Yorkshire Post Newspapers.

Lynes had chosen four A-level arts subjects as well as General Studies and
O-level Latin; we all thought he was mad but, of course, he coped. Life in
the sixth form was quite different from how I had imagined it. Firstly, the
school had decided to experiment with a different set of teachers compared
with the traditional ones for A-level sciences. The new arrangements
worked adequately for Physics and Chemistry but the Maths teaching turned
out to be a disaster, due to unfortunate circumstances beyond anyone's
control. It began with the tragic death of Jack ('Trog') Ripley, aged thirty-
eight, at the end of the first term. Whilst a new Maths teacher was rapidly
sought, poor old Brian Holroyd, a young, inexperienced Maths teacher, had
to take charge of the Applied Maths lessons whilst being no more than a
lesson ahead of the class. As our confidence and interest started to wane,
'Grannie' Gornall, our Pure Maths teacher, gave me a rollicking for fooling
about, thereby providing the rest of the class with further amusement as a
disenchanted, six-foot youth was told to pull his socks up by a five-foot

'Grannie'. Eventually, a former Maths teacher at Thornes House, Joe Glick, a dapper, chirpy fellow with a well-trimmed moustache and high reputation was persuaded out of retirement to put us back on course. Unfortunately, he had barely settled into his old routines before suffering a serious illness. Although we had four different Maths teachers during the two year A-level course, there was quite a lot of time when we didn't have a teacher at all, so we failed miserably to complete the syllabus. The only good outcome for those of us who survived this unfortunate episode of 'Do it Yourself' was that it proved invaluable experience during our further education, when working alone became more the norm.

Life in the sixth form meant taking on more responsibilities, as

Lower Sixth Science Form, 1959/60. Back row, left to right: David Royle, Trevor Smith. Front row, left to right: Derek Chappel, Michael Paterson, Kathleen Lomax, Keith Stewart (form tutor), Richard Pitts, Stephen Fox, Keith Barraclough. Geo Holdsworth & Son.

prefects, in house leadership and in various school teams. There was also a strong emphasis on general education and outdoor activities, usually with the girls. Sixth form scientists were predominantly male, but it is to the school's eternal credit that we were not allowed to be closeted in our laboratories, fiddling with Bunsen burners and sweeping up globules of mercury from broken thermometers. Music, modern languages, theatre and

Thornes House School's First XI football team, 1959/60. Back row, left to right: John Briggs, Ken Parker, Keith Barraclough, David Lynes, Peter Leese; front row, left to right: John Speight, Alan Beck, Rodney Young, Peter Alexander, Roger Whincup, Mike Henton, Derek Chappel. GEO HOLDSWORTH & SON.

the arts flourished at Thornes House and were key features of our general education in the sixth form – at least, that was the school's intention.

We had regular classes on modern English literature in which we were introduced to 'kitchen sink' novels by a rather attractive student teacher who chose to sit on a desk at the front of the class in a short skirt, one long leg wrapped around the other, directly in our line of sight. Whilst the teacher studiously dissected the motives of John Braine's character, Joe Lampton, other randy males in front of her were preoccupied with analysing whether there was enough room at the top of her nylon stockings to reward their sharp eyes with major prey: a flash of bare thigh …

There were no distractions in our other General Studies classes, facilitated by headmaster, Cliff Bracewell, who encouraged us to sit the O-level and A-level examinations in the subject. One of our first encounters with General Studies was the General Election, which had been called for 8 October 1959. Despite their unpopularity after the Suez crisis, the Conservatives were now faring much better under Prime Minister Harold Macmillan, mainly from an upturn in the economy. Their tactics for this election were very clear from the slogan: 'Life's better with the Conservatives, don't let Labour ruin it'. Our natural inclination was to favour the Opposition, after eight years of Conservative government. However, although I suspect this was also Cliff's inclination, he taught us to be more rational in our judgements and to take stock of the various manifestos and candidates. It was very clear when the two local candidates visited the school that they were like chalk and cheese.

The local Conservative candidate was Michael Jopling, who was fighting his first parliamentary seat against the incumbent Labour MP, Arthur Creech Jones, defending a fairly safe majority of 9,745. It wasn't just their politics that were in opposition. Jopling was a dashing, floppy-haired twenty-eight-year-old; Creech Jones was a balding, bespectacled sixty-eight-year-old Victorian, old enough to be Jopling's grandfather. Creech Jones had been in national politics since before the Second World War, long enough to establish a sound reputation in the Trade Union Movement and colonial affairs. Jopling had relatively little political experience beyond serving on local government committees of the Rural District Council of Thirsk, North Yorkshire, where he farmed 500 acres of land at Ainderby Quernhow.

Jopling's energetic campaign was based on the Conservative slogan, and he exuded an air of confidence that only a private education at an independent school could have bestowed. However, this bluster from someone with such a privileged background didn't go down too well at Thornes House, and Jopling was quite peeved when upper sixth former, Pete Alexander, displayed a Labour poster during the photo shoot. Creech Jones was also given a tricky time, especially when Keith Flood and head boy John ('Jake') Paterson quizzed him about the infamous Ground Nut scheme that had been initiated by Attlee's post-war Labour government, of which Creech Jones had been a cabinet member as Secretary of State for the Colonies. The government had invested a fortune in a harebrained scheme to grow ground nuts (peanuts) in Tanganyika on a massive scale, without taking due account of the difficulties of introducing mechanisation into Africa, as well as the problems of its basic geography, notably the inadequate condition of the soil and the low annual rainfall. The scheme failed miserably and was abandoned in 1951 with the loss of some £50 million, resulting in considerable embarrassment for the Labour cabinet, including Creech Jones.

After the school visit, someone in the General Studies class pointed out that Creech Jones had been imprisoned as a conscientious objector during the Great War, but I can't recall war hero Cliff Bracewell, MC adding anything to the discussion about that sensitive topic. In his favour Creech Jones was reputedly a thinking man's socialist, a founder member of the Fabian Colonial Bureau, which had been established to plan for the liberation of the British Colonies. Cliff's wife, Dora, was also a member of the Fabian Society but there was no evidence of Cliff being a member, despite his obvious 'left of centre' leanings.

In the actual contest, Jopling never had a chance in this Labour stronghold, where it was said that Trade Unionists and Labour party members loitered outside some of the polling booths, to indicate to those voters who were unable to read, which line of the ballot paper they should mark with their cross. On polling day the good weather also favoured the Labour party when a huge 82 per cent of the Wakefield electorate turned out. Both Conservatives and Labour increased their number of votes, with Creech Jones's majority decreasing only very slightly from 9,745 to 9,591. However, it was a different story across the country, with the Conservatives increasing their overall majority to a hundred seats, putting them and their leader, 'Supermac', into a third successive term of office. The way forward was to be guided by yet another Conservative government.

When it came to my turn to introduce a General Studies topic

The Rt. Hon. Arthur Creech Jones, Labour MP for Wakefield, 1954–1964. NATIONAL PORTRAIT GALLERY, LONDON.

in November 1959, Cliff gave me the subject of motorways, following the opening of the new M1 motorway from London, St Albans to Rugby in the Midlands, completed on time and on budget. I don't recall the exact details of my introductory talk, but I expect it contained many useless facts and figures with little penetrating insight, rather like my report on the new school building three years previously. However, I do recall Cliff's penetrating question about the likely impact of a motorway on the city of Wakefield, if the M1 continued north into the West Riding conurbation, beyond the then planned destination of Doncaster further south. It would take years for the answer to emerge but it was typical of Cliff that he should be already thinking about the road ahead and its consequences.

Then, there was the entertainment of German lessons. Given that we were finding Maths, Physics and Chemistry difficult enough in our native language, the chances of us ever being able to understand any relevant scientific German seemed rather remote, so German lessons were treated rather light-heartedly. We had enjoyed learning O-level French in the live theatres run by the likes of 'Pop' Hill, Jean Holden and 'Oscar' Smith, so 'Walter' Rennie had a lot to live up to in the teaching of a foreign language. Ever the pedagogue, 'Walter' was more than up to the task, but he had a slightly different approach from the French Department.

'Walter's' slender frame would be bent almost double as he staggered into the classroom under the weight of an enormous tape recording machine, equipped with huge spools of tapes, set up to play back recorded songs in the German language, each bearing a basic grammatical message, ranging from the declensions of the definite article, to the case following German prepositions. The lyrics were sung by a very clear, relaxed crooner, accompanied by a pianist with a very delicate light touch, not unlike that of Charlie Kunz, a well known jazz pianist who was famous for his unique relaxed style. We gradually realised that we were not listening to Bing Crosby and Charlie Kunz from a professional recording studio, but a series of home-made efforts by Bill 'Walter' Rennie who had composed, sung, accompanied and recorded the songs himself: a man of many talents.

I was rapidly learning that a small sixth form meant that most of us had

My best recollection of one of 'Walter' ('Spike') Rennie's German songs, with acknowledgement to the originator. BILL RENNIE.

to be roped in to perform some task or other for major school functions; keeping one's head down was not an option. Thus it was with the school play during the autumn term of 1959. I still didn't have the courage for the stage, and there was never any danger that English teacher, Vic Prooth, would select me for an acting role in his production of Noël Coward's *Blithe Spirit*. However, an A-level science student with a good mark in O-level Physics and some basic knowledge of Ohms Law was obviously seen as a prime candidate for the stage lighting crew, thereby providing succession planning for next year's play when leading electricians, Pete Alexander and John Speight from the upper sixth, would have left. Vic Prooth was not the sort of producer to argue with: he was a stocky, thick-set ebullient figure, not unlike a bespectacled version of the boxer, Freddie Mills, used to getting his own way albeit by the powers of persuasive speech rather than by any pugilistic means.

There were many rehearsals, and I soon became familiar with the backstage electrical gear, including a set of huge sliding resistors (rheostats) for dimming sections of the lights manually at the appropriate times in the performance. John Speight was given the difficult task of playing exactly on cue a recording of Vera Lynn singing 'We'll Meet Again' on a wind-up gramophone. After repeated use, the borrowed record inevitably became scratched, necessitating considerable grovelling and explanation to its owner after the performances.

Blithe Spirit is a long and difficult play, demanding marathon acting performances, concentration by the prompts, subtle make-up and novel stage effects. Although Vic Prooth became concerned that he had bitten off more than he could chew, he was a tenacious producer and the first night was extremely successful. The 12 December edition of the *Wakefield Express* was full of praise. John ('Bud') Briggs gave an exceptional performance as Charles Condomine, without having dropped a single line in a marathon performance. Even the stage and lighting crews were commended, but the *Wakefield Express* doesn't report what happened during one of the later performances, when the failure of the lighting crew to tot up the wattage of all the stage lights had especially dramatic consequences.

I had just got used to the idea of playing God as I cast light on my little world with a flick of a switch here and a slide of a rheostat there, when at a moment of maximum illumination a fuse blew, bringing me down to earth and plunging the stage and school hall into darkness: only one pathetic light bulb glowed defiantly over the stage on a separate circuit. For once, 'Bud' Briggs was lost for words. Worse still, the Mayor of Wakefield was in the audience. He had not got to where he was by being a shrinking violet, however. Taking matters into his own hands, he leaped onto the stage and declared in a broad Yorkshire accent that the show was so good, it must go on and, if necessary, he would call out the Wakefield Fire Brigade to illuminate the stage. Meanwhile, a fuming Vic, arms flailing, demanded that the scientists should fix the problem instantly. I was completely transfixed by embarrassment and fear; the rest of the crew were nowhere to be seen or heard, and I feared they had 'done a runner', leaving me to take the flak from Vic and to wave some magic wand. The 1958 senior boys' 100 yards sprint champion, Pete Alexander, and disc jockey, John Speight had, indeed, both hared off but only to the main fuse box outside the hall. By a stroke of good fortune, senior master Jack Davies was aware that a senior engineer from the Yorkshire Electricity Board was in the audience and he managed to persuade him to open the sealed box so that the blown fuse could be replaced with some thicker wire! After about twenty minutes, the lighting was restored, the play continued and now all we had to worry about was the possibility of an overloaded circuit overheating and the drama of having to call out the fire brigade, not to illuminate the stage, but to yet another school fire. At this point, God decided to avoid a repeat of 1951 by restraining his powers and operating the lights with less intensity than 'full wick'. Despite this debacle, my experiences of school theatre did not end with *Blithe Spirit;* I was involved with the lighting of *Pygmalion* the following year, with John 'Bud' Briggs as Higgins and head boy Keith Flood as Mr Doolittle.

As the 1950s came to an end, the local council spent all of £200 on festive decorations and illuminations for the Bull Ring, cathedral and the town hall clock; hardly a signal that the age of austerity was over. The licensing authorities were somewhat more generous when they extended drinking hours from 10.30 p.m. to 11 p.m. on Christmas Eve and Boxing Day, but they excelled themselves by granting an extension from 10.30 p.m to 12.15 a.m. to celebrate the New Year, the first time for years that pubs were open through midnight. Despite this opportunity for revelry, the local police and fire brigade reported a quiet holiday period which had been wet rather than cold and white.

There were now plenty of opportunities for enjoyment in and around the city. Many young people with jobs and money would visit Mecca's new Locarno Ballroom which had opened in Southgate in the centre of Wakefield on 28 November 1959. The Australian rugby league tourists were its first foreign guests on the opening night, after suffering a defeat at the hands of Trinity in an exciting match in front of 17,600 spectators. It was the sort of place where Trinity rugby players might be seen on a more regular basis, smartly clad in their navy blue blazers with the city emblem, the fleur-de-lis on the breast pocket. T'Mecca, as it eventually became known, was a much 'posher' place than Wakefield's other dancehalls, such as the Embassy down Market Street. With a sprung maple wood dance floor, dance bands, a range of other music and refreshment bars, t'Mecca fully justified its description as a proper ballroom. Those not wishing to dance could saunter upstairs and spot the local talent from a balcony overlooking the floor. 'The Gents' was now known as the 'Stag Room' whilst ladies visited the 'Boudoir', typical of the upmarket appeal of the Mecca brand at that time.

'T' Mecca', Southgate, Wakefield. City of Wakefield MDC Libraries Photographic Collection.

There were no fancy 'Stag Rooms' or 'Boudoirs' in St George's Church hall, Lupset, where I and many Wakefield sixth formers gathered for the regular Saturday night youth club dance to quickstep, foxtrot and jive to the latest hits bellowing out from a record player. Yet, the social dynamics were the same as those at t'Mecca, t'Embassy and every other dancehall at that time: clusters of expectant girls, 'done up to the nines', patiently waiting to be asked to dance; groups of lads in their best suits and ties trying to look relaxed and pretending to be absorbed by the music, whilst occasionally puffing on a fag and nervously eyeing up the girls from a distance, petrified to approach them for fear of refusal and almost certain humiliation from their mates. During this agonising stand-off, a few of the more pragmatic girls would start to dance with one another, usually around their handbags placed on the dance floor. At this point some of the lads might resort to a pint or two of Dutch courage, either from a bar in t'Mecca or, in the case of St George's, down the road at the Lupset Hotel. In t'Mecca, the name of the game was for the lads to latch onto a girl before smooch time at the end of the evening, when the lights dimmed and the huge glitter ball above the dance floor started to rotate, reflecting light across the ballroom from spotlights directed at its myriad tiny mirrors. At St George's, the critical signal was usually the playing of 'Smoke Gets in Your Eyes' by the Platters. If you weren't 'fixed up' by then, it was either the last bus or the consolation of fish and chips with your mates on the long walk home.

The social dynamics were somewhat different on the school trip to the Lake District, where we were staying in wooden huts at the Wall End Cooperative Holidays Association in Langdale during the 1960 Easter holiday. We were accompanied by male and female members of the teaching staff whose main duty was to keep the boys in their huts and the girls in theirs, but we managed to cross the threshold far more successfully than on an unsupervised dance floor. In the evening, John Speight's hut was usually bursting at the seams. During daylight, the field next to the huts served as a useful pitch for a game of touch and pass under the watchful eye of Gwynne Davies, a top class rugby league referee and recent addition to the school's PT staff.

After supper, the teaching staff were quite happy for us to retire to the nearest pub, the Old Dungeon Ghyll Hotel, but we had a frosty reception from the landlord, Sid Cross who, after pointing out that some of us were obviously under-age, simply pointed us to the door. Sid Cross was a well-known climber in these parts, famous for being the first to ascend Great Eastern on Scafell with Maurice Linnell in the 1930s and, in circa 1950, for establishing the Langdale Mountain Rescue Service, a volunteer group based at the Old Dungeon Ghyll Hotel. There was no way Sid was going to risk losing his licence and livelihood for the sake of a few underage drinkers. Meanwhile, we all retired half a mile down the valley to the New Dungeon Ghyll Hotel where we were all served without any problem.

I had managed to have some elementary training on local rock outcrops before going to the Lake District, but the long 'Bracket and Slab' route up Gimmer Crag was rather different. This was my first rock climb under the classification of 'Severe', and by the time I was half way up, it had started to rain heavily, not unusual in the Lake District but something for which I was totally unprepared. What had been a surprisingly trouble-free climb was now fraught with danger: foot and hand-holds that previously had ample grip were now as smooth as ice and about as cold; big heavy boots soaked up the rain and became like lead weights; non-waterproof, ice cold wet trousers clung to my legs; bare hands became numb with cold. My anorak was actually waterproof but a wet woolly hat would have offered no protection to the head in the event of a fall. Worst of all, my lifeline, a nylon rope that appeared to be rather thin at the best of times, now looked like a piece of wet string, incapable of holding my weight. A jovial soul, bespectacled Jimmy Ferguson in flat hat, shouted from above that the climb was now so wet that it was almost certainly upgraded to the 'Very Severe' category. My confidence shattered, I did not have any clarity of thought to rationalise this perilous situation. I now know that there were basically two alternatives: the negative one of succumbing to the fear and probably becoming another statistic in Sid Cross's logbook; or the positive one of keeping calm and inching my way upwards. Encouraged by form tutor and Physics teacher, Keith ('Rocky') Stewart and my mates at the top, I had chosen the latter and somehow grappled my way up, maybe with them also pulling on the rope. Over fifty years later I can still recall the elation after having triumphed over fear and despair.

Scafell Pike, 9 April 1960. From left to right: John Speight, Jimmy Ferguson, David Salt, David Royle, John Paterson, (front), Michael Paterson, (back), Peter Alexander (extreme right). K. G. Barraclough.

On Saturday, 9 April, we hiked to Scafell Pike. On our way back in the late afternoon some of us ran all the way down the Band to Wall End, anxious to find out the final score in the match between Trinity and Featherstone Rovers, which was no ordinary local derby but a rugby league Challenge Cup Semi-final at Odsal stadium, Bradford, in front of more than 55,000 spectators. It wasn't just the lads in the school party who were interested in the result: upper sixth former Gwenda Severn had more than a passing interest in Trinity's progress to London's Wembley stadium for the Cup Final. Gwenda was the current 'Miss Trinity', and at a recent beauty competition at t'Mecca she had also been crowned 'Yorkshire Rugby League Queen'.

By the end of the fifties Wakefield Trinity had all the key components in place to become a dominant force in rugby league for the next decade. Trinity had continued to add to its talented youngsters from the mid-fifties, but youth alone was never going to be enough to reach the very top in this game, even though twenty-year-old Neil Fox was already an international and breaking many club point scoring records. Trinity needed to add further capabilities, in particular, better management and tactical nous on and off the field. On the field they needed guile, some tough, ball winning forwards, and a natural leader who would drive the team forward, especially when the 'going got tough'. In the professional sport of rugby league, the key to acquiring such a blend of skills was money.

It was said that the new Trinity chairman, businessman Stuart Hadfield, had 'a bob or two' from his dealings as a coal distributor. Cash was also flowing into the club from improved cup runs, increased season ticket sales and increased attendances, long before Hadfield's elevation from the committee in July 1959. The Trinity club had made a profit during the previous year, despite a huge outlay on new players. Wakefield locals were getting behind their team and there were collective fund-raising activities in an increasing number of supporters clubs throughout the district. Trinity had also introduced a successful Pools scheme and were making investments in ground improvements: by 1958 a covered stand had been erected at the Agbrigg End which became my favourite standing position with my mates, 'back o' t'sticks'. During the following season in 1958/59, investment was made in a new all-white strip, tastefully embellished with two bands of blue and one of red, a psychologically smart move, making the Trinity team look as imposing as the top teams from Lancashire, notably Wigan and St Helens.

The first key acquisition of new Trinity players had occurred in December 1957, when Ken Traill had signed from Halifax. Traill was a master tactician, one of the best passers and kickers of a rugby ball, capable of 'reading' a game from his position at loose forward where he had excelled at Bradford Northern during the immediate post-war era, when rugby league was blessed with a plethora of world class players in this position. Ken Traill was coming to the end of his playing days, but it was a master stroke when the management committee appointed him as player-coach at the end of the 1957/58 season. During the same season Trinity had also signed full back Gerry Round and a local stand-off half from Lupset, Harold Poynton, who had played rugby league as a schoolboy but, after completing National Service, was languishing in the Wakefield and District Amateur Football League, playing centre forward for British Ropes Ltd. After only two games in the A-team, my mates and I saw him trot out at Belle Vue on 1 February 1958, to make his first team debut against league leaders, St Helens. Poynton appeared an unlikely rugby figure. With shirt collar turned up against the cold air, hollow cheeks, deep set eyes and receding forehead with slicked back blond hair he looked a terrified, frozen creature, but he proved otherwise during the actual game. Fearless in the tackle and a natural footballer, Poynton's main assets were his guile and animal cunning as he mesmerised opponents with his devastating handling skills. By coincidence, another local former footballer also made his first team debut that day: nineteen year old Geoff Oakes from 'back o' t'Alec' had previously played in goal at Thornes House Grammar School, and was now one of the tallest hookers in professional rugby league. Trinity won 17–12.

Not all Trinity's acquisitions were so successful. The club had been tempted into the South African rugby union market following the outstanding success of St Helen's South African winger, Tom van Vollenhoven.

However, Trinity's new recruits, 'the Iron Man of South African Rugby Union', forward Ivor Dorrington, and 6 feet, 3 inches, Springbok triallist winger, Jan Lotriet, were huge disappointments: Dorrington looked as if he had never passed a rugby ball before and, despite his size, Lotriet lacked 'bottle' and was too easily tackled into touch. Just when the Trinity committee were being berated by the fans for having 'more brass 'n' brains', they unearthed a little gem, Springbok centre Alan Skene, who more than made up for his countrymen's shortcomings. Despite a very slight frame, Skene was a reliable defender with pace, a delightful outside swerve and a perfectly timed pass, usually to his wingman, Freddie Smith. Trinity now had the ideal foil for Neil Fox and, with Poynton pulling the strings, the Fox/Skene centre partnership was the best in the land by 1959.

Trinity still needed to add ball winning experience and fire to the forwards, although local youngsters, Albert 'Budgie' Firth, Les Chamberlain, Geoff 'Knocker' Oakes and Malcolm Sampson were shaping up well. The first significant signing of the 1958/59 season was Welshman Don Vines from Oldham, a tough, fiery forward with pace and ball handling skills. We used to laugh at the way Vines hitched up his shorts at the sides to show off his enormous thighs. Although he was a wrestler off the field, Vines was anything but a 'showboater' on it. Early in the 1959/60 season, veteran international prop forward Jack Wilkinson signed from Halifax, to strengthen Trinity's ability to win enough ball for their scintillating backs. 'Wilkie' proved to be another fine buy, but the real coup in early 1959 was the transfer of local star international, Derek Turner, from Oldham for £8,000, at the time a world record fee for a forward.

Although not the biggest loose forward in the game, Turner had everything: pace, power, organisational skills, fierce tackling ability, and even film star looks. His only weakness was a short fuse, often ignited by local rivals such as Featherstone Rovers, who knew how to get him sent off. When Turner became Trinity's captain at the start of the 1959/60 season, he applied this fierce competitive edge in a positive way, and his unremitting drive, will to win and never-say-die attitude became unique features of the team's increasing success. Here was Trinity's talismanic leader, the vital cog in a machine that would drive them to greatness. If Wakefield folk had been asked in 1960 whom they would trust to get them out of a tricky physical confrontation, most would have chosen the heroic warrior, Derek 'Rocky' Turner.

By the start of the 1959/60 season such was the attraction of the revitalised Trinity that the aggregate attendance for the first three home league fixtures against Wigan, Leeds and St Helens was 50,000 spectators. There was also a surge of optimism in the city that this was going to be the season when Trinity won some major silverware. In those days that meant the Rugby League Challenge Cup, after fourteen years of disappointments since the last triumph at Wembley.

Trinity had beaten Featherstone Rovers in the 1960 Challenge Cup Semi-final, and on 14 May, my mates and I travelled to a sun-drenched Wembley stadium for the Final, graced for the first time by the presence of Her Majesty the Queen and His Royal Highness the Duke of Edinburgh. Trinity's opponents were Hull, weakened by injury, but this probably had little influence on the outcome as Trinity ran riot in a record score of 38–5, with Neil Fox bagging a record number of 20 points. 'Rocky' Turner was presented with the trophy by Her Majesty the Queen, and we all cheered until we were hoarse. On the following Monday we joined the throng of 40,000 lining the Wakefield streets, from Westgate Railway Station to the Town Hall, as the Trinity team held the Cup aloft a brewery wagon, bedecked with red, white and blue flags, rosettes and a smiling Miss Trinity, who received a special cheer from us.

Derek Turner, captain of the triumphant Wakefield Trinity team, displays the Rugby League Challenge Cup to packed crowds at Wembley Stadium. *Wakefield Express.*

Although there was the anticlimax of a defeat against Wigan in the

Championship Final the following weekend, at last Trinity and their supporters had been rewarded for all their hard work and investment. The way forward for Trinity in the 1960s was very clear: onwards and upwards.

As far as my own way forward was concerned, I wanted to go to university, but was unsure whether I was good enough and had no idea what to study within the general field of science and engineering. I was grappling with DIY Maths, and not devoting enough time to Chemistry and Physics. There were too many new distractions such as coffee bars, pubs, music, girlfriends and playing a range of sports, as well as taking on numerous responsibilities at school, where I had virtually no free

Wood Street, Wakefield, 16 May 1960. *WAKEFIELD EXPRESS.*

periods. I had also become too cocky after sailing through O-levels.

In 1961, long before the expansion of higher education recommended in the 1963 Robbins Report, there were only 111,000 university students in England and Wales, and less than 15 per cent of applications to university were successful: demand for places exceeded supply and competition was tough. At Thornes House, advice on higher education was virtually nonexistent. The school had no 'career specialist' and the only advice I can recall is that I would find it harder to obtain a university place to study a pure science subject than an 'applied science'. Bearing in mind this pearl of wisdom, I started to investigate the range of possibilities within technological subjects and came across metallurgy, largely through chatting with older school pals Hughie Everson and John Speight, who by 1960 were already studying the subject at Birmingham University. My best subject at school had always been Chemistry, a pure science, so in the end I split my applications into: Chemistry at the Universities of Leeds and Manchester and Metallurgy at Birmingham and Sheffield. All courses accepted me, some after an interview, subject to attaining my three A-levels with marks of 60 per cent or better. Oxbridge entrance was not usually discussed at Thornes House in the 1950s, even for exceptionally bright students like Melvyn Lynes and John Briggs, who were certainly good enough, but the school had no Oxbridge links, no *savoir faire* and no regular teaching of Latin, at that time an Oxbridge entrance requirement at O-level standard. Eventually, a pupil from a school year below us, Martin Taylor, gained entrance to Cambridge University.

My A-level marks were good enough for university entrance but not for a scholarship. The hard work was rewarded by offers from all four universities, and I chose Birmingham. Most of the upper sixth form went on to some form of higher education, either at university, medical school, college of advanced technology or teacher training college. The thirteen plus transferee Derek Chappel, who had failed his eleven plus interview by describing an orange as a sphere, went on to Hull University to read Maths. From the arts side Sheila Spence went on to Leeds University. Kathleen Lomax, the only girl in the upper sixth science class went on to medical school. Melvyn Lynes, John Briggs, Jimmy Ferguson, David Murray and Keith Flood all ended up at Manchester University. Melvyn gained a State Scholarship to read French, with five A-levels, including two distinctions; he had also passed his O-level Latin, all within two years. John Briggs had grasped the opportunity of a third year in the sixth form and gained an Open Entrance Scholarship and State Scholarship to Manchester University to read Physics, having attained four A-levels with three distinctions.

In October 1961 we all went our separate ways, the latest clutch of first generation students to leave home, and their immensely proud, mainly working-class parents. We didn't have to borrow any money or pay anything towards our higher education fees. Those of us without scholarships received a means tested maintenance grant from the local authority, which in my case was £276 p.a., close to the maximum for outer London. I thought I was the luckiest person in the world: master of my own destiny, and being paid for the pleasure. Dad hired a little Ford Anglia to take me, a large suitcase and a present from Auntie Olive, a brown leather briefcase, down the A61 and A38 to Birmingham, through so many towns and cities that Mum worried whether we would ever get there. I had already been to the University of Birmingham for an interview, but Mum and Dad had never seen a university campus before and were overawed by its sheer size and scale. They were also somewhat bemused by one or two 'strange-looking folk', prompting Dad to joke that I would be returning home for Christmas with a beard and a pair of 'those blue working trousers'; he could never bring himself to call them jeans. As I awaited my final instructions before parting company and immediately celebrating my independence in the Guild of Undergraduates' bar, Dad became contemplative, as if he were formulating a grand farewell speech, but he just shook my hand, smiled and told me to 'make the best of it'; 'it' being the opportunity he never had. Mum started to fuss about how I would cope with doing my own washing. I told her not to worry and gave her a hug. A tear trickled down her cheek.

References and Further Reading

The 18-plus explosion, the Universities, and the Technical Colleges, A. J. Jenkinson, Journal of Vocational Education and Training, 15:31, (1963) 158–169.

University Entrance and Success Rate – The Cabinet Papers, 1915–1979, Before and After the Second World War. The National Archives.

Hansard: Students Grants, HC Deb 01 February 1982, vol. 17, cc33-4W.

CHAPTER 12

Epilogue

It would be remarkable if Wakefield and its surrounding district had not changed dramatically in the last fifty years; most places have, especially those 'up north'. A combination of political, economic and social pressures has transformed the diverse industrial city of the 1950s into a place that is barely recognisable to those of us returning after a long period of absence, with images of the fifties still firmly embedded in our memories. It starts with the visual impact of the changed landscape on the approach to the city. Collieries and their winding gear that once guarded the city like sentries have disappeared; the grey colliery yards and muckheaps of the past have been transformed into green spaces for sports, leisure and recreational activities. The tall cathedral spire can still be seen from miles away, but it is now joined by modern high-rise flats and hotels on the city centre skyline. Further south, the twin cooling towers and chimney of the power station that once dominated the skyline are no more. In the sprawling suburbs, widened roads and many new commercial and residential developments catch the eye, but the smoke stack industries are long gone.

Wakefield's core industry, coal mining, and the industries dependent on it have disappeared, as they have throughout the country. 'King Coal' is dead but its heritage is extremely well preserved in England's National Coal Mining Museum at the former Caphouse colliery in Overton, on the western outskirts of the city. Loss of competitive advantage in textiles and engineering led to a huge decline in Wakefield's other major industries and the closure of many mills and factories. The end of the age of steam signalled the end of the engine sheds in Belle Vue. Boundary changes and the reorganisation of local government in the 1970s also had an adverse effect on Wakefield: it lost its administrative independence when it became part of a metropolitan district covering neighbouring towns, which also had a voice on the new council. Wakefield is still the headquarters of the successor to the West Riding Constabulary, the West Yorkshire Police, but it lost its other traditional seat of power when the West Riding County Council and its short-lived successor, the West Yorkshire County Council, were disbanded. With so many upheavals across a wide range of jobs in industry and administration, unemployment became a continual problem, and Wakefield had to seek a new identity. Regeneration became an imperative for local government, supported by UK and European government initiatives.

By a stroke of good fortune, perhaps also with a dash of strategic management, Wakefield found itself in the corner of one of the most important motorway networks running the length and breadth of the country. Just as Cliff Bracewell had mused in 1959, the north-south M1 motorway had, indeed, reached Wakefield (by 1968) and the nearby east-west M62 motorway was completed by the mid-seventies. Thus, towards the end of the twentieth century Wakefield's new road transport network became as important as the turnpikes, canals and railways of previous centuries. Wakefield became readily accessible from three junctions on the M1 and two junctions on the M62, resulting in the district becoming a favoured location for distribution centres, business centres, hotels and retail developments, all sources of new employment opportunities in a service economy; new jobs in 'logistics' started to appear in the district. As car ownership continued to increase, those who were unable to find work in Wakefield might now be able to travel further afield for jobs in the large conurbations of Sheffield to the south and even Manchester to the west; the thriving town of Leeds and the huge West Yorkshire conurbation were within easy reach. Electrification of the mainline railway meant that even London was less than two hours from Wakefield Westgate Station, also renovated, albeit without its iconic Victorian clock tower. The heart of Wakefield is still undergoing major surgery but its arteries are in better shape than ever; even the old turnpike of Denby Dale Road now plays its part as a busy dual carriageway transporting commuters and goods to and from the M1 motorway. But what is Wakefield for? Is it a place to get out of, or a place to get into?

By day, shopping is the main activity in modern retail centres such as the Ridings, the New Market Hall and Trinity Walk. Supermarkets came to Wakefield in the 1960s; the first ones were of modest size, then they became huge complexes. Access to the retail experience is everything, so due attention has been paid to the construction of relief roads such as Marsh Way which, along with the new car parks and pedestrian zones, give me the feeling of being in a completely different city! It's the same story on the edge of the city centre: the south side of Ings Road, now a busy dual carriageway, provides access to retail parks with yet more stores, a multiplex cinema and fast food outlets, all announcing themselves with huge coloured logos on bland modern buildings in what became known as 'Shed City'. Even as early as 1960, Wakefield had lost around half of the ten cinemas that it had in 1949 and now they are all gone; the remains of the old Regal in Kirkgate present a sorry sight.

By night Wakefield fulfils its traditional role as a drinking centre, with numerous clubs and 'fun-pubs', particularly along Westgate. In sharp contrast to this, Westgate in the fifties was the location of more serious activities, notably banking and the law. The 'Westgate Run' has developed a reputation as the star attraction for many outside visitors with the sole intention of becoming paralytic by downing a drink or two in every pub. Many leave their 'visiting card', a constant reminder to those with the job of cleaning up the mess that this is hardly a means of regenerating the 'Merrie City'.

Local community groups work tirelessly to preserve the city's cultural heritage and to ensure the new identity imposed by regeneration programmes is in harmony with its historic past – a difficult task and obviously not without tension. A local Civic Society was established in 1964 in response to the redevelopment of the city when many of its significant buildings had been demolished. Local voluntary groups are dedicated to specific projects. One of these is the Friends of Wakefield Chantry Chapel, which raises funds for the upkeep of the chapel, ensures it is in good repair and made available to visitors. Many of Wakefield's other significant buildings and institutions have survived, notably Wakefield Prison, the Cathedral, the two railway stations and many historic buildings in Wakefield's civic centre in and around Wood Street: the Town Hall, County Hall, Court House and Wakefield Museum. Further north, the Georgian area of St John's is also instantly recognisable. After a triumphant return to a refurbished Bull Ring, following thirty-five years of exile on Denby Dale Road, the statue of Queen Victoria was yet again removed in 2009 to facilitate further renovations in the city centre before a new site was found in Castrop Rauxel Square, Rishworth Street. A new bus station has replaced the one in Union Street that we all thought was so swish in 1952. As far as health care is concerned, only Clayton and Pinderfields Hospital survived the 1950s, the latter benefiting from a new £300 million building which was opened in 2010.

The local Rhubarb Triangle faced increasingly strong competition in the post-war era, as refrigerated transportation made foreign produce readily available. Production declined, and the regular rhubarb trains to London stopped in 1964. However, forced rhubarb has long been a part of Wakefield's heritage and, although it is now grown on a much smaller scale than in the past, it remains the vegetable the city is renowned for growing. The forcing sheds of E. Oldroyd & Sons Ltd. are a tourist attraction and there is now a Wakefield Festival of Food, Drink and Rhubarb! TV 'celebrity chefs' extol rhubarb's nutritional value.

Wakefield's famous Victorian novelist George Gissing is celebrated in the Gissing Centre in Thompson's Yard, off Westgate, where he lived as a boy. Other famous local writers Stan Barstow and David Storey drew on their 1950s experiences for their first novels, both published in 1960 and subsequently made into films: Barstow's *A Kind of Loving* and Storey's *This Sporting Life.*

Choral singing continues to thrive. Margaret Markland conducted the Thornesian Guild of Singers until she retired in 1972. It eventually became known as the Yorkshire Philharmonic Choir in 1999 and is now one of the premier choirs in the North of England, performing mainly in Wakefield Cathedral and Dewsbury Town Hall.

Local groups are involved in a wide range of cultural and sporting activities. Music, theatre, visual arts and a range of sports seem to be flourishing. In 2010, Wakefield was named as the UK's third 'most musical city' by the PRS (Performing Rights Society) for Music. Wakefield Jazz holds its gigs at what is claimed to be one of the best jazz venues in the country, the Wakefield Club, a new centralised facility in College Grove, also used by many local sports clubs and Wakefield Camera Club, which still attracts keen photographers. The principal occupants of College Grove in the fifties, Wakefield Cricket Club and Wakefield Rugby Union Football Club, both folded. Cricket is still played throughout the district, and rugby union continues to be played by the Sandal Club, south of the city. There are also many local amateur rugby league teams in the district.

It is tempting to denounce Westgate as a cultural desert when experiencing the boorish behaviour of the Saturday night drinkers, but theatre and the arts are now more prominent in this part of the city than they ever were in the 1950s. Wakefield's Theatre Royal and Opera House was rescued from extinction by community action in 1986; a new Art House in Drury Lane now provides studios for aspiring artists, and the Westgate Studios in the Prudential Building of Westgate is home to an eclectic mix of artists. A new cooperative venture has been launched to restore the ailing Unity Hall, originally a nineteenth century centre for Wakefield's Industrial Co-operative Society, to a vibrant twenty-first century hub for the arts, conferences and new business innovators.

DIVA is a local agency for Development Initiatives for the Voluntary Arts, aiming to increase opportunities for voluntary groups and individuals to participate in the arts. The local Civic Society has produced a guide,

Wakefield, City of Sculpture and Public Art, which helps visitors discover the wealth of sculpture and public art in and around the city centre. Wakefield's most significant development in the visual arts is, undoubtedly, the new £35 million gallery, the Hepworth Wakefield, which opened in May 2011, displaying a unique collection of Barbara Hepworth's works.

Located on the newly developed Waterfront on the south bank of the River Calder, David Chipperfield's unusual grey/blue concrete structure is one of the largest purpose built galleries outside London. Inevitably, it has its detractors, and to erect such an expensive building at a time of austerity was a bold move – some thought perhaps a foolhardy one. The strategy to make Wakefield a cultural hub as a means of regenerating the district is also ambitious, but quite persuasive. Many key elements are already in place in the city and surrounding district. The Yorkshire Sculpture Park, a few miles southwest of the city in the village of West Bretton, is an international centre for art in a scenic gallery without walls and includes a collection of some of Henry Moore's works. Ten miles north in Leeds is the Henry Moore Institute, and his work often features in exhibitions at Leeds Art Gallery. Further east is Moore's birthplace, Castleford, which also pays homage to one of Britain's most acclaimed sculptors. Great art endures economic, political and social change, and after a long period when two of the world's greatest sculptors were rather neglected by the district of Wakefield, they have been reclaimed by the area that provided their inspiration at the beginning of the last century. Moore and Hepworth have returned home. This is a welcome change in itself, but it also provides some exciting contributions to the area's renaissance.

Continuing my journey south of the River Calder, I find that the White Bear at Bridge End, Lunn's bakery at the beginning of Doncaster Road and the old Graziers hotel at the entrance to Belle Vue have all disappeared. The thin wedge-shaped building of the Alexandra is still there but it is no longer a pub. Many of Belle Vue's Victorian buildings have disappeared completely: St Catherine's Church (destroyed by fire in 1993), St Catherine's Church School, the two cemetery chapels, Oxford Street Wesleyan Chapel and Doncaster Road Methodist Chapel. Many of the original terraced houses in and around Denmark Street and 'back o' t'Alec' have been replaced, but some Victorian housing has survived, notably around Regent Street, Oxford Street and Wesley Street, many now clad in bright colours and festooned with cables and satellite TV dishes. Our cobblestoned cricket pitch and iron grate wicket can still be seen in Back Regent Street where young boys of the large Asian community now play. They have fewer dog turds to negotiate, but there's plenty of other litter, especially the plastic and metal of used food and drink containers. The air is cleaner: the stink of smoke has gone.

Wakefield's industrial decline is poignantly displayed alongside one of its major successes, at the end of Elm Tree Street, 'back o' t'Alec'. A vast area of flat scrubland is all that remains of the site that was once the home of the engine sheds and power station. Now, there's no smoke, no steam and not a soul in sight; it is eerily quiet. In direct contrast, the neighbouring factory of Joseph Rhodes Ltd. is still going strong as one of Wakefield's few manufacturing industries still remaining from the 1950s. As a winner of the 2010 Queen's Award for Innovation in the development of metal pressing equipment, Joe Rhodes continues to be a 'Colossus' and a beacon of hope for the future; Wakefield could do with a few more Joe Rhodes.

Business premises now occupy the old t'Spit building which closed its doors as a cinema in 1960. Opposite, the modern complex of the rebuilt St Catherine's Church Centre provides community care, a café, conference rooms and an exhibit of the stone remains of the old Victorian church, as well as a place of worship; it has a much broader appeal to the community than in the past.

Wakefield Trinity 'Wildcats' still play the professional game of rugby league at a furious, non-stop pace, now as members of the Super League. Forwards are no longer distinguishable from backs; they all appear as big and fast as each other in their flashy red, white and blue kit, embellished with sponsors' logos and fearsome images of wildcats. Attendances are now much smaller than those in the heydays of the past when there were fewer activities competing for spectators' leisure time. Super League is mainly a summer sport, thirsty work for the players and also their vociferous supporters who can now buy alcoholic refreshments in the ground. There is no let up in the entertainment; at every opportunity live music is blasted out of a powerful PA system whilst leggy young dancing girls, dressed in rather flimsy costumes, confidently 'strut their stuff'. It's all so different from those far off days of 1953 when their timid grandparents' generation meekly performed country dances whilst dreaming of playing rugby on the sacred turf. I never fulfilled that boyhood dream.

The Trinity teams of the modern era have not yet achieved the supreme heights of those in the 1960s when they won the Rugby League Challenge Cup three times and the Rugby League Championship twice. Wembley became a second home for Trinity and their supporters; my student friends and I went to all four of Trinity's cup final appearances there in the 1960s. It was a glorious period for rugby league in Wakefield. As a former player, local writer David Storey had experienced the tough, uncompromising environment of professional rugby league which he used as the backdrop to *This Sporting Life,* the winner of the 1960 Macmillan Fiction Award. When the novel was made into a film in 1963, the Wakefield Trinity players and the Belle Vue ground featured in many of the clips. I recall being an 'extra' in the crowd when the Trinity team, led by 'Rocky' Turner, gave lead actor Richard Harris a genuinely rough time during the filming of some of the action at Belle Vue.

The Australians generally dominate the game of rugby league, but the local 'Big Fella' Neil Fox surpassed them all, having scored a world record number of 6,220 points in a glittering career that spanned four decades, a record that will surely stand for all time. Neil is a local legend: he was inducted into Rugby League's Hall of Fame; was awarded an MBE, and the Freedom of the City of Wakefield; he even had a local bus, a street and a housing estate named after him.

The Belle Vue rugby ground is now known as the Rapid Solicitors Stadium, but not only the name has changed: the Agbrigg End is now occupied by hospitality suites and, after the fire disaster at Bradford City football ground in 1985, the handsome wooden Victorian stand had to be demolished. Advertisements now plaster every available surface of the ground, rendering it more colourful than before; the lush green pitch is in much better condition than it ever was in the 1950s. However, this tired old stadium and infrastructure cannot meet the stringent requirements of the Super League authorities, and Belle Vue's future hangs in the balance: Trinity must either improve its ground or move to a new abode.

The large Asian community of Agbrigg has its own mosque at the bottom of St Catherine's Street, where many of the old terraced houses remain. The Duke of York pub and Sandal Railway Station are still there. Sandal Council School is still located in Belle Vue Road, now as Sandal Magna Community Primary School but, after 120 years' service, the school's old Victorian building was recently demolished to make way for a new structure. The small trees we planted below the playground in 1953 as a 'permanent commemoration' of the Coronation have long gone, as have eleven plus examinations, free school milk, swimming lessons at t'owd baths and many competitive sports, including interschool athletics at Wakefield Greyhound Stadium. In nearby Sparable Lane, it is a relief to see Sandal Library still there, but it now looks much smaller and more vulnerable than it did sixty years ago. Further west in Portobello, W. E. Rawson Ltd. is a rare survivor of the changes in Wakefield's industrial landscape.

The twelfth century Sandal Castle is now well worth a visit, another example of the area's heritage that has been carefully nurtured from the time it was just a crumbling ruin in the 1950s. A new community group, the Friends of Sandal Castle, helps to promote and preserve this historical site. Finds from the 1964–1973 excavation are displayed in a visitor centre, and from the castle's motte there is an excellent panoramic view of the Calder Valley, the city to the north, the district of Thornes and Lowe Hill in Wakefield Park to the northwest, and the 250 acre development of Pugneys Country Park to the west.

Previously an opencast mine and sand and gravel quarry, Pugneys Country Park now has two lakes, a modern water sports centre and a café. The larger lake is a 100 acre facility for sailing, windsurfing, canoeing and kayaking; those not wishing to take to the water can either stroll around the lake and enjoy its beautiful surroundings or observe the wildlife in the smaller lake's nature reserve. The creation of a water sports and recreation centre from an industrial site is a good example of Wakefield's ability to adapt its available resources to meet modern requirements.

In the district of Thornes some old dwellings were demolished in the widening of Denby Dale Road. The Greyhound Stadium has also disappeared; the triangular site between the railway lines is now occupied by industrial units. However, many parts of Thornes have not changed significantly, especially Wakefield Park, St James's Church and many surrounding residential areas, including Avondale Street, Tew Street, Cotton Street and Horne Street. In Avondale Street a fish and chip shop is still on the corner with Tew Street and, after more than fifty years, Dad's brickwork on the garden walls and front porch of number 21 is still intact.

There is now a community group, the Friends of CHaT (Clarence, Holmfield and Thornes Parks), aiming to maintain the heritage of Wakefield Park. In Clarence Park, the bandstand has been renovated, following efforts by a local voluntary group, the Music Collective, in partnership with the local council. There is now a regular programme of events and a free music festival in Clarence Park. Nearby in Holmfield Park, Holmfield now goes under the name of Holmfield Arms as part of a hotel and restaurant chain. Here, a restaurant and bar have replaced the school tuck shop; large flat panel television screens displaying Sky Sports programmes grab the attention in place of blackboards chalked up with 'Pop' Hill's huge letter 'S'; our old playground is now a car park. In Thornes Park, the beautiful walled rose garden and lake are still there and there is a newly constructed skate park and children's play area. At the Horbury Road end, our old sloping football pitches have been levelled and are now part of Wakefield Council's athletic stadium, home to Wakefield Harriers. Wakefield Park seems to have a much broader appeal than it ever did in the 1950s, but it is no longer home to a secondary school.

The fifty-six-year-old Thornes House buildings now form part of Wakefield College which comprises a sixth form centre and further education college. Its days as a secondary school ended when it fell victim to 'falling rolls' in a badly planned, poorly implemented comprehensive education system which, at a stroke, had also killed off 'social mobility'. The latter was a key advantage of its grammar school days when intake was based on ability across a much wider catchment area. What a shame that Wakefield's model tripartite education system of the 1950s was never developed by improving its secondary modern schools and transfer system, instead of meddling with the bit that worked effectively! Thornes House Secondary School had lasted only seventy years; QEGS, Wakefield Girls' High School and Silcoates are still going strong as independent schools, having survived the nation's experiments in secondary education.

Some of us often felt inferior to pupils at the other two grammar schools in Wakefield, simply on the basis of the superior eleven plus results of their intake, but the diversity of achievements and activities of many Old Thornesians speak volumes for the school's ability to provide a well rounded education. Amongst my contemporaries, many succeeded in various walks of life: teaching, the civil service, local government, business, administration, science, engineering, medicine, acting, the Church and the law; some carried on the established tradition of Thornes House and pursued careers in music. Lists of old students' successes are far too long to highlight individually; some can be found in old editions of the *Stork* and Nora George's account of the school's history. Two of the most successful Old Boys of my generation left at sixteen, and deserve a special mention: Clive ('Benny') Brooke joined the trade union movement and was elevated to the peerage as Baron Brooke of Alverthorpe, in recognition of outstanding public service; Rodney ('Wacker') Walker, my old junior school rugby opponent and Thornes House classmate, was knighted for his outstanding services to sport.

Rodney left Thornes House School in 1959 with four O-levels, and became a successful businessman and entrepreneur. After making his fortune in the construction industry, he devoted considerable time and effort to the leadership of various national sporting organisations, charities and lost causes, including leadership of the campaign to re-open Wakefield's Theatre Royal and Opera House. Rodney was awarded a knighthood in 1996, a City of Wakefield Lifetime Achievement Award in 2007 and the

Freedom of the city in 2012. Wakefield Trinity Wildcats owe much to this generous philanthropist; in 2010 Sir Rodney bailed them out by paying their outstanding tax bill, reported to be £164,000. He is currently chairing the Wakefield and District Community Stadium Trust, aiming to secure a new home for the club. Sir Rodney may not have gleaned much from the formal lessons at Thornes House Grammar School, but he has certainly lived up to the old school motto, 'In Fellowship'.

Sadly, many other school friends and contemporaries passed away before they were able to realise their full potential. The premature deaths of Melvyn Lynes, aged fifty-two, and Marianna Wagner, aged twenty-seven, were particularly tragic. At Sandal Council School we had often wondered about the origins of Marianna's Germanic surname. Nearly sixty years later I found out.

Marianna's grandfather, Wilhem Wagner, was German, and came to Selby, Yorkshire, to work as an engineer during the early part of the twentieth century. At the outbreak of the Great War he was interned, but he eventually married an English girl from Selby. After their son Walter was born in 1918, the family returned to Germany where Walter was raised, eventually becoming an apprentice carpenter on leaving school in 1932. When Hitler came to power, Walter was compelled to join the Hitler youth movement and swear his allegiance to the Nazi party. As the youth movement gradually took on a more sinister complexion from its initial Boy Scout-like organisation, Walter became increasingly concerned about the rise of German nationalism and his own involvement in it. One day in 1936, telling no-one but his English mother, he cycled the hundred miles or so to Hamburg and took passage on a merchant ship bound for Hull, close to his ultimate destination of Selby, the home of his English aunt. He had left behind an anxious English mother, an angry German father and his younger, German-born siblings. Walter gradually learned English and ended up in Wakefield, working as a joiner at shopfitters Drake and Waters. He married Blanche Scholey in 1940 and two years later they had a daughter, Marianna, who was born a few weeks before me. With such a strange background, not to mention a strong German accent, in the early days of the Second World War Walter found it difficult to prove that he was not a German spy; he was interned and intensively questioned but, eventually, proved his innocence and was called up into the British Army. He had, of course, been born in England and held a British passport. Walter became a sergeant in the Intelligence Corps, with the specific task of interrogating German prisoners of war. Meanwhile, his younger brothers were fighting on the opposite side in the German army: one was captured on the eastern front and held in a Russian prisoner of war camp. It wasn't until after the war in 1947 that Walter was able to visit his parents and younger siblings whom he hadn't seen for over ten years. There was a happy reunion with his mother but his father, Wilhem, never forgave him for going over to the 'other side' and refused to speak to him again. Internment in England during the Great War had obviously made a lasting impression on Wilhem, resulting in feelings of frustration and anger towards his son for turning his back on Germany and leaving for England. After acting so courageously as an 18-year-old, it was a double tragedy for Walter to be shunned forever by his father, then to lose his daughter in her prime from the effects of influenza. Walter died in 1990 and his ashes were scattered on Marianna's grave in Wakefield Cemetery. Truth is stranger than fiction.

After six years as a student, I embarked on a research career at the University of Birmingham, the University of Oxford and the Central Research Laboratories of Siemens A.G. in Munich, West Germany, before settling down in what my parents called 'a proper job' at a government scientific research laboratory, the Royal Signals & Radar Establishment in Malvern, Worcestershire. There, I met another Old Thornesian, Michael White, a physicist from the University of Bristol, who had ended his first year at Thornes House at the time of the fire in 1951. In Munich I had learned to speak German, and I entertained my wife Jane and her linguist friends with renditions of 'Spike's' German grammar songs. Interestingly, they thought the songs were marvellous teaching aids and that 'Spike' had been years ahead of his time! In 1979 my old school pal, John Briggs, also went to work in Germany as professor of Theoretical Physics at the University of Freiburg, and has been there ever since. Another old school pal, John Speight pursued a career in solid state electronics and after working in the USA ended up in senior management at BT; he was my best man when I married Jane in 1972.

With many Old Thornesians scattered across the globe, meetings and reunions tended to be quite rare and confined to small groups. Purely by chance in about 1980 I came across a group in a Worcestershire pub celebrating a birthday. They were complete strangers to me but I struck up conversation with them because I was intrigued by their Yorkshire accents and, again by remarkable coincidence, it also happened to be my birthday. I was amazed when it turned out that they had been pupils at Thornes House Grammar School, Wakefield, in the late 1940s/early fifties period. When I informed them that I was also an Old Boy of the same school, albeit in a younger age group, one individual made an astonishing revelation in such a genuine manner that I had no reason not to believe his every word, although he declined to give any details to substantiate his claim: 'The fire that destroyed the school in 1951 was not an accident; it had been started deliberately by a schoolboy with a grudge ...' No records of criminal proceedings have been found but the story is consistent with the report in the 21 July 1951, edition of the *Wakefield Express* that detectives had discovered that sometime during the incident an unsuccessful attempt had been made to open the school safe and that the fire appeared to have originated from two places. Truth is stranger than fiction.

Also by remarkable coincidence, major controversy now surrounds the arrest and subsequent death sentence which was passed down to Alfred Moore for the murders of Dad's West Riding Police colleagues, PC Gordon Jagger and Detective Inspector Duncan Fraser, on the same weekend as the fire at Thornes House, over sixty years ago. The dying PC Jagger had apparently picked out Moore in a nine man identity parade at the hospital but the gun was never found. Alfred Moore's death by hanging turned out to be highly controversial and was one of the probable miscarriages of justice that by 1969 had led to the permanent abolition of the death penalty. In 2006 the case was examined by a former detective, Steven Lawson, who claimed that there was no forensic evidence linking Moore to the murders and that he had probably been 'set-up'. A campaign was started for a posthumous pardon for Alfred Moore. Truth is stranger than fiction.

After suffering significant deprivation in their younger days, many of my parents' generation who had survived the Second World War experienced a better life in their later years. Dad didn't live long enough to hear the noise-free music reproduced by a compact disc but he eventually owned a car, a second hand Rover P4 which spent a lot of time in his workshop, being taken to bits and reassembled, for no apparent reason other than to satisfy his endless curiosity for the workings of a new toy. During my time at university in the 1960s, the entrance hall of number 21 Avondale Street eventually housed a large black telephone which Mum proudly announced every Sunday night as 'Wakefield, treble three eight' (later, 'seven treble three eight') in a voice as loud and clear as the speaking clock.

Travel became a regular, relaxing undertaking for my parents, rather than a nervous expedition. They were able to visit their new grandchildren: Thomas, born in Munich and Daniel, born in Oxford. Closer to home, Elaine's children Andrew and Steven also kept them on their toes. On 30 September 1976, Mum and Dad moved house to nearby Skelmanthorpe, with the intention of retiring closer to their roots. Former Wakefield Trinity hero, 'Rocky' Turner of Derek Turner Ltd., undertook the removal for the sum of £24·30, including £1·80 for a new tax known as value added tax at a rate of 8 per cent. However, joint retirement in their new home was short-lived: Dad died of lung cancer aged sixty-nine and, after suffering a stroke, Mum died, aged seventy-seven. The painful era of family funerals began as aunts and uncles also passed away.

Now, as a senior member of the family, I have to refrain from being a grumpy old man, lecturing my children and grandchildren about the good old days because, of course, they were not all good. Although by 1959 Britain had been transformed from the austere, regulated, class conscious and shackled society of 1950 to a more affluent and more physically- and socially mobile consumer society, there were still many aspects of life that had not changed for decades and which are now regarded as at best old-fashioned and at worst unacceptable. Many of my age group had to wait until the sixties for sex to be 'invented' following the actual invention of the contraceptive pill. Sexual oppression, gender inequality and sexism were the norm in the fifties and, although there is still room for improvement, current attitudes bear no relation to the situation sixty years ago. We now live in a more caring society, supported by liberal laws, especially on human rights. Fear and deference, so typical of the 1950s, have been reduced substantially. Minority groups such as homosexuals, communists, ethnic minorities and disabled people suffered considerable discrimination in the fifties when, unlike nowadays, they did not have their rights adequately protected by law. Racism was rampant throughout the land. In 1950 it was bad enough arriving in Belle Vue with a Lancashire accent; it is difficult to imagine how true immigrants felt a few years later.

Our standard of living has improved enormously in the past sixty years but the notion of reaping reward only after the investment of effort, 'earning it before spending it', has largely disappeared. In the 1950s there was always 'something for something'; getting something for nothing was the way of life for criminals and gamblers. Waiting for reward was the norm and, to many such as my parents, deliberately extending the wait was seen as a means of enjoying the reward even more; as I described, delayed gratification was a significant feature of many aspects of life in the 1950s. Although hire purchase schemes were available then, it wasn't until much later that the 'must have it now' syndrome or 'instant gratification' became the expectation for everything. I am not sure what Dad would have made of instant digital photography or the availability of instant information via the Internet that now lures us into buying goods that we don't really need with money we don't have: 'instant gratification' via 'instant credit'. It was the insatiable appetite for consumerism – greed by any other name – that led to the recent credit crunch and debt crisis, phenomena unheard of in the 1950s. However, my generation cannot claim the moral high ground here. Desire was the main driver for the consumer boom in the late fifties; the only difference was, we usually couldn't access the necessary technology and financial credit to fulfil our desires: 'Let he who is without sin cast the first stone!'

Once we had survived rationing and other inconveniences during childhood in the 1940s and early fifties there were no major impediments to the good life for most of us. The great political and social reforms of post-war Britain gave us enormous improvements in healthcare and the opportunity of a completely free education in schools, colleges and universities. We never had to be conscripted to fight in an armed conflict; very few had to worry about unemployment in an unprecedented period of economic growth; many became wealthy, simply through investment in property; we travelled up and down the country in cars that we once thought we would never own; we jetted across the world to lands we once thought we would never see. Many retired on fat, inflation-proof pensions and we all enjoyed the benefits of a national health service, free at the point of use. Some, rightly, label us the Golden Generation, but before we wallow too much in our good fortune, we should remember that the next generations will probably not be so lucky. It was the Golden Generation that collectively drove the demand for post-war consumerism and sowed the seeds of the future; we increasingly feasted on finite world resources and fuelled the irreversible changes now taking place to our one and only planet, its resources and its climate. Of course, we didn't know the consequences of our collective actions at the time, but they are now starkly and undeniably set out before us, compelling reasons for us to remind ourselves constantly of an old American Indian proverb: 'Treat the earth well – it was not given to you by your parents, it was loaned to you by your children.'

ACKNOWLEDGEMENTS

When I started this project as a complete novice, I sought guidance from Wakefield-born local historian, Kate Taylor. I am immensely grateful to Kate for her unstinting support as my mentor and critic over the past three years. An Internet 'brainstorming' session with Kate led to the book's main title, and I was delighted when she agreed to write the foreword.

I am also extremely grateful to my wife, Jane, and my sister Elaine and her husband, Nigel Staples, for their help and enduring patience during the book's long gestation period.

Many local and national organisations and their staff have been most helpful, notably the City of Wakefield Metropolitan District Libraries, Wakefield Museum, St Catherine's Church, Wakefield, the *Wakefield Express* newspaper, the John Goodchild Collection, the Wakefield Trinity Wildcats, the webmaster of the Thornes House School website, www.thorneshouse.org.uk, the West Riding Registry of Deeds, the West Yorkshire Police, the Fabian Society and the National Monuments Record. I am grateful to them for providing information in various forms and, in some cases, for permission to reproduce photographs. I am grateful to all copyright holders and surviving relatives for permission to reproduce their photographs. Andy Simons is gratefully acknowledged for support with imagery.

I thank my old friend, John Speight who helped me with many aspects of our shared past, provided valuable advice and kindly read through a draft manuscript. I am also grateful to Sir Rodney Walker and David Hinchliffe for their valuable help and advice and, along with Emily Gardiner, Geoff Oakes and Gareth Thomas, for reviewing the final manuscript. Many old friends and acquaintances have helped me in various ways, e.g. with the provision of photographs, literature, advice, anecdotes and information: Eric Abbiss, Mollie Atkinson, Jean Boocock (Holden), John Briggs, Les and Jenny Burkitt, Derek and Judith Chappel, Hughie Everson, Jimmy Ferguson, Bob Guiry, Bryan Heeley, Alan Kenworthy, Barbara Lazenby (Hawes), Andrew Lynes, Keith Oldroyd, John Parr, Brian Perkin, David Royle, David Rushton, John Shepherd, Jeff Sidebottom, Malcolm St John Smith, Val Speight, Geoff Stephenson, Anne Taylor (Sutton), Mary Tibbles, Michael White and Martin Wright.

I have made many new friends and contacts during the project and am most grateful for their help and advice: Jack Alderson, Simon and Anne Austerfield, Len Bedford, Marie Brian, June Geldart (Bracewell), John Hargreaves, Christine Hudson, Mrs Land, Chris Leach, Jean and Brian Morton, Violet Vokins, Colin Walker and Neil White. Other new contacts kindly provided help and advice with particular photographs and copyright matters: Steve Armitage, John Banks, Brian Davidson, Alwyne Gill, Steve Harris, Mrs G. Holdsworth, Robert Johnson, William Perraudin, Andrew Roper, Robin Saidman and Tony Sharkey.

Last, but not least, I thank all the staff of Aspect Design for their co-operation.

Index of People